Super Science Fair Sourcebook

Other books by Maxine Haren Iritz

Blue-Ribbon Science Fair Projects

Science Fair: Developing a Fun and Successful Project

Winning the Grand Award: Successful Strategies for International Science and Engineering Fair Competition

Super Science Fair Sourcebook

Maxine Haren Iritz

LEARNING TRIANGLE PRESS

Connecting kids, parents, and teachers through learning

An imprint of McGraw-Hill

New York San Francisco Washington, D.C. Auckland Bogotá Caracas Lisbon London Madrid Mexico City Milan Montreal New Delhi San Juan Singapore Sydney Tokyo Toronto

McGraw-Hill

A Division of The ***McGraw-Hill*** *Companies*

pbk 3 4 5 6 7 8 9 BBC/BBC 9 0 0 9 8

Library of Congress Cataloging-in-Publication Data

ISBN 0-07-032849-8

McGraw-Hill books are available at special quantity discounts to use as premiums and sales promotions, or for use in corporate training programs. For more information, please write to the Director of Special Sales, McGraw-Hill, 11 West 19th Street, New York, NY 10011. Or contact your local bookstore.

Acquisitions editor: Judith Terrill-Breuer
Editorial team: Robert E. Ostrander, Executive Editor
Sally Glover, Book Editor
Jodi L. Tyler, Indexer
Production team: Katherine G. Brown, Director
Lisa M. Mellott, Coding
Janice Ridenour, Computer Artist
Toya B. Warner, Computer Artist
Rose McFarland, Desktop Operator
Design team: Jaclyn J. Boone, Designer
Katherine Lukaszewicz, Associate Designer

SFP2
0328498

Contents

A word to parents

It has been eight years since I worked on my very first science project book. That book, "everything you've always wanted to know about science projects," was followed by two more books that described and analyzed student projects on the beginning and advanced levels.

Since then, much has changed, but more has remained the same. Computers, which were simply an aside in my first book, have since become so much faster, more sophisticated, and accessible that for many students, computers are a powerful tool when working on a science project. However, many of the factors that were important eight years ago (and before that) are still important now—thorough research and experimentation, good record keeping, interest, integrity, and dedication. Therefore, this new sourcebook addresses students with and without access to computers. The science fair experience is of great value in so many ways that it should be available to all students, even those with limited resources.

As has been true for the last 40+ years, Americans are concerned about education, especially math, science, computers, and engineering. We've found out that even under the best of circumstances, education often doesn't always keep up with technological advances. As a result, loss of jobs, economic decline, and a sense of displacement from society often create greater demands on parents, students, teachers, and the educational experience as a whole.

These days, it seems that education is like the weather; everyone complains about it. "Can't read, can't write, can't compute, can't function" seem to be the common gripes. Without engaging in an editorial, I believe that if any of these critics visited a local science fair, they would be forced to reconsider their opinions.

One way to encourage and reward an active, hands-on interest in science is the annual science and engineering fair. Now a feature of elementary, intermediate, and secondary schools, science projects call upon students to integrate many facets of their talents, abilities, and acquired knowledge.

Projects exhibited at a science fair require students to do research and conduct experiments in order to prove a hypothesis. When finished, these projects, together with displays, are entered in individual school fairs, where winners from each category advance to a regional science fair. The most outstanding projects proceed to state or international competitions, where recognition, scholarships, trips, and other prizes can be considerable.

As parents, you're probably reading this book because your child is planning to do a science project and is looking forward to competing in a science and engineering fair. For some students, the project is an unwelcome chore, required for a grade in science class. Others, already interested in some aspect of science, are looking forward to doing their projects.

Although valuable and rewarding, a science project requires a major commitment of time and effort for the better part of a school year. If it is a first project, it is most likely the largest single effort the student has ever made. Along the way, first-timers need encouragement, moral support, and often some very specific assistance.

Preparation can often take up to a year of intense effort, from the crucial first step, the selection of a topic appropriate to the interests and abilities of the student, to the construction of the display at the project's conclusion. Errors can be costly, both in terms of money spent for supplies and equipment and the time and energy diverted from the ultimate goal.

Parents are essential to the success of a project, especially for a first-timer. Unfortunately, many parents might not know how to best help their youngsters, especially if parents have never done a project themselves. One goal of this book is to help parents help their youngsters achieve not only success, but also enjoyment and satisfaction from the entire science fair experience. Teachers, although an important resource, are often so busy with their many students and their projects that they are spread rather thin and cannot always deal with the detailed problems of each student's experiment.

This book presents a clear guide on how to complete a successful science project. To do so, the text leads you through the steps involved, giving some concrete examples from "real-life" projects. The book also includes information and advice from teachers, judges, participants, and their families, advice geared towards guiding you down the easiest road to success and helping your child avoid the pitfalls. From the very first step, choosing a topic, until judging day at the science fair, this book covers just about anything and everything you need to know.

Whether or not your children decide to focus on careers in science, computers, or engineering, you'll find that the experiences your children have and the lessons they learn while doing a science project will have lasting benefits. One young man who worked on several science projects in junior and senior high school was faced with a large sociology project during his freshman year in college. Most of his classmates were in a panic, but he was quite calm. "It's just another science project," he said.

NOTE: Before you plan an experiment using live vertebrates or tissue samples, check your state and local regulations.

1 Introduction

At least half of you students reading this book are hoping that it will create a miracle and show you how to quickly and painlessly create a winning science project. It seems so overwhelming, with so many things to do. Besides, it might be half of your science grade. So this is stress!

Some of you might be among the lucky ones who want to do a project. Perhaps you're interested in some area of science and already have chosen your project idea. Maybe you just like to compete and match your abilities against your peers.

Whatever your reasons or motivation, if this is your first project, it might be your first independent study. Working on your own is one of the most important benefits of doing a project. Although you'll have help from parents, teachers, and other resources, this project will be entirely your responsibility (in many cases, you'll even be responsible for finding help). You'll do the planning and scheduling as well as executing the research and experiment. Although you will use many of the procedures and techniques that you've learned in science lab, you'll have the freedom to set your own pace.

The first, and possibly the most important, phase of the project is selecting your topic. This gives you the opportunity to investigate the ISEF categories and explore the general topics included in the various scientific disciplines. While going through the process, you'll find out which topics interest you the most. Perhaps you'll learn about subjects you never thought about before.

Another important element is the background research paper. Throughout high school and college, you'll be graded on the ability to write a well-researched and presented paper. For many of you, the research paper will be graded not only by your science teachers, but also by your English teacher.

Completing a project will give you real "on-the-job experience" in carrying out an experiment using sound scientific methods. In your school labs, your teachers generally specify the steps to follow for each experiment and provide the materials you need to work with. Teachers are always on hand to ensure that the procedure is carried out safely and properly.

When completing your project, you must design your experiment, find the materials, specify the procedures, safely do the experiment, and record and measure your observations, making sure that you properly adhere to scientific methods.

When the experiment is finished, you'll have to compile and tabulate your results. To do this, you might need mathematical or statistical skills, as well as the ability to graphically show your results. Finally, you'll develop your conclusions based on the results of the experiment. This will demonstrate your ability to relate the facts you have researched with the results of your experiment.

In your concluding statement, you can also speculate on the possible benefits to society that your results might present. Here you can also mention any plans you might have to continue working in that area. Sometimes, students become so fascinated with their subject area that year after year, they continue expanding on their research topic until, by the time they're 12th graders, they've become experts in their field.

One young man, Benjamin C. Preisner, started in ninth grade with a project to determine if caffeine produced color changes in frogs. That summer, he saw a television special on Parkinson's patients, put the two ideas together, and began a series of projects on the effect of caffeine on Parkinson's patients. Each project generated more interest, including grants from the United Parkinson's Foundation and the National Parkinson's Foundation. Figure 1-1 shows Ben's project display.

Doing a science project might satisfy the artist in you, too. Creating a display, which will illustrate and present a summary of your project, should show you and your work to its best advantage. Producing an effective backboard will call on your design, artistic, and photographic skills. Figures 1-2 and 1-3 show some attractive and original project displays.

If this is your first science fair, you're probably wondering what judges look for. At all levels, judges agree that the steps and methods used in the experiment are usually more important than your results or whether you prove your theory.

If you advance beyond your school fair, you'll probably get to spend a few days at the city, county, or state fair. There, fair organizers usually offer guided tours to areas of interest, such as museums, hospitals, universities, or laboratories. Professionals are sometimes available for counseling about scientific careers. Finally, you'll also get the chance to meet new and interesting people. In the process, you'll discover within yourself a poise and grace you never knew existed.

Although it is by no means necessary to have a home computer to do a successful science project, I have described, in extensive detail, how to use the computer to make your work easier, suggesting ways to use your system at all stages of project development. For those of you who do not have your own system, several students said they were able to use their school computer labs after hours or on Saturday.

1-1 *Does Caffeine Have an Effect on L-Dopa Therapy in MPTP Treatment in Mice?—Backboard.*

Although we are definitely in the information age, I don't want anyone to think that a computer is required for success. I've included several winning projects that were done manually on a limited budget.

For many of you, a science project is the largest, most complex piece of work you've ever attempted. Although the individual parts of the project might not be difficult, to complete the whole task you'll need to use a combination of

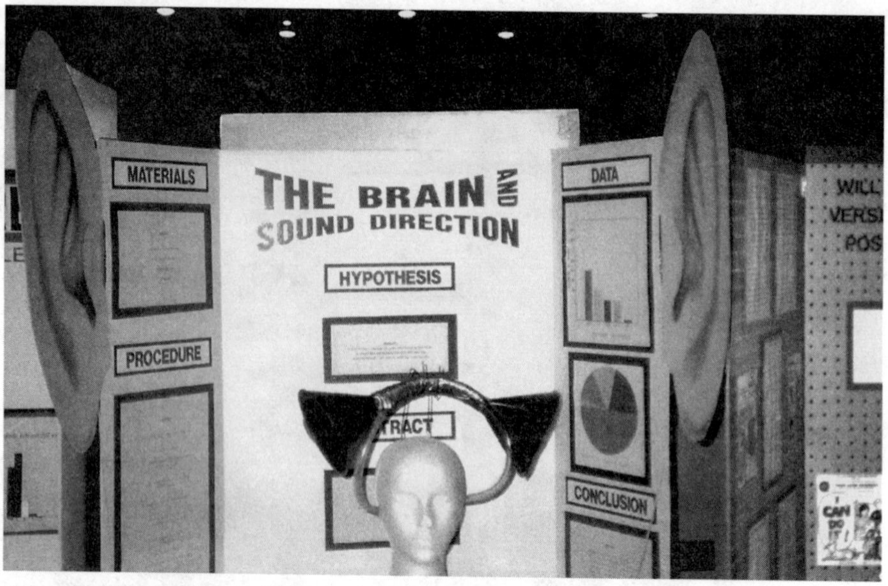

1-2 *The Brain and Sound Direction—Backboard.*

1-3 *The Effects of Cultivation on the Strength of Redwood—Backboard.*

skills, some of which you never even knew you had. Other attributes, such as creativity and flexibility, are a little harder to pin down, but these are qualities that will also be helpful. If you don't start the project with these abilities, you'll have many of them by the time you finish.

While you're working on your project, you'll also develop a better knowledge of yourself. With so many different aspects of a science project, you'll learn whether you love research, hate libraries, are afraid of handling chemicals, get excited when the statistics come out just the way you want them, relate to plants, or get turned on creating an attractive display.

You'll also get a strong feeling for the way you like to work: Thursday the 23rd between 2 a.m. and 4 p.m., or any time between the first day of school and President's weekend? Some people like a firm, structured schedule, with every task broken down to its smallest element and assigned to a specific time slot. Others are very well disciplined and can pace themselves and set their own goals. There are those, however, who like to live dangerously. They perform well only when they have a fast-approaching deadline, with more work than they can reasonably handle (to the frustration and panic of their parents and teachers). Some people prefer to do one task at a time, and others can work on many things at once. For most of you, a science project is the first opportunity to learn how you work best.

This book presents fully developed science projects in a variety of categories. However, the projects are grouped to illustrate the many ways you can get science project ideas. Incidentally, all the projects shown are actual projects that students have developed, from day one to science fair, and through all the steps in between. As you will see, some of these projects are fairly easy to do, while others are quite complex. Not all of these projects are top prize winners, but they are all top-notch projects done by students just like you.

You'll see every step in the development of these projects—from vague concept to science fair display. For each project, you'll learn how students found their topics, conducted project research, and developed the questions and hypotheses.

You'll see how students got organized to begin their experiments, and bought, begged, borrowed, or built their supplies and materials. By seeing how others succeeded, you'll also learn how to conduct an experiment or write and test a computer program. You'll see the results and find out how each student reached his or her conclusion. We'll also illustrate how each experiment, device, or program was displayed to its best advantage. Finally, we'll include some helpful hints for organizing and working on your own projects.

This book was written for you, the student, to make the science project experience an enjoyable and fulfilling educational experience. Because it is probably your first undertaking of this type, you might doubt whether you can do it. Many other students have approached their projects with the same mixture of fear and uncertainty. However, with an open mind, a lively curiosity, and a willingness to dig in and work, they have created effective, scientifically acceptable, award-winning projects.

For many of you, the learning will extend far beyond the areas of science to writing, art, mathematics, and research. I hope you will also find a true sense of pride, confidence, accomplishment, and a true joy of learning.

Like any other long-term effort, a science project is filled with many small victories, false starts, bursts of activity, periods of procrastination, sleepless nights, and stomachs full of butterflies. Through it all, regardless of awards or grades, everyone who completes a project is a winner.

Remember that the main objective is learning. One student, who worked on a large-scale project for several years, said, "Spending so much time on a science fair project might be hard to imagine, but if you're intensely curious about something, the time you spend answering it for yourself will give you more knowledge and experience than you would have gotten from a text. The purpose of science is to help us understand everything around us and within us. Do your project knowing that your time was spent well, developing a greater understanding of who you are, where you are, and what your purpose is here." Look at your science project not as an assignment but as an adventure. Happy exploration!

2

Choosing a topic

All science projects begin with an idea, an inspiration, and the ability and enthusiasm to complete a project. Actually, for many of you, science project ideas start even before that, when your science teacher announces that you will do a project if you have any hopes of passing the class. So before you even take the first step, you should get yourself mentally prepared to accept the challenge.

Probably the hardest part of any project is finding a topic. You don't want something so simple that even a child of four could do it, but neither do you want something that requires the talents of a rocket scientist. You don't want to rehash a topic that's been entered (several times) in every science fair since your mom was in school, but you can't pick something so obscure that you can't find any information. If there is one factor that is essential to the success of all science projects, it is the choice of topic. Some of the exhibitors, especially those competing for the first time, said that finding a subject was the most difficult part of the entire experience. Most students wanted an idea that was original, or at least not overdone. Everyone wanted a concept that excited their curiosity, but they also wanted an experiment that wouldn't be too difficult.

The best project idea for you is one that you're interested in. You will be involved with your science project for almost the entire school year. If you find a topic that's interesting, you'll probably have fun, too. And if you're having a good time, the odds are that you'll finish successfully.

Okay, so you're interested in sports, music, cars, food, and boys (or girls). And so is everyone else, which brings us to the next problem—finding something unique. You might have a particular hobby or interest that will give you an idea. Do you play chess, water-ski (or snow-ski, for that matter), fish, or sew? There might be an idea in one of those pursuits. For example, see chapter 3 for a discussion of some projects, in all categories, based on sports. Figure 2-1 shows the project display for a "sports" project.

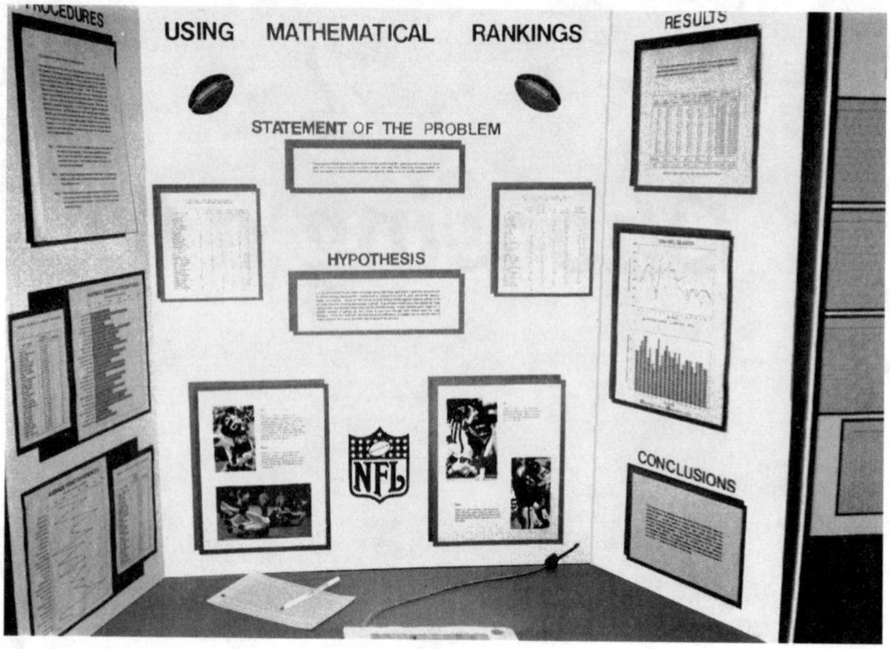

2-1 *Using Mathematical Rankings—Backboard.*

One way to find out if your idea is original is to look at programs from previous science fairs to see what's been done frequently. Your teachers will also be glad to tell you what projects they don't want to see. If you're lucky, you'll get a list of "banned" projects before you're committed to a topic.

Some of the best sources of ideas are your math, science, or computer classes, especially something you're currently studying. This way you'll already know something about the topic. Also, your textbook might contain additional sources of information. However, don't limit yourself to math, science, and computer classes. Even classes in social science might suggest an excellent topic idea. For example, a class discussion on subliminal advertising led to an animal behavior experiment that measured the effect of sound on mouse appetite. History courses that deal with prehistory might lead to a project dealing with fossils, ancient ship design, or dating ancient artifacts, as shown in Fig. 2-2.

Another place to look for an idea is in your family. There's nothing wrong with doing a project on the strength of different types of wood if your mom is a carpenter. For most projects, you'll need some sort of assistance, and there's no place like home! Some students have developed excellent projects because they became interested in a parent's profession or hobby. As long as you don't have someone else doing your work, there's nothing wrong with getting your idea or inspiration from someone you know.

A word of warning, however. Well-meaning friends and relatives might propose or try to impose ideas, and even offer their assistance. Before you make a decision, be sure that you want to do this project and that you have the ability to complete it on time. A project that relies solely on the knowledge and work of parents, friends, and relatives will not help you to achieve any of your goals in doing a project. If you are uncertain, discuss the idea with your teacher or ad-

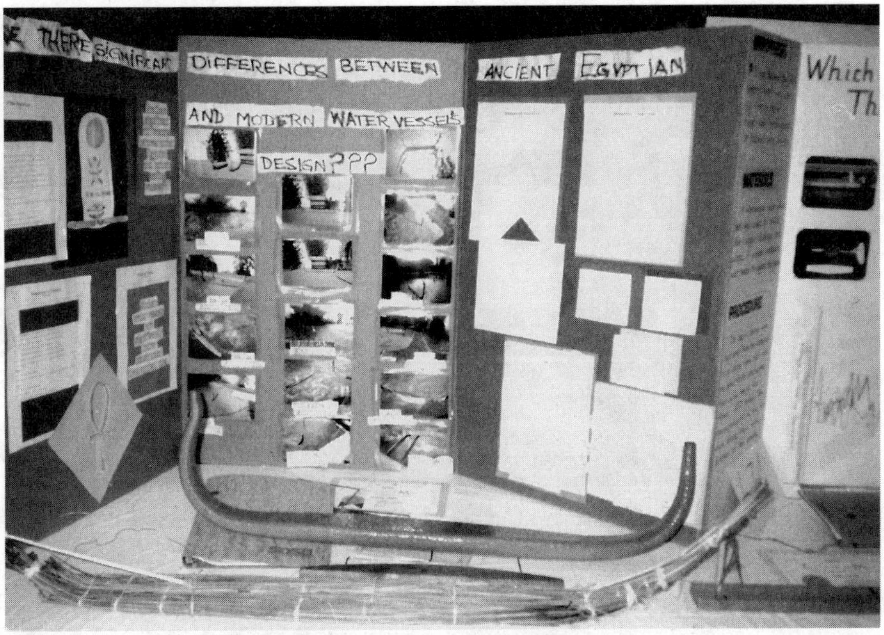

2-2 *Ancient Egyptian and Modern Vessel Design: Are There Significant Differences?—Backboard.*

viser. He or she will be glad to talk with you and might even point out something (either positive or negative) that you hadn't yet thought of.

Advertisements are excellent sources of project ideas, and today's TV jingle can be the inspiration for tomorrow's science project. "Whiter, cleaner, brighter," says the ad. Really? How? Perhaps a science project will show you. In some local science fairs, a new category in consumer and product testing has been created to address this type of project. Figures 2-3 and 2-4 show projects that deal with product testing.

Many students get their ideas from the news of the day and often want to use their projects to right some social wrong. It's important to realize that your eighth-grade project will probably not discover the cure for cancer or fix the hole in the ozone layer. However, you could do a project that addresses some important concerns on a smaller, more local scale. You can certainly analyze the smog or pollution in your area, or try to measure the effects of second-hand smoke, as you will see in chapter 15. Also, the work that you do now might be the beginning of greater efforts later on. The main reason for limiting the scope of the experiment is to make sure that you can actually do the project. You might also find a question that arouses your curiosity in a newspaper or magazine. Areas of science, especially those that are important in your particular locality, are often discussed in feature articles. Weekly news magazines deal with the areas of health, aerospace, the environment, and other scientific fields, particularly when new problems, discoveries, or theories are presented. The best way to find a topic is to be aware of and receptive to your environment. The world around you offers many opportunities for topics.

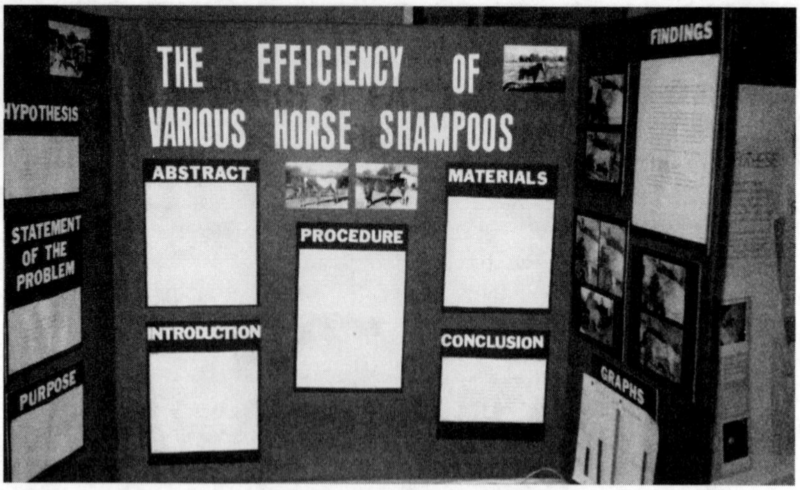

2-3 *The Efficiency of Various Horse Shampoos—Backboard.*

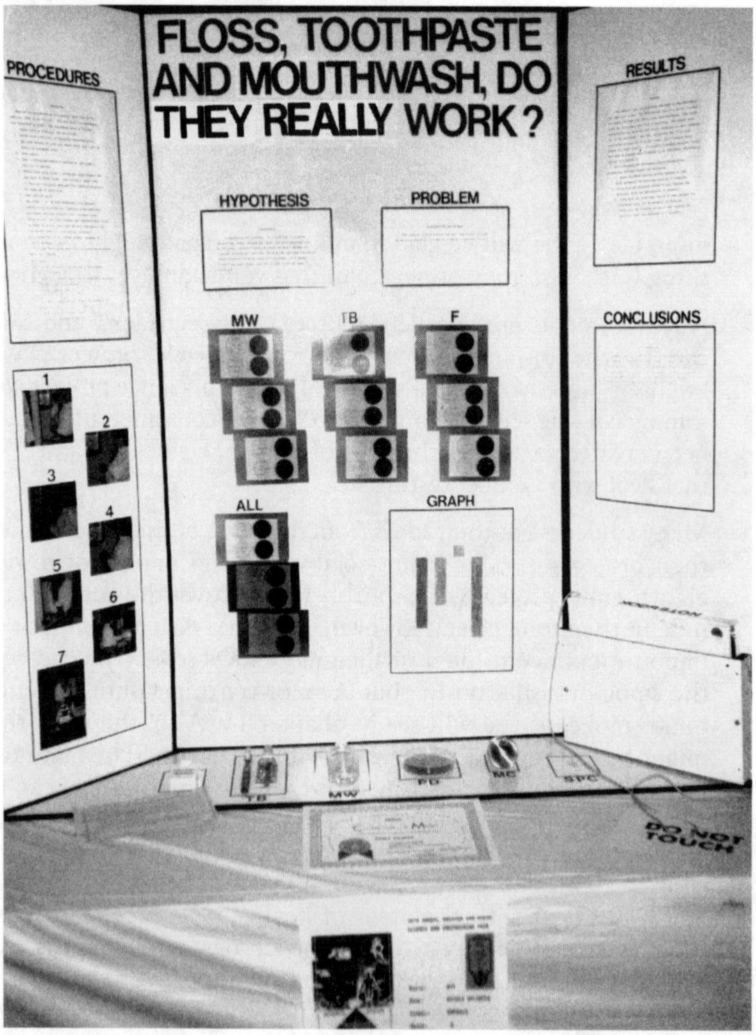

2-4 *Floss, Toothpaste, and Mouthwash: Do They Really Work?—Backboard.*

Besides finding a topic that you like, be sure to select a subject with which you feel comfortable and confident. Although the main purpose of doing a science project is to explore new techniques and learn new things, it is best to pick a topic in which you have at least a basic understanding. This is not a good time to do a crash self-study course in your most difficult subject. For example, if math is giving you trouble, a topic requiring complex and sophisticated calculations is unwise.

Also, make sure you have the time and ability to complete the project before you go any further. Your teacher can help you take a realistic look at your project idea and decide if it's within your scope.

Besides the list of "tired old projects" that you'll no doubt get from your teacher, there are a few more areas where you must proceed at your own risk. In the past, many experiments in the animal behavior and zoology categories relied on the use of live specimens. Although these types of topics were fascinating and fun, this introduces another dimension into your science project plan.

Each year it becomes more difficult to enter projects that use live vertebrates in experiments. Animal rights groups have influenced ongoing research and how animals are used in student experiments and projects. Judges might want evidence that animals were handled correctly and explanations of any deaths in your experimental or control groups. Irregularities can prevent you from exhibiting at a science fair. Therefore, unless you have a professional adviser who can certify that there is no mistreatment of the animals at any time during your project, find another project idea. (Your family will probably be pleased, too!)

In talking with exhibitors and coordinators from all over the country, we have also found that some local fairs use different standards for judging experiments using live specimens. To be sure that your project will be acceptable if you move ahead in competition, adhere to the standards required by Science Service, who conducts the International Science and Engineering Fair. By doing this, you will be able to compete anywhere. You can get a copy of the ISEF rules by sending $.50 to:

Science Service
1718 N Street N.W.
Washington, DC 20036

Carefully consider whether you can and will commit the time and effort to care for these animals. Fortunately for you and your family, the project will probably involve small animals, but even the smallest live vertebrate requires special handling. Another factor in deciding whether you want to do an experiment of this type is to determine exactly how many specimens you need. You might need a rather large number, kept in separate groups, for your experiment to be scientifically valid. Before beginning this type of experiment, be sure you have the facilities to keep three cages of 20 mice, with each cage completely segregated.

To do this properly, learn all you can about the animals' care, feeding, habits, required temperature, and what you need to do to keep them clean. You must also find out about the reproductive cycles and characteristics of the species in order to plan for possible periods of gestation and birth. For example, when dealing with mice or other rodents, it is extremely important to remove the males when a litter is born, to prevent them from eating the newborns! Many students using rodents have therefore limited their specimens to one sex (provided, of course, that reproduction is not a factor to be considered).

Another word to the wise: Be sure to get your parents' approval before embarking on such an experiment. Nothing will terminate your project faster than an unknowing parent entering the house to find 600 (or even 60!) mice running around. Talk to your mom and dad. You will need their cooperation. If you do get their approval, be conscientious in keeping the animals and their quarters clean. Also, make sure that the animals are always properly confined and kept isolated from family pets. Help and cooperation will fast disappear in a home that smells like a neglected cage in a travelling zoo!

If it turns out that caring for live vertebrates isn't your cup of tea, this doesn't exclude you from doing a project in animal behavior or zoology. You can try insects or fish to conduct certain experiments. On the other hand, you can use vertebrates in a project when not needing to experiment on them for long periods of time. In a project that explored the connection between allergies and obesity in dogs, the only "live" tests on the dogs were pinch tests to determine the body fat content. Bottom line? Unless you have great dedication and commitment, choose another topic.

You will also need to follow stringent ISEF rules and certifications for projects involving human subjects. Any experiment that might cause potential physical or psychological damage must be done under supervision. Some topics might be obviously unacceptable, such as depriving people of sleep or nourishment for long periods of time. However, there are many projects you can do, such as the two projects presented in chapter 15. As you will see, the experiments required the subjects to perform two very normal functions—breathing and seeing.

Problems affecting teenagers are often the impetus behind projects. There are always projects involving concentration and stress. The attention given to eating disorders or attention deficit disorders also motivated several projects recently. Drug-related problems have inspired many projects on the effects of alcohol, caffeine, and nicotine impairing a spider's ability to weave its web. However, it is sometimes hard to predict if an experiment will give offense. A few years ago, a controversy erupted concerning an experiment where adults were given alcoholic beverages and then tested on a video game (incidentally, the more they drank, the worse they scored). Although the project won at a school science fair, a screening committee later disqualified it. The judges determined that the tests, which were done without supervision, could have caused physical or psychological harm. Because the project's hypothesis was to prove the harmful effects of drinking and driving, MADD (Mothers Against Drunk Driving) disagreed with the ruling, but the judges stood firm and disqualified the project.

So before you begin a project that uses human subjects, check with your teacher, or if you can, discuss it with your local screening committee. If possible, take the "pulse" of your community if there's a possibility that the project might be too controversial. If you're committed to the idea but still have doubts about whether it will be acceptable, check and recheck the ISEF rules. If you decide to go ahead, find a professional who will supervise your work and certify that you followed proper procedures. Still in doubt? Find another topic.

In spite of these few warnings, there's a whole world of ideas just looking for a home in your science project. The next few chapters take a look at several projects, from the easy to the complex, from the commonplace to the unusual, that students just like you have developed. From rockets to rebounds, from viewing through a telescope to viewing through a painting, the projects shown in Figs. 2-5 through 2-8 display a variety of ideas. You'll see that regardless of your interests or expertise, there's something just waiting for you.

2-5 *The Perfect Rebound—Backboard.*

Categories

Many categories of projects compete in science fairs. Categories cover all scientific and engineering disciplines, ranging from botany to zoology, and everything in between. See appendix A for ISEF project categories. If you already have a project idea, it would be good idea to see what category it might fit into. If, on the other hand, you have no idea at all, examining the various categories might at least give you some insight into the general area you want to work in.

A program from a past science fair contains a great deal of valuable information about the different categories. Usually the projects competing in each category are listed, along with the name and school of each exhibitor. One of the first things you might notice is that some categories have many more entries than others. This, especially at the junior-division level, occurs for several reasons.

2-6 *Blast Off—Backboard.*

One important reason is that these popular fields are covered in the junior-high-school science classes. Availability of background information in that particular category is another reason for having more projects in that area. Finally, in certain areas, the subject matter is more relevant to the students' lives—for example, human behavior, computers, or medical science. However, these reasons, which make a certain area of study easier and more popular, also mean stiffer competition in those categories.

Your topic does not necessarily have to be original for your project to be a success, but teachers and judges will look for a creative approach. Therefore, if you plan to use an idea that has been done often, look at it from a fresh angle. Although information is more readily available in these areas, you might need to work harder to manage an original viewpoint. Categories, as defined by the International Science and Engineering Fair, are rather specific. Particularly for senior division projects that will hopefully make it to ISEF competition, it is

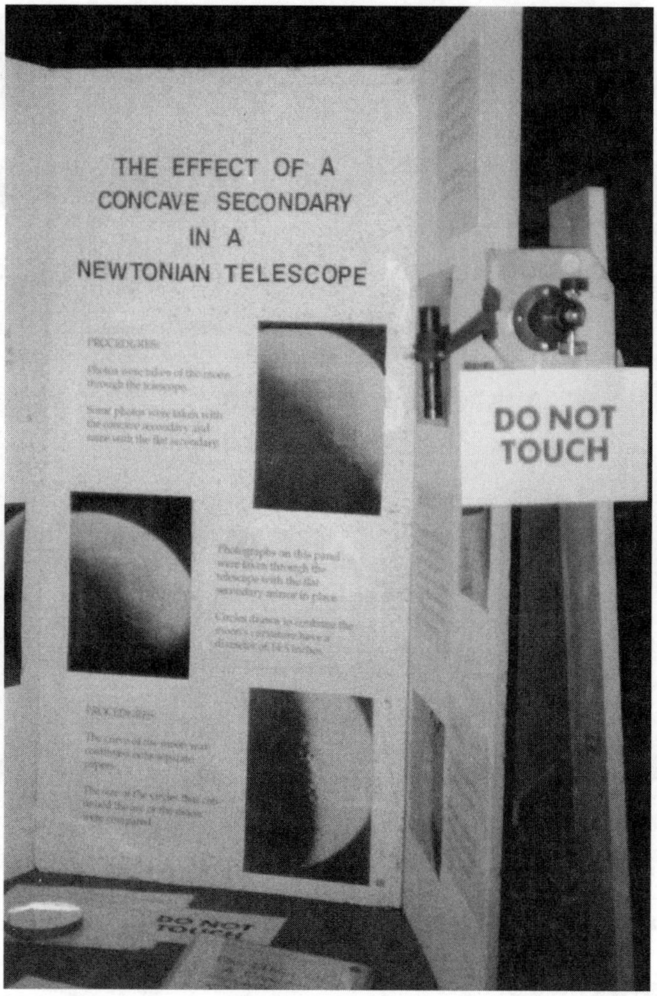

2-7 *The Effect of a Concave Secondary in a Newtonian Telescope—Backboard.*

important to adhere to these categories. However, local science fairs sometimes define things differently, particularly for junior-division projects. The 1995 Greater San Diego Science and Engineering Fair defined these categories:

Behavioral and social sciences

- Eating Disorders: Are You Dying to Be Thin?
- Does Smell Affect Memory?
- Different Methods of Finding Hidden Pictures
- Graphology: The Art of Handwriting Analysis—Fact or Fiction?
- Can a Dog Reduce Stress in 3rd Graders?

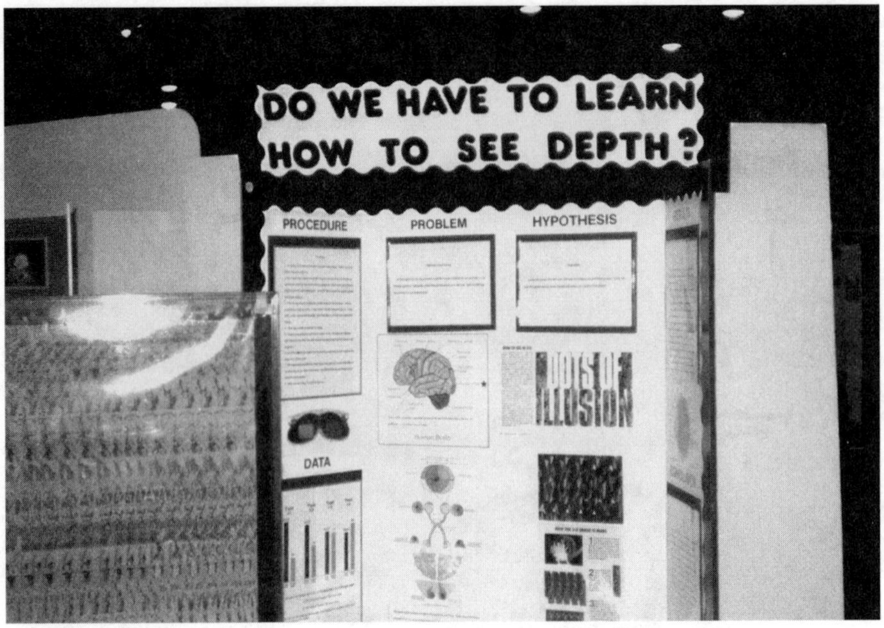

2-8 *Do We Have to Learn to See Depth?—Backboard.*

Biochemistry

- Can We Spontaneously Create Life?
- Radioprotective Effect of Black and Green Tea on DNA Strand Breaks
- Effects of Temperature on the Structure of DNA

Botany

- Effects of Pretreating Corn Seeds Prior to Germination
- Effect of Acid on the Molding of Cheese
- Flower Child
- Fertilizers: Chemical Versus Organic
- Does Aspirin Prolong the Life of Cut Flowers?

Chemistry

- Is the First Drop as Good as the Last?
- Fire Retardation
- Water, Water Everywhere: Which Is Best to Drink?
- Which Juices Contain the Most Vitamin C?
- What Stinks? The Truth About Lemon Scent

Computer Science

- Fashions Unlimited: A Computer Program
- Voice Recognition Systems: Effect of Age and Sex on Voice Recognition
- Creation of Virtual Scientific Laboratory Software
- Can an Easy-to-Use Internet Menu Program Be Created?
- Artificial Intelligence: An Analysis of Natural Selection

Earth and Space Sciences

- How Safe Is Christmas?
- The Veil of Darkness
- Effect of a Concave Secondary in a Newtonian Telescope
- Spying on Satellites
- To Rain or Not to Rain

Engineering

- Is it Possible to Recycle Bath and Shower Water?
- What Color Paint Is Most Reflective?
- Which Surfaces Best Resist the Adhesiveness of Chewing Gum?
- Inexpensive Homemade Filters for Laser Lights
- The Flexibility of Rubber Bands
- Shotgun Pellet Efficiency: Steel Versus Lead

Environmental Sciences

- Oil Spills: Danger in the Sea
- Are Safe Pesticides Really Safe?
- Does Garbage Decompose Faster Above or Below Ground?
- Comparative Study of Compounds Found in Rural and Urban Lakes
- Effects of Acid Rain on Building Stone
- Recycling Waste into Energy
- Pollution in Our Bays
- Ocean Pollution

Mathematics

- Probability Analysis: An Experiment with Dice
- Mathemagics: Magic Squares—Orthomorphic Groups for Target Years
- Magic Hexagons: Algebraic and Computed Solutions

Medicine and Health

- Gels and Creams: Which Sunscreen Is Best?
- Color Perception in the Peripheral Field of Vision
- Leonardo da Vinci's Human Proportions: Fact or Fiction?
- Effects of Antacid Dosage on Stomach Acidity
- Protective Effects of Antioxidants Against Nicotine
- Taste: Inherited Versus Cultural

Microbiology

- Effect of UV Light on Living Microorganisms
- Efficacy of Soap Versus Disinfectant Soap in Handwashing
- Which Cleaner Kills the Most Household Bacteria?
- Harmless Herb?
- Ginseng: The Real Cure?
- Effects of Cigarette Smoke on Sea Urchin Embryo Development

Physics

- Natural Versus Synthetic Dyes
- Have You Ever Seen a Guitar Note?
- Can Friction Be Measured with a Toy Truck?
- Solar Power
- Edible Batteries

Zoology

- Slime
- Wild Bird Food Preferences
- Which Is Most Attractive to Bees—Fragrance, Color, or Flavor?
- Which Common Household Compound Repels Ants Best?
- Hermit Crabs: A Behavioral Study

Consumer science/product testing

- How Much Air Is in Your Ice Cream?
- The Coca-Cola/Pepsi Project
- How Accurate Is the Calorie Content on Food Labels?
- The Effects of Chlorine Bleach on White Cotton Sock Longevity
- Nail Polish: How Much Is Enough?
- T-Shirt Wearability—Is Cost the Primary Factor?
- Plop, Plop, Fizz, Fizz, Oh What a Relief It Is!
- Analysis of Sourdough Starters

In talking with science fair participants, we found a variety of reasons for choosing a particular topic. Some wanted to find a simple project with quick results, where others simply wanted something unique. Often, students were drawn to a category, such as computers, and then looked for a project idea. Others were inspired by their parents' occupations, and yet others looked for an idea that would attract a lot of attention.

Can I do it?

Once you find a topic (or have several possibilities), it's a good idea to analyze the feasibility of your plans. You must decide whether you can actually complete the project in the time available. Here's a checklist to help you decide:

- Is the information that I need readily available?
- Where can I find the information?
- If the information is not available locally, where is it?
- How long will it take to get?
- Will I need to pay for my information? (Government agencies or industry might charge for their data).
- If I need special books, can I check them out of the library, or must I use them there?
- Will I need professional advice? From whom (specifically)? Are they willing to help? Will it cost anything?
- What supplies will I need?
- Can I build some of the things I need? Do I need help?
- Can I borrow some of the supplies and equipment I'll need?
- What will my supplies cost?
- Do I have the money for my supplies and equipment?

- Can I finish in the time allowed? If not, can I break the project idea into smaller segments?
- Is there anything about the experiment my family might object to?

Answering these basic questions will, at least, give you a rough idea of whether you can complete this project. If you have any doubts, consult your teacher or adviser. However, if you are sure that this is the topic for you, now is the time to consider it in more detail.

Safety first

If you are dealing with chemicals or electricity, make sure your personal experiment will be safe.

Some questions that you should ask are:

- Electricity
- Is battery power adequate?
- If I plan to use house current, is there sufficient wiring?
- Can I avoid overloading circuits?
- Will everything be properly insulated and grounded?
- If I must use line voltage, do I need an electrician?
- Do I need the approval of an electrical inspector?
- Do I need to notify the local power company?
- Is the power the right kind (110 versus 220 versus 550), or do I need transformers or converters? Are they readily available?
- Chemicals
- Are the substances readily available, or do I need special permits to acquire them?
- Is anything I plan to use or make considered a toxic substance?
- Do I need approval of state, local, or federal authorities (such as the EPA) to do my experiment?
- Are there any unstable compounds that could possibly cause explosion? Will these compounds, either alone or in combination with other substances, form toxic gases or start fires that might cause injury or property damage?
- Will I need special containers?
- Do I need protective gear (goggles, aprons, gloves) to work with this substance?

Caution: With an electrical or chemical project, always seek adult assistance or supervision to ensure a safe experiment and environment.

Dollars and cents

Before making a final decision, estimate all of your total costs. It is not necessary to spend a huge amount of money to be successful, nor must you have access to a sophisticated million dollar computer to do a thorough and creative experiment. Some very successful projects that have advanced all the way to international competition have been done with minimal expenditure, whereas others require a great deal of money. Students reported that their projects cost anywhere from $15 up to infinity.

Often you can borrow laboratory equipment, computers, and other machines, or you can use them on high-school and university campuses when classes are not in session. If you think you will need facilities of this type, arrange for them before you commit too heavily to your idea. If you can do that, you'll spend minimal amounts of money compared to the value of the equipment that you use. One young man told us he spent approximately $400, but he used over $12,000 worth of equipment and supplies.

Try to be as accurate and complete as possible when making your estimate. For many exhibitors we interviewed, the project ended up costing more than they had anticipated. The biggest exception to this was where the experiment was a continuation of a prior year's project. Then it was easier to predict the expenses, especially because the student had already bought what he or she needed. Again, talk to your parents and find out whether they're willing to fund your project or might have ideas on cheaper solutions.

When you're making your estimate, include everything, from the supplies for the experiment to the materials for the graphs and the display board. Often, people forget that art supplies might be the most expensive portion of the project. As we'll discuss later, an impressive display can't hurt, but it also can't improve a project that was done poorly. In any event, making an estimate, and perhaps budgeting or saving for these expenses, will help you avoid unpleasant surprises at the last minute.

Finally, get the approval of your science teacher or adviser. Sometimes you'll need him or her to sign a form agreeing to the experiment. Now that you've selected your topic, let's begin!

3 Fun and games

When you're looking for an idea for a science project, one way to start is with the things you're interested in, even if they are completely unrelated to science. Are you interested in music, sports, games, or books? There might be an idea for a project buried somewhere in there.

For many of you, sports are the most important thing in your life right now. Whether you're participants or fans, sports occupy a great deal of your thoughts. Wooden bat or aluminum? The best type of cleat? Sod or Astroturf? Batting averages? Yards rushing? Any of these questions might be the start of a great science project.

In just one metropolitan science fair, let's look at the many projects in various categories based on sports.

Computer science

- Can Computers Predict the Outcome of Football Games?
- When Does a Baseball Player Reach His or Her Peak?

Engineering

- Sail Shapes
- Effect of Core Composition on Softball Liveliness
- Teflon-Coated Hockey Skates
- Are Shinguards Effective When Kicking a Soccer Ball?
- Which Combination of Bearings and Lubricant Makes for Faster Skateboards?
- Baseball Bats: Wood or Aluminum?
- Which Shoe Has the Most Shock Absorbency?

Environmental science

- Mountain Biking's Impact on Canyon Erosion

Mathematics

- Correlation Analysis Provides the Key to Winning Basketball Games
- The Keys to Winning Football Games
- The Best Angle to Take a Shot on Goal
- Optimal Standing Position for Hitting Curve Balls

Medicine and health

- Baseball Soccer and Football—Which Causes the Most Injury Among Teens?
- Fishhooks in Fingers: Which Removal Method is Best?
- Relationship of Pro Football Injuries to Position, Experience, and Weight

Physics

- Which Bat Hits the Ball Farthest?
- Is the Ball Juiced?
- Roller Hockey: The Search for the Perfect Puck
- Effect of Launch Angle on Baseball Travel Distance
- Achieving Maximum Distance When Kicking a Soccer Ball
- Effects of Weight Change on a Golf Club
- The Golf Ball Challenge

"For it's root, root, root, for the home team..."

You don't have to be an athlete to do a project about sports. In fact, an armchair quarterback, or any other type of fan who avidly reads the sports pages, follows the home team, or quotes statistics, probably has loads of project ideas running around his or her head.

Matthew Duke is just such a sports fan. (But don't be fooled. He's no couch potato; he's an athlete as well.) As a home-team enthusiast, he wanted to find out whether the home-field advantage was really fact or simply fiction. He decided on a mathematics project to determine whether the home team is a statistical favorite. The question and hypothesis are shown in Fig. 3-1. Matthew's background paper was more of an introduction than background research. In it, he described the factors that might cause a home-field advantage.

In outdoor sports, the weather is often a factor because the home team is more accustomed to the local conditions. For example, the New Orleans Saints might be at a disadvantage playing during a snowstorm in Green Bay, Wisconsin. The playing field can be another factor that might favor the home team, especially when some fields use artificial turf and others are made of natural grass. The fatigue and jet lag involved in travelling to other cities could also cause a team to perform more poorly away from home. Finally, the enthusiasm

Question	Hypothesis
Is there a home field advantage in sports?	In any professional athletic competition, a team's performance, and likely the outcome of the game, will be affected by whether the game is played at home or away, with the home team having an advantage over the visiting team.

3-1 *Home-Field Advantage—Question and hypothesis.*

of the home team fans (or the hostility of those same fans towards the visiting team) could be another factor in the home-field advantage. By choosing basketball and soccer, sports that are played indoors on a regulation court, Matthew eliminated the weather and playing field factors from consideration.

Very few materials were used for this project, as shown in Fig. 3-2. The variables and controls, and the experimental and control groups, are shown in Fig. 3-3. To determine how many games from each league to use for his project, Matthew sent for schedules from the NBA (National Basketball Association) and MISL (Major Indoor Soccer League). During the course of the project, which ran from 11/27/89 through 12/9/89, Matthew collected scores from 236 basketball games, which represented 20.77% of the NBA season, and 49 soccer games, which represented 23.56% of the MISL season. He selected a number of games as close to ⅕ of a season as possible so that each team would have an equal proportion of home and away games.

Materials
1. Daily newspaper 2. PC 386 computer 3. dBase IV software 4. Macintosh computer 5. Microsoft works

3-2
Home-Field Advantage—Materials.

Variables	Controls
Experimental Scores of MISL and NBA games **Measured** • Average home score • Average visiting score • Average winning score	Proportion of home and away games for each team.

3-3 *Home-Field Advantage—Variables and controls.*

Each day, Matthew got the scores from the San Diego Union. To record the data, he set up two files using a database program, dBase IV, on his personal computer. Database programs store and organize information so that all data or any selected portion of the data can be arranged, retrieved, and analyzed at any time. With dBase IV, he created two files, one for soccer and one for basketball, that defined the information he needed to enter. For each game, he recorded the home and visiting team names and scores and the winning score. The file structure for the soccer games is shown in Fig. 3-4, and the file structure for the basketball games is shown in Fig. 3-5.

When all the scores were entered, Matthew ran data queries on the files to list the scores and compute the average home score, visiting score, and winning score. The database query for soccer is shown in Fig. 3-6, and the resulting list is shown in Fig. 3-7. The database query for basketball is shown in Fig. 3-8, and Fig. 3-9 shows a portion of the basketball season listing.

```
. USE SOCCER
. LIST STRUCTURE
Structure for database: C:\DBASE\SOCCER.DBF
Number of data records:       49
Date of last update    : 12/08/89
Field  Field Name  Type       Width    Dec    Index
    1  HOME_TEAM   Character      3               Y
    2  VIS_TEAM    Character      3               Y
    3  HOME_SCORE  Numeric        2               N
    4  VIS_SCORE   Numeric        2               N
    5  HOME_WIN    Character      1               Y
    6  DATE        Date           8               N
    7  WIN_SCORE   Numeric        2               Y
** Total  **                     22
```

3-4 *Home-Field Advantage—dBase IV panel, soccer.*

```
. USE BBALL
. LIST STRUCTURE
Structure for database: C:\DBASE\BBALL.DBF
Number of data records:      230
Date of last update    : 12/09/89
Field  Field Name  Type       Width    Dec    Index
    1  HOME_TEAM   Character      3               Y
    2  VIS_TEAM    Character      3               Y
    3  HOME_SCORE  Numeric        3               N
    4  VIS_SCORE   Numeric        3               N
    5  HOME_WIN    Character      1               Y
    6  DATE        Date           8               N
    7  WIN_SCORE   Numeric        3               Y
** Total  **                     25
```

3-5 *Home-Field Advantage—dBase IV panel, basketball.*

```
DATA BASE QUERIES – SOCCER

.USE SOCCER
.
.COUNT FOR HOME_WIND="Y"
      32 records
.
.COUNT FOR HOME_WIN="N"
      17 records
.
.AVERAGE HOME_SCORE
      49 records averaged
      HOME_SCORE
           4.29
.
.AVERAGE VIS_SCORE
      49 records averaged
      VIS_SCORE
           3.57
.
.AVERAGE WIN_SCORE
      49 records averaged
      WIN_SCORE
          5.08
.
.?(4.29+3.57)/2
          3.94
```

3-6 *Home-Field Advantage—Database query, soccer.*

He also wrote an analysis program, listed in Fig. 3-10, to calculate the summary statistics for each team. These statistics are percentages of games won at home and away, and the average points earned at home and away. Figure 3-11 illustrates the summary statistics for soccer, and Fig. 3-12 shows an example of the results of the analysis for basketball. Figure 3-13 summarizes the project procedures.

When the calculations were complete, Matthew transferred his results to Microsoft Works on a Macintosh computer. He created pie charts showing the percentage of home games won and lost for both soccer and basketball. He also created bar graphs, which illustrate the average home and visiting scores. To illustrate the MISL results, Fig. 3-14 shows the pie chart and Fig. 3-15 shows the bar graph. To display the NBA statistics, Fig. 3-16 shows the pie chart, and Fig. 3-17 shows the bar graph. Matthew summarized the results and drew his conclusion, as shown in Fig. 3-18. The results clearly show that statistically, there is a home-field advantage, which proves the hypothesis.

HOME_TEAM	VIS_TEAM	HOME_SCORE	VIS_SCORE	HOME-WIN	WIN_SCORE	DATE
STL	KAN	2	3	N	3	10/27/89
DAL	SAN	9	3	Y	9	10/28/89
KAN	STL	6	5	Y	6	10/28/89
WIC	TAC	4	3	Y	4	10/28/89
BAL	CLE	6	3	Y	6	10/29/89
KAN	TAC	5	4	Y	5	10/31/89
CLE	WIC	4	5	N	5	11/02/89
BAL	WIC	7	6	Y	7	11/04/89
DAL	STL	5	4	Y	5	11/04/89
TAC	SAN	4	3	Y	4	11/04/89
TAC	CLE	5	1	Y	5	11/03/89
SAN	KAN	4	3	Y	4	11/03/89
BAL	TAC	3	2	Y	3	11/09/89
CLE	TAC	5	0	Y	5	11/10/89
STL	WIC	2	5	N	5	11/10/89
WIC	BAL	3	9	N	9	11/11/89
DAL	KAN	5	4	Y	5	11/11/89
STL	CLE	4	3	Y	4	11/12/89
SAN	DAL	6	2	Y	6	11/12/89
WIC	DAL	0	3	N	3	11/17/89
SAN	STL	7	4	Y	7	11/17/89
SAN	TAC	4	3	Y	4	11/18/89
CLE	WIC	10	4	Y	10	11/18/89
BAL	KAN	4	2	Y	4	11/18/89
DAL	STL	3	4	N	4	11/19/89
BAL	DAL	3	7	N	7	11/21/89
KAN	CLE	3	4	N	4	11/22/89
WIC	SAN	4	2	Y	4	11/22/89
STL	TAC	2	5	N	5	11/22/89
CLE	DAL	8	3	Y	8	11/24/89
KAN	SAN	4	3	Y	4	11/24/89
WIC	KAN	8	2	Y	8	11/25/89
SAN	BAL	4	5	N	5	11/25/89
TAC	STL	4	6	N	6	11/25/89
DAL	BAL	3	2	Y	3	11/26/89
SAN	KAN	5	4	Y	5	11/28/89
CLE	BAL	4	3	Y	4	12/01/89
STL	SAN	0	4	N	4	12/01/89
WIC	DAL	4	3	Y	4	12/01/89
BAL	CLE	2	3	N	3	12/02/89
DAL	KAN	6	4	Y	6	12/02/89
SAN	WIC	3	5	N	5	12/02/89
TAC	STL	4	5	N	5	12/02/89
KAN	DAL	3	1	Y	3	12/08/89
STL	BAL	2	5	N	5	12/08/89
TAC	WIC	6	5	Y	6	12/08/89
BAL	STL	5	1	Y	5	12/09/89
DAL	SAN	4	1	Y	4	12/09/89
TAC	CLE	2	4	N	4	12/09/89
		4.29	3.57		5.08	
		2.01	1.64		1.64	

3-7 *Home-Field Advantage—Soccer data listing and averages.*

```
DATA BASE QUERIES - BASKETBALL


.USE BBALL
.
.COUNT FOR HOME_WIND="Y"
     163 records
.
.COUNT FOR HOME_WIN="N"
      67 records
.
.AVERAGE HOME_SCORE
     230 records averaged
     HOME_SCORE
         108.80
.
.AVERAGE VIS_SCORE
     230 records averaged
     VIS_SCORE
        102.15
.
.AVERAGE WIN_SCORE
     230 records averaged
     WIN_SCORE
        115.29
.
.?(108.8+102.15)/2
         105.48
```

3-8 *Home-Field Advantage—Database query, basketball.*

On the backboard, shown in Fig. 3-19, Matthew used his graphs, charts, tables, and printed material, and several sports photographs, to create an attractive display. Matthew enjoyed doing his project because it dealt with sports and also proved his hypothesis. He also learned a lot about computers and became quite expert at using dBase IV, a complex database program.

He intends to expand on the project next year by including different sports, such as football, baseball, and hockey, and by using a greater portion of the sports season.

HOME_TEAM	VIS_TEAM	HOME_SCORE	VIS_SCORE	HOME-WIN	WIN_SCORE	DATE
BOS	CLE	102	89	Y	102	12/01/89
NJ	MIA	101	77	Y	101	12/01/89
IND	ORL	125	110	Y	125	12/01/89
WAS	PHI	107	90	Y	107	12/01/89
ATL	UTA	114	103	Y	114	12/01/89
PHO	LAC	111	90	Y	111	12/01/89
LAK	DET	97	108	N	108	12/01/89
POR	GOL	123	110	Y	123	12/01/89
WAS	UTA	98	100	N	100	12/02/89
ATL	PHI	100	92	Y	100	12/02/89
CLE	MIN	74	101	N	101	12/02/89
HOU	DAL	103	106	N	106	12/02/89
SAN	CHA	118	110	Y	118	12/02/89
DEN	POR	146	113	Y	146	12/02/89
PHO	NY	112	122	N	122	12/02/89
SEA	DET	120	95	Y	120	12/02/89
LAC	SAC	114	84	Y	114	12/02/89
GOL	MIL	101	98	Y	101	12/02/89
LAK	NY	115	104	Y	115	12/03/89
ORL	POR	121	95	N	121	12/04/89
NY	PHI	110	103	Y	110	12/05/89
CHA	BOS	101	114	N	114	12/05/89
MIA	POR	107	113	N	113	12/05/89
CLE	UTA	80	96	N	96	12/05/89
CHI	DEN	119	99	Y	119	12/05/89
MIN	NJ	92	90	Y	92	12/05/89
DAL	GOL	107	88	Y	107	12/05/89
SEA	HOU	133	123	Y	133	12/05/89
LAK	LAC	111	103	Y	111	12/05/89
SAC	MIL	118	103	Y	118	12/05/89
BOS	NY	113	98	Y	113	12/06/89
PHI	MIA	121	98	Y	121	12/06/89

3-9 *Home-Field Advantage—Basketball data listing and averages.*

HOME_TEAM	VIS_TEAM	HOME_SCORE	VIS_SCORE	HOME-WIN	WIN_SCORE	DATE
ORL	ATL	110	118	N	118	12/06/89
DET	WAS	115	107	Y	115	12/06/89
IND	DEN	136	117	Y	136	12/06/89
SAN	GOL	121	119	Y	121	12/06/89
CHA	POR	86	96	N	96	12/07/89
UTA	DAL	107	97	Y	107	12/07/89
LAK	PHO	100	96	Y	100	12/07/89
LAC	CLE	105	88	Y	105	12/07/89
BOS	DEN	103	102	Y	103	12/08/89
PHI	DET	107	101	Y	107	12/08/89
MIA	ORL	122	114	Y	122	12/08/89
ATL	POR	127	120	Y	127	12/08/89
IND	CHI	106	104	Y	106	12/08/89
HOU	NJ	94	99	N	99	12/08/89
DAL	SAN	93	99	N	99	12/08/89
PHO	MIL	123	98	Y	123	12/08/89
GOL	SAC	121	126	N	126	12/08/89
NY	BOS	124	92	Y	124	12/09/89
WAS	LAK	103	101	Y	103	12/09/89
CHA	DEN	93	106	N	106	12/09/89
ATL	MIN	104	91	Y	104	12/09/89
DET	IND	121	93	Y	121	12/09/89
CHI	PHI	125	105	Y	125	12/09/89
SAN	NJ	109	92	Y	109	12/09/89
UTA	HOU	104	98	Y	104	12/09/89
SEA	LAC	104	100	Y	104	12/09/89
LAC	CLE	101	108	N	108	12/09/89
		108.80	102.15		115.29	
		13.90	11.80		56.50	

3-9 *Continued*

```
ANAL.PRG 12/29/89

STOP = "F"
DO WHILE STOP "F"
  CLEAR
  *TEAM = "A TEAM'S NAME"
  *LNAME = "FULL TEAM NAME"
  ACCEPT "ENTER TEAM NAME: " TO TEAM
  ACCEPT "ENTER FULL NAME FOR TEAM: " TO LNAME
  HCNT = 0
  VCNT = 0
  HPTS = 0
  VPTS = 0
  HAVE = 0
  VAVE = 0
  HPER = 0
  VPER = 0
  HWIN = 0
  VWIN = 0
  HAVPTS = 0
  VAVPTS = 0
  HPERWIN = 0
  VPERWIN = 0
  GO TOP
  DO WHILE .NOT. EOF()
    IF HOME_TEAM = TEAM
      HCNT = HCNT + 1
      HPTS = HPTS + HOME_SCORE
      IF HOME_WIN = "Y"
        HWIN = HWIN + 1
      ENDIF
    ENDIF
    IF VIS_TEAM = TEAM
      VCNT = VCNT + 1
      VPTS = VPTS + VIS_SCORE
      IF HOME_WIN = "N"
        VWIN = VWIN + 1
      ENDIF
    ENDIF
    SKIP
  ENDDO
  HAVPTS = HPTS / HCNT
  VAVPTS = VPTS / VCNT
  HPERWIN = HWIN / HCNT
  VPERWIN = VWIN / VCNT
  CLEAR
  SET PRINT ON
  ?LNAME
  ?"  "
  ?"PERCENT WON AT HOME :    ",HPERWIN
  ?"PERCENT WON VISITING :   ",VPERWIN
  ?"AVERAGE PTS AT HOME :    ",HAVPTS
  ?"AVERAGE PTS AS VISITOR :",VAVPTS
  ?"  "
  ?"  "
  SET PRINT OFF
  ACCEPT "I WANT TO STOP (T/F):" TO STOP
ENDDO
```

3-10 *Home-Field Advantage—Analysis program.*

SAN DIEGO SOCKERS

PERCENT WON AT HOME :	0.71
PERCENT WON VISITING :	0.17
AVERAGE PTS AT HOME :	4.71
AVERAGE PTS AS VISITOR :	2.67

CLEVELAND CRUNCH

PERCENT WON AT HOME:	0.80
PERCENT WON VISITING :	0.50
AVERAGE PTS AT HOME :	6.20
AVERAGE PTS AS VISITOR :	3

KANSAS CITY COMETS

PERCENT WON AT HOME:	0.80
PERCENT WON VISITING :	0.14
AVERAGE PTS AT HOME :	4.20
AVERAGE PTS AS VISITOR :	3.14

TACOMA STARS

PERCENT WON AT HOME:	0.50
PERCENT WON VISITING :	0.17
AVERAGE PTS AT HOME :	4.17
AVERAGE PTS AS VISITOR :	2.83

ST. LOUIS STEAMERS

PERCENT WON AT HOME:	0.17
PERCENT WON VISITING :	0.43
AVERAGE PTS AT HOME :	2
AVERAGE PTS AS VISITOR :	4.14

DALLAS SIDEKICKS

PERCENT WON AT HOME:	0.86
PERCENT WON VISITING :	0.33
AVERAGE PTS AT HOME :	5
AVERAGE PTS AS VISITOR :	3.17

3-11
Home-Field Advantage—Analyzed data, MISL.

LOS ANGELES LAKERS

PERCENT WON AT HOME :	0.91
PERCENT WON VISITING :	0.57
AVERAGE PTS AT HOME :	112.27
AVERAGE PTS AS VISITOR :	101.71

PORTLAND TRAILBLAZERS

PERCENT WON AT HOME:	0.91
PERCENT WON VISITING :	0.50
AVERAGE PTS AT HOME :	113.18
AVERAGE PTS AS VISITOR :	103.63

SEATTLE SUPERSONICS

PERCENT WON AT HOME:	0.89
PERCENT WON VISITING :	0.25
AVERAGE PTS AT HOME :	117.22
AVERAGE PTS AS VISITOR :	112.88

3-12
Home-Field Advantage—Analyzed data, NBA.

PHOENIX SUNS

PERCENT WON AT HOME:	0.70
PERCENT WON VISITING :	0
AVERAGE PTS AT HOME :	115.30
AVERAGE PTS AS VISITOR :	108.40

GOLDEN STATE WARRIORS

PERCENT WON AT HOME:	0.44
PERCENT WON VISITING :	0
AVERAGE PTS AT HOME :	110
AVERAGE PTS AS VISITOR :	104.33

LOS ANGELES CLIPPERS

PERCENT WON AT HOME:	0.67
PERCENT WON VISITING :	0
AVERAGE PTS AT HOME :	107.67
AVERAGE PTS AS VISITOR :	97.67

Procedures
1. Built database files to support information requirements. 2. Collected daily scores from all NBA and MISL games from 10/27/89 through 12/09/89. 3. Entered scores into dBase IV format. 4. At end of ⅕ season: a. Designed and printed database reports to show data collected. b. Queried database to show and tabulate summary data for: 1) Home score. 2) Visiting score. 3) Winning score. c. Designed computer program to analyze data d. Created graphs to reflect summarized and analyzed data.

3-13 *Home-Field Advantage—Procedures.*

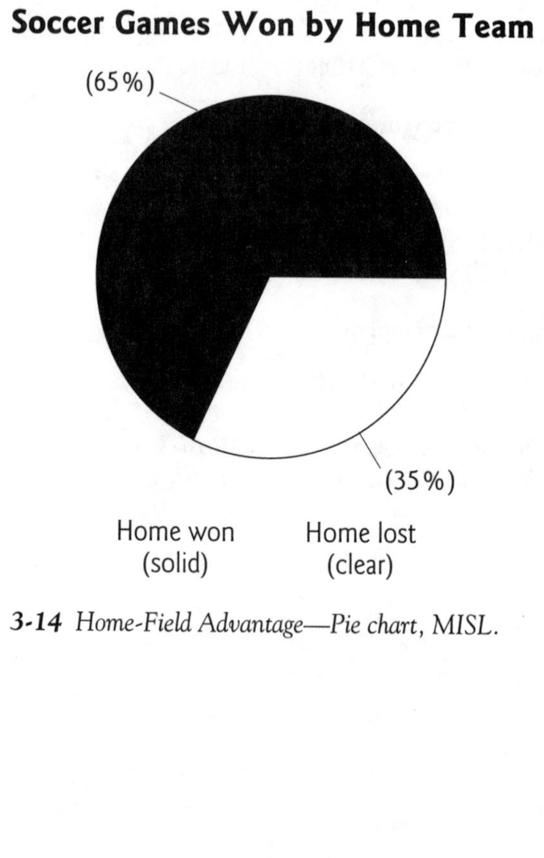

3-14 *Home-Field Advantage—Pie chart, MISL.*

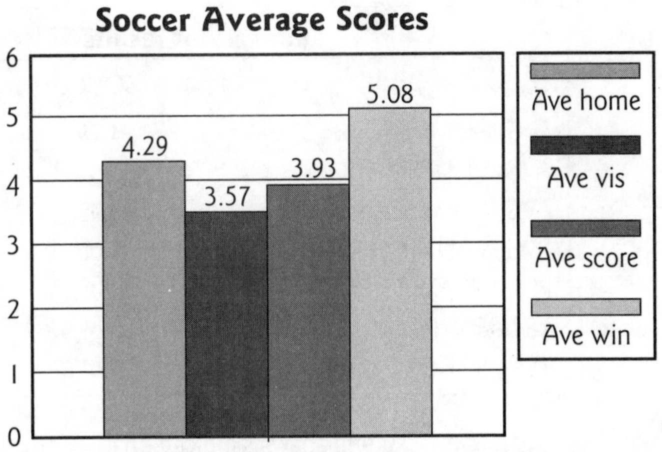

3-15 *Home-Field Advantage—Bar graph, MISL.*

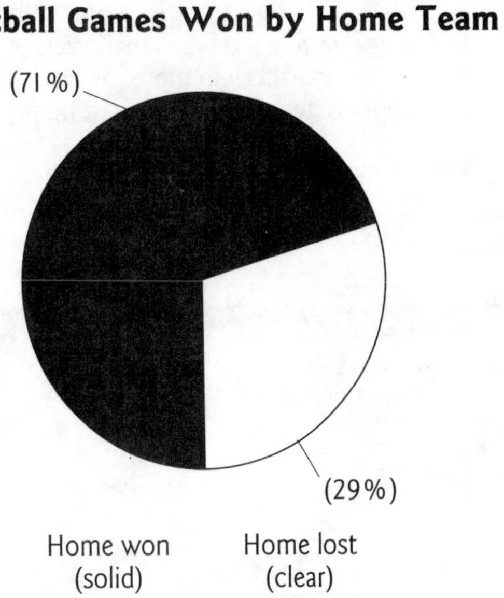

3-16 *Home-Field Advantage—Pie chart, NBA.*

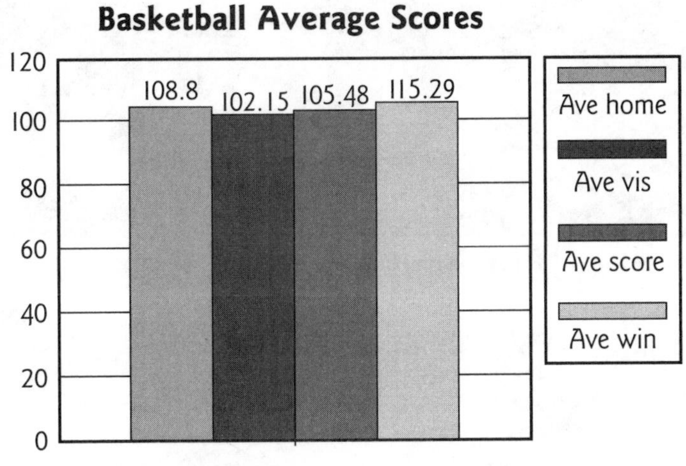

3-17 *Home-Field Advantage—Bar graph, NBA.*

Summary of results		
	SOCCER	BASKETBALL
AVG. HOME SCORE	4.29	108.8
AVG. VISITORS SCORE	3.57	102.15
AVG. TEAM SCORE	3.93	105.48
AVG. WINNING SCORE	5.08	115.29
PCT. WON BY HOME TEAM	65%	71%
TEAMS WIN MORE AT HOME	7 of 8	27 of 27
TEAMS SCORE BETTER AT HOME	5 of 8	22 of 27

The data and resulting analysis indicate that:

1. Home teams win more games.
2. Home teams score more points.
3. The average home score is greater than the average visitors score.
4. Average visitors score less than average score.
5. Majority of teams win more games at home.
6. Majority of teams score better at home.

3-18 *Home-Field Advantage—Results and conclusions.*

3-19 *Home-Field Advantage—Backboard.*

In the swim

As you have seen, major league sports are great sources of project ideas for many students. However, other sports also yield many effective topics. Talina Konotchik, a speed swimmer, managed to parlay her passion into an award-winning science project, "Which Swimsuit Material Has the Least Drag in the Water?"

Swimmers, she said, are always trying to shave a few seconds off their time. To that end, even the swimsuits they wear have an effect on the swim time. The material that produced the least drag, or resistance of an object in the water, would make the fastest suit. In the natural world, among marine animals, drag is reduced by streamlining the body and reducing friction.

Talina did part of her research using an encyclopedia on CD-ROM. "It gave me access to more material without leaving home," she said. By using a word processor to produce her report, and a spreadsheet to record, tabulate, and graph the results, she felt that the computer was a great help in getting the project done well and on time.

The object of the experiment, then, was to test a variety of swimsuit materials, as stated in the hypothesis, shown in Fig. 3-20. Talina got nine fabric samples from Speedo, a swimsuit manufacturer specializing in racing gear. Incidentally, don't hesitate to write to manufacturers for samples. They're usually quite willing to help.

PROBLEM

The purpose of my project was to find the fastest swimsuit for competition. The suit with the least drag would make one swim faster in the water so I was trying to find the material with the least drag.

HYPOTHESIS

I think the metallic sample will go the fastest because it is very smooth and its texture is like that of a porpoise or other marine animal. I don't think that the patchwork material samples will go very fast, because there is a lot of material for the water to hold onto and make the sample drag in the water. I think that if the material is similar in both directions, the one that is placed vertically will go faster than horizontally.

3-20 *Which Swimsuit Material Has the Least Drag?—Problem and hypothesis.*

Each material sample was sewed into a pocket that would hold a penny. The sample was dropped into a clear plastic tube of water, and the sample's passage through the tube was timed. A description of Talina's materials is in Fig. 3-21, and her procedures are shown in Fig. 3-22.

Each fabric sample was tested 10 times, but three of the fabrics were tested in the direction opposite to the fabric's natural stretch, for a total of 13 samples. The test showed that sample #1, the horizontal striped fabric, was the fastest, and the slowest was #7, the patchwork fabric. The charted and graphed results are shown in Figs. 3-23 through 3-25. Figure 3-26 shows the backboard.

MATERIAL #	DESCRIPTION	MADE OF
1	Black w/white stripes—horizontal	70% Nylon 25% Lycra 5% Polyester
2	Black w/white stripes—vertical	"
3	Black—horizontal	79% Nylon 21% Spandex
4	Black—vertical	"
5	Purple—horizontal	87% Nylon 13% Lycra
6	Purple—vertical	"
7	Patchwork—horizontal	55% Polyester Microfiber 45% Cotton
8	Patchwork—vertical	"
9	Yellow	85% Nylon 15% Lycra
10	Blue	90% Cotton 10% Lycra
11	Metallic	80% Nylon 20% Lycra
12	Denim	100% Cotton
13	Green	78% Nylon 22% Lycra

3-21 *Which Swimsuit Material Has the Least Drag?—Description of material samples.*

PROCEDURES

1) Sew each swimsuit material into a 6 in. by 1 in. pocket.
2) Put a penny in each pocket.
3) Mark the plastic tube .2 meters off the top and bottom of the tube.
4) Fill the tube with water.
5) Have one person drop the sample (with the penny in it) down the tube.
6) When the sample passes the first mark start the stopwatch.
7) When the sample passes the second mark stop the stopwatch.
8) Record data.
9) Empty the tube of water into a bucket to get the weight out.
10) Repeat steps 4–9 ten times for <u>each</u> sample material.

3-22 *Which Swimsuit Material Has the Least Drag?—Procedures.*

material number	trial number 1	2	3	4	5	6	7	8	9	10	total	average	std. dev.
1	3.94	3.59	3.32	3.53	3.91	3.69	3.34	3.78	3.13	3.53	35.76	3.58	0.25
2	5.37	5.35	3.72	4.75	4.88	3.97	3.56	3.75	3.25	4.28	42.88	4.29	0.72
3	5.59	5.07	4.22	4.06	4.15	3.69	3.69	4.66	4.56	4.50	44.19	4.42	0.56
4	6.41	5.06	5.07	4.88	5.00	4.81	4.75	5.47	5.09	4.53	51.07	5.11	0.49
5	7.28	5.81	5.04	5.06	4.56	4.97	4.43	4.28	5.59	4.69	51.71	5.17	0.84
6	4.65	4.53	4.38	4.78	4.22	4.00	4.40	4.53	4.19	3.53	43.21	4.32	0.34
7	8.91	8.72	6.66	8.82	7.78	8.69	8.28	8.25	7.72	7.37	81.20	8.12	0.69
8	4.66	5.22	5.40	4.91	5.22	5.15	5.37	5.00	5.25	5.44	51.62	5.16	0.23
9	3.50	3.88	3.79	3.66	3.63	3.59	3.50	3.90	3.63	4.06	37.14	3.71	0.18
10	4.47	4.28	3.97	4.25	3.50	3.71	3.68	3.97	3.66	3.75	39.24	3.92	0.30
11	5.06	4.34	3.65	4.00	3.91	4.35	3.87	4.35	3.93	4.16	41.62	4.16	0.37
12	3.91	3.21	5.34	3.32	3.35	3.47	4.78	3.91	3.68	3.32	38.29	3.83	0.67
13	3.78	4.22	3.84	3.87	3.85	3.78	3.87	3.47	3.57	3.71	37.96	3.80	0.19

material number	average	std. dev.	av. + sd	av. – sd
1	3.58	0.25	3.83	3.33
2	4.29	0.72	5.01	3.57
3	4.42	0.56	4.98	3.85
4	5.11	0.49	5.60	4.61
5	5.17	0.84	6.01	4.33
6	4.32	0.34	4.66	3.98
7	8.12	0.69	8.81	7.43
8	5.16	0.23	5.39	4.93
9	3.71	0.18	3.89	3.54
10	3.92	0.30	4.23	3.62
11	4.16	0.37	4.54	3.79
12	3.83	0.67	4.50	3.16
13	3.80	0.19	3.99	3.61

3-23 *Which Swimsuit Material Has the Least Drag?—Results.*

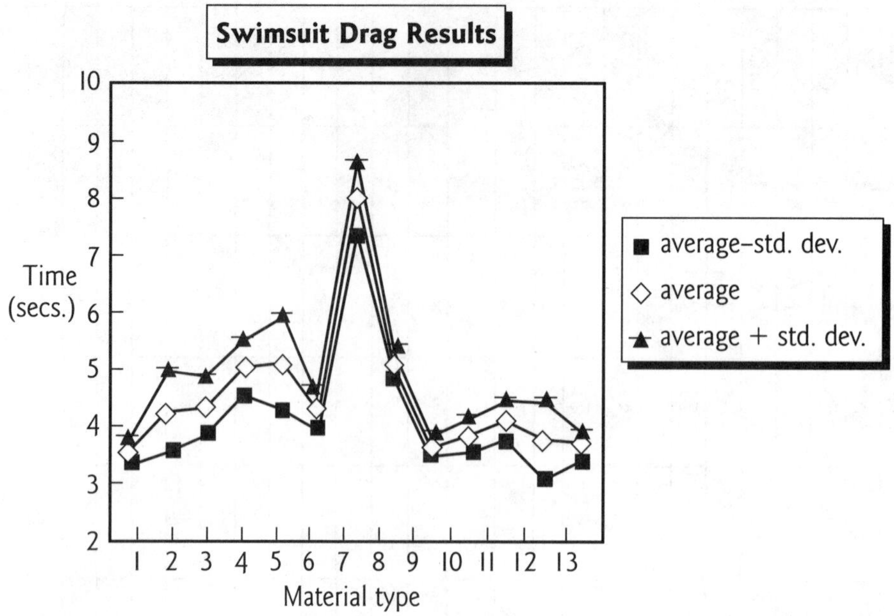

3-24 *Which Swimsuit Material Has the Least Drag?—Drag results.*

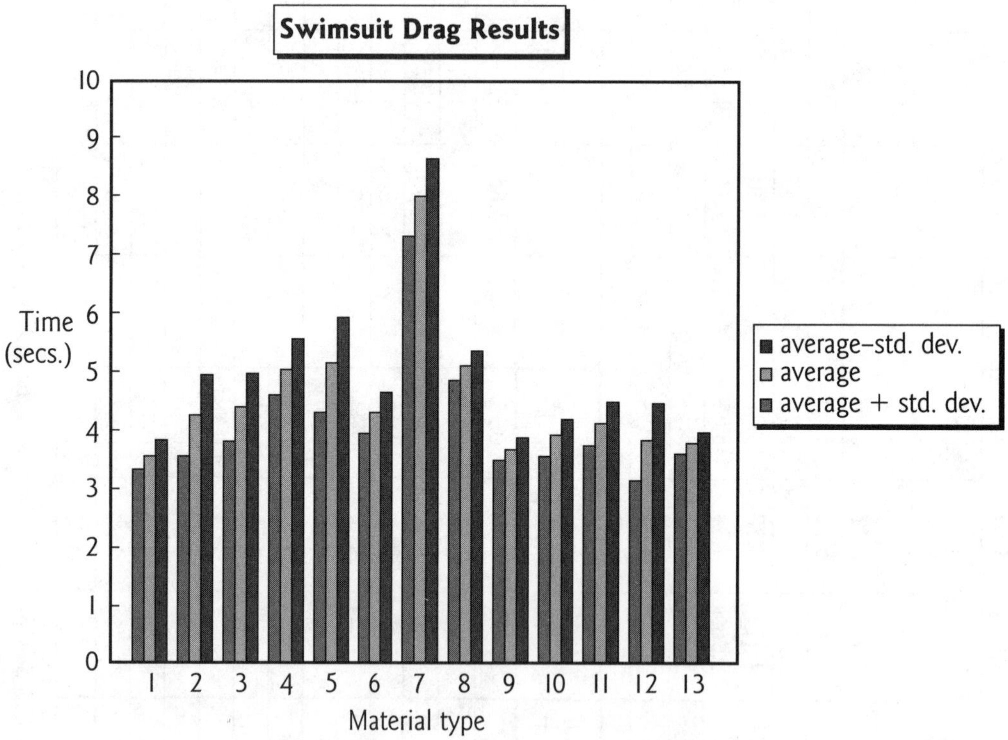

3-25 *Which Swimsuit Material Has the Least Drag?—More drag results.*

3-26 *Which Swimsuit Material Has the Least Drag?—Backboard.*

The project conclusions were that the thinnest- and lightest-weight material had the least drag. The hypothesis was proven in terms of the material with the most drag, but Talina's guess was wrong when she tried to predict the fastest material. To make the results more valid, Talina said that she would select materials that are the same weight. She would also use a longer tube to get greater variations in the results.

Talina's project display was certainly programmed to attract maximum attention. Made of hot-pink foam core with the nine swimsuit samples attached, the display would make anyone sit up and take notice. And take notice they did; Talina won first place at her school and county science fair and a place as the sweepstakes alternate in the physical sciences. Would she do it again? You bet; it was fun and rewarding.

That's the way the ball bounces

Another interesting project about sports arose from a dinner-time conversation that Aaron Barclay had with his family. How high does a tennis ball bounce? Does it bounce higher on a hard court, on clay, or on grass? An engineering project measured the bounce of tennis balls, launched from the same height at equal velocity, to determine that a hard court creates the highest bounce. Like Matthew's project, Aaron took advantage of the latest high-tech gear. He conducted the entire experiment in a little over an hour, while his father videotaped the results! The backboard for the project, entitled "Court Surface Effect on Tennis Balls," is shown in Fig. 3-27. So whatever you're into, for fitness or for fun, you can find a science project.

Helpful hints

- If you're interested in sports, you can find ideas in many categories: physics, engineering, mathematics, or even zoology.
- Take advantage of any technology that is available to you, but you do not need a computer, a video camera, or other sophisticated equipment to conduct an experiment and do a good project.

3-27 *Court Surface Effect on Tennis Balls—Backboard.*

4
What no home can be without

Some good project ideas can come from the simplest, most obvious sources. Just looking around the house, examining the food that you eat, the clothes that you wear, and the tools, products, and appliances that you use can give you an idea. These projects can fall into almost every category, from human behavior to chemistry to engineering. The following projects will demonstrate that you do not need to turn to complicated or obscure topics to find your science project. Some excellent project ideas often come from some common, everyday items.

Jolly Orville

Nguyen Vy was rather unenthusiastic about a science project, but she wanted something that related to everyday life. She came up with a list of ideas in several categories, but since one of Vy's main interests is cooking, she really wanted a topic in that field. After thinking of several ideas, Vy decided to test how well popcorn popped under different conditions.

Her teacher conducted several brainstorming sessions, both with the entire class and with individual students. As a result of these sessions, Vy planned to test room-temperature popcorn and frozen popcorn to see which popped better.

Originally she thought she would freeze the popcorn for 20 minutes, but, together with her teacher, decided that a longer freezing time would be better. They determined that the popcorn should be frozen for three days.

Vy conducted most of her research in the school library, using the encyclopedias. She also found an Orville Redenbacher recipe book, which was helpful. While doing research, Vy took notes on sheets of paper. When it was time to write the research paper, she looked for related ideas and numbered them so that she could easily arrange them into paragraphs. Vy tried to use the word processor on the Apple computers at school, but decided instead to produce a handwritten draft of the paper, edit it, and then type a final copy.

The project question and hypothesis are shown in Fig. 4-1, and the variables and controls are shown in Fig. 4-2. This project used two experimental groups, and no control groups, as shown in Fig. 4-3.

Because of the number of batches tested, this experiment was time-consuming. However, Vy completed her project with a minimum of materials and expense, as shown in Fig. 4-4. She was able to conduct the entire experiment at home, and she needed help only from her mother as "safety inspector."

To ensure that she did enough testing, Vy conducted her experiment 12 times with frozen popcorn and 12 times with room-temperature popcorn. For each trial with frozen popcorn, she took 200 kernels and froze them for three days in an uncovered bowl. Then she placed the kernels in a pot and popped them without oil for two minutes. She quickly poured the popcorn into a bowl and transferred the popped kernels to a bag. Vy counted the unpopped kernels left in the bowl, subtracted the number from the original 200 kernels, and recorded the number on her experimental log.

Vy used exactly the same procedure with the room-temperature popcorn. She conducted the 24 trials over a period of three weeks. Any time she was interrupted, or an experiment failed due to spillage or other circumstances, she discarded the sample and started again. Vy's procedures are summarized in Fig. 4-5.

Question	Hypothesis
Does frozen popcorn pop better?	Popcorn at room temperature pops better.

4-1 *Cool It, Orville Redenbacher—Question and hypothesis.*

Variables	Controls
Experimental Temperature of popcorn **Measured** Number of popped kernels Number of unpopped kernels	• Popping time • Popping method • Type of popcorn

4-2 *Cool It, Orville Redenbacher—Variables and controls.*

Experimental Groups
• Frozen popcorn • Room-temperature popcorn

4-3 *Cool It, Orville Redenbacher—Experimental and control groups.*

Materials
1. Jolly time popcorn
2. Cooking pot
3. Bowls
4. Paper bags

4-4 *Cool It, Orville Redenbacher—Materials.*

Procedures
1. Popped 200 kernels of popcorn in a pot without oil for 2 minutes
2. Poured popcorn into a bowl
3. Transferred popped kernels into a bag
4. Counted unpopped kernels left in bowl
5. Subtracted number of unpopped kernels from 200 and recorded the resulting number of popped kernels in the experimental log

4-5 *Cool It, Orville Redenbacher—Procedures.*

When all testing was complete, Vy totalled the numbers for popped and unpopped kernels in each category and calculated the average and mean number of kernels popped. She then graphed the results for frozen popcorn, as shown in Fig. 4-6, and room-temperature popcorn, as shown in Fig. 4-7. After analyzing the data, the experiments showed that popcorn kept at room temperature popped better by an average of 3¾ kernels out of 200.

Vy's backboard consisted of three equal-sized panels, using paper attached to plywood stretcher frames. She drew up a plan of what belonged on each panel, but when it was time to create the backboard, she simply attached the material, including bags of popcorn, where it fit best. Finally, partly inspired by the recipe book she found in the library, she entitled her project, entered in the engineering category, "Cool It, Orville Redenbacher."

In one way, the backboard was the most difficult part of the project, since she had to stay up late to finish it. Views of Vy's backboard are illustrated in Figs. 4-8, 4-9, and 4-10.

How would Vy improve her project? The first thing that occurred to her was to conduct more testing to further validate her results and conclusions. Another project? Perhaps, but if she does one, Vy is ready to try something more scientifically challenging.

And what did she get out of it? The project gave her scientific experience in conducting the experiment, and artistic expression in creating the backboard. She also won her first license, poetic license, by titling the project "Cool It, Orville Redenbacher," when she actually used Jolly Time popcorn!

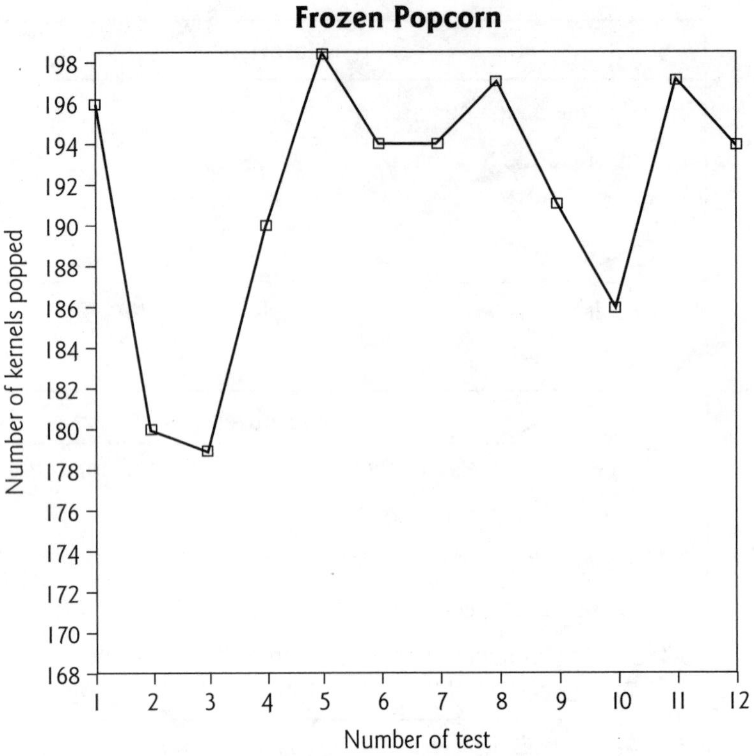

4-6 *Cool It, Orville Redenbacher—Graph of frozen popcorn.*

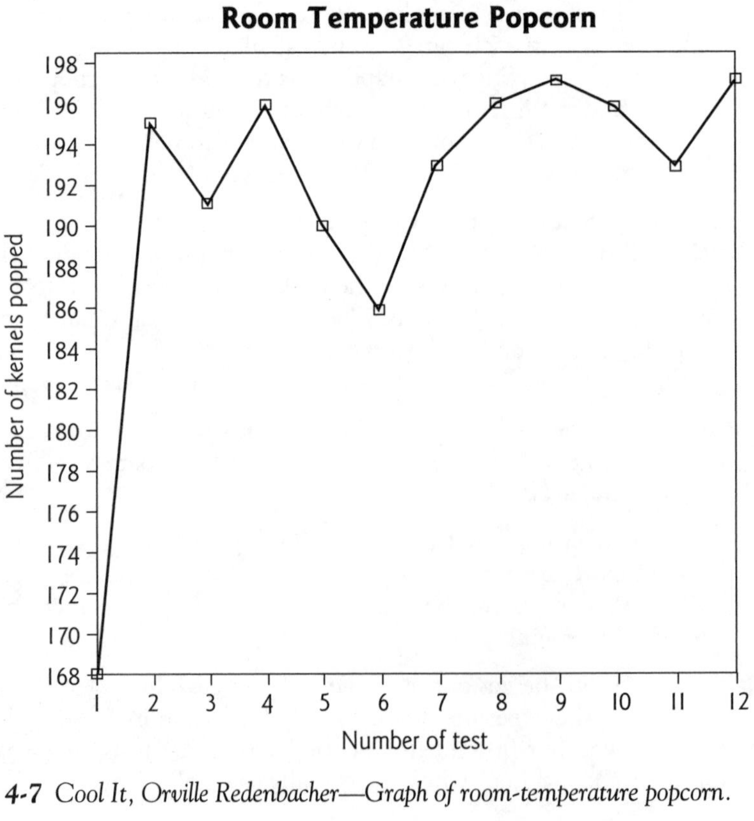

4-7 *Cool It, Orville Redenbacher—Graph of room-temperature popcorn.*

4-8 *Cool It, Orville Redenbacher—Backboard.*

4-9 *Cool It, Orville Redenbacher—Backboard.*

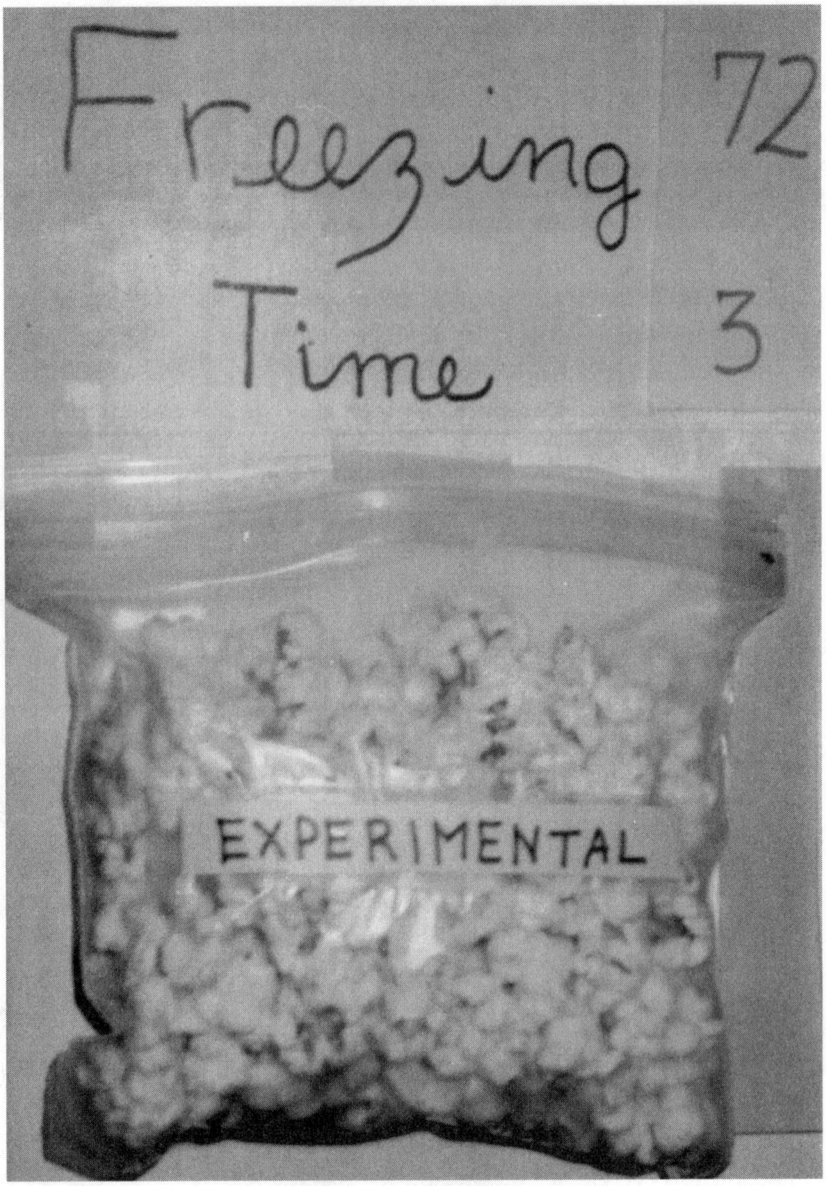

4-10 *Cool It, Orville Redenbacher—Backboard.*

Which wood would you pick if you could...

Another physics project that evolved from family concerns was Justin Evenson's project, "Water Absorption in Nine Selected Woods." While his family was enduring the joys and tribulations of home remodeling, Justin wondered why certain woods were chosen for specific uses, and why a redwood fence (a material popular in the area) needed to be replaced with a more durable material.

It turned out that the single most important factor in choosing wood for outdoor use was the amount of water the wood could absorb. To determine, which woods to test, Justin consulted the contractors involved in the home remodeling and decided to use cedar, cherry, Douglas fir, mahogany, maple, oak, pine, poplar, and redwood. As part of his background research, he gathered some basic facts about each type, as shown in the sample in Fig. 4-11. He then developed the statement of problem and hypothesis, as shown in Figs. 4-12 and 4-13.

For this project, Justin's procedures were quite specific. After gathering the woods, he measured, cut, and sanded them to create uniform samples. All the pieces of wood were completely submerged in water in a large barrel. At the same time each day, Justin took the samples out of the water, weighed them, recorded the results, and replaced the samples in the barrel, adding water if necessary to cover all the samples. Justin's procedures are shown in Fig. 4-14.

After 23 days, Justin entered the data in Excel, a popular spreadsheet program, and produced his results, showing the total amount of water absorbed, and the amount of water as a percentage of weight. Figure 4-15 shows the weight per observation day of all types of wood, and Figs. 4-16 and 4-17 show samples of the graphs for each type of wood individually. Before drawing his conclusions, he graphed the comparative weight gain in a variety of ways, as shown in Figs. 4-18 and 4-19.

Pine

Basic Description: Pine has a rounded crown with a large trunk, Height is between 30 meters to 46 meters and its diameter is between .8 meters to 1.2 meters. Pine is often much taller than 46 meters.

Habitat: Pine grows in moist soils in high mountains, usually with other conifers.

Range: Pine grows in the Cascade mountains and coast ranges from Washington to California.

Common uses: Pines uses include timber, pulp, tar, and is used as ornamental pieces.

Poplar

Basic Description: Poplar is a tree with narrow conical cones of slender, upright branches. It is 15 meters high and .5 meter in diameter. Poplar is a short lined fast growing tree.

Habitat: Poplar grows in moist soils of valleys, mountain streams, sandbars and flood plains, and on low slopes.

Range: Poplar grows across North America to tree line in Alaska to British Columbia. It also grows south to Pennsylvania and west to ?????, and in Colorado and the Rocky Mountains.

Common uses: Poplar is used in light construction, paper pulp, and crate making.

Conclusion: Poplar is a sappy, fast growing, porous, loose grained wood. Its primary use is paper pulp.

Redwood

Basic description: Redwood is the world's tallest tree. Its height can be over 10 meters tall, and its diameter is usually 3 meters to 4.6 meters. It has a reddish brown trunk and is enlarged and buttressed at the base of the trunk.

4-11 *Water Absorption in Nine Selected Woods—Information about samples.*

STATEMENT OF THE PROBLEM

For years certain woods were selected for particular projects, such as, shipbuilding, fence construction, ornamental objects, etc. Shipbuilders would, in the past, select a certain type of wood for the bottom of boats. Probably the wood was found through trial and error, to be the best suited. Carpenters use woods for their appearance, hardness, and the ability of some species to resist pests, such as, termites. This project will look at 9 different species of wood and their ability to resist absorption of water. The results of this project can be used to determine with accuracy which specie of wood is best for use in a wet damp environment.

4-12 *Water Absorption in Nine Selected Woods—Problem.*

HYPOTHESIS

Cherry wood will absorb more water than other varieties of natural wood.

4-13 *Water Absorption in Nine Selected Woods—Hypothesis.*

PROCEDURES

1. Gathered research on the topic of wood absorption and related topics.
2. Developed hypothesis.
3. Purchased scale that reads in grams to the nearest 1/10 gram.
4. Obtained 9 varieties of wood.
5. Cut all varieties to the same dimensions to within plus or minus 1 millimeter.
6. Sanded all wood with 150-grit sandpaper to obtain uniform surface.
7. Weighed wood samples to obtain dry weight.
8. Obtained large plastic jar.
9. Filled plastic jar with tap water.
10. Put all wood varieties in plastic jar and completely submerged.
11. Remove all wood every 24 hours, plus or minus 1 hour, for the purpose of weighing the samples.
12. Wipe each piece of wood to remove any excess water.
13. Weigh wood.
14. Replace wood samples into plastic jar with old water.
15. Add additional water to plastic jar as needed to top off and assure that all samples are completely submerged.
16. Repeat steps 11 through 15 for 23 repetitions.

4-14 *Water Absorption in Nine Selected Woods—Procedures.*

Varieties		Weight Per Observation Day																						
of Wood	Day Dry	Day 1	Day 2	Day 3	Day 4	Day 5	Day 6	Day 7	Day 8	Day 9	Day 10	Day 11	Day 12	Day 13	Day 14	Day 15	Day 16	Day 17	Day 18	Day 19	Day 20	Day 21	Day 22	Day 23
Cedar	41.0	53.0	55.7	57.9	59.5	61.5	62.7	64.0	65.2	66.3	67.2	68.3	69.5	70.1	70.2	71.1	71.8	72.3	72.8	74.2	73.7	74.0	74.3	74.6
Cherry	69.3	81.7	85.7	89.4	91.9	95.0	96.8	98.3	99.9	101.3	102.5	104.0	105.2	105.9	106.3	108.0	108.2	108.9	109.9	110.6	110.9	111.7	112.2	113.3
Douglas Fir	76.8	86.3	88.5	91.0	92.3	94.4	95.6	96.7	97.5	98.6	98.9	99.9	101.0	101.3	101.5	103.3	102.8	103.2	103.5	105.1	104.3	104.4	105.0	105.6
Mahogany	84.3	91.5	93.7	95.9	57.2	98.9	100.0	101.0	101.8	102.7	103.3	104.5	105.3	105.5	106.5	106.9	107.1	107.6	108.2	109.4	108.5	109.2	109.9	110.5
Maple	103.0	118.4	123.9	128.3	131.4	136.1	139.1	141.5	143.5	144.9	146.3	147.2	148.6	149.0	150.2	150.3	150.9	151.9	152.5	154.4	153.5	153.9	154.4	155.0
Oak	99.5	115.4	120.5	125.0	127.7	130.7	132.9	134.6	136.0	137.4	138.9	140.1	141.7	142.3	143.3	144.3	145.4	145.7	146.3	147.6	147.4	148.2	148.6	149.9
Pine	45.1	63.5	63.9	65.8	68.1	72.5	75.4	78.4	81.5	83.1	84.6	84.8	86.4	85.7	85.5	85.5	86.7	87.0	87.1	88.9	87.4	86.8	87.6	88.3
Poplar	49.7	83.8	90.9	97.9	101.7	107.1	110.8	113.4	115.3	117.0	118.7	119.0	120.9	121.1	121.1	122.6	123.6	124.4	124.9	127.0	125.2	125.5	126.4	127.4
Redwood	42.0	82.2	54.5	56.8	58.7	61.3	62.6	64.1	65.1	66.0	66.9	68.1	68.8	69.6	70.3	71.1	71.5	72.2	72.8	74.7	73.7	74.1	74.2	75.3

4-15 *Water Absorption in Nine Selected Woods—Daily observations.*

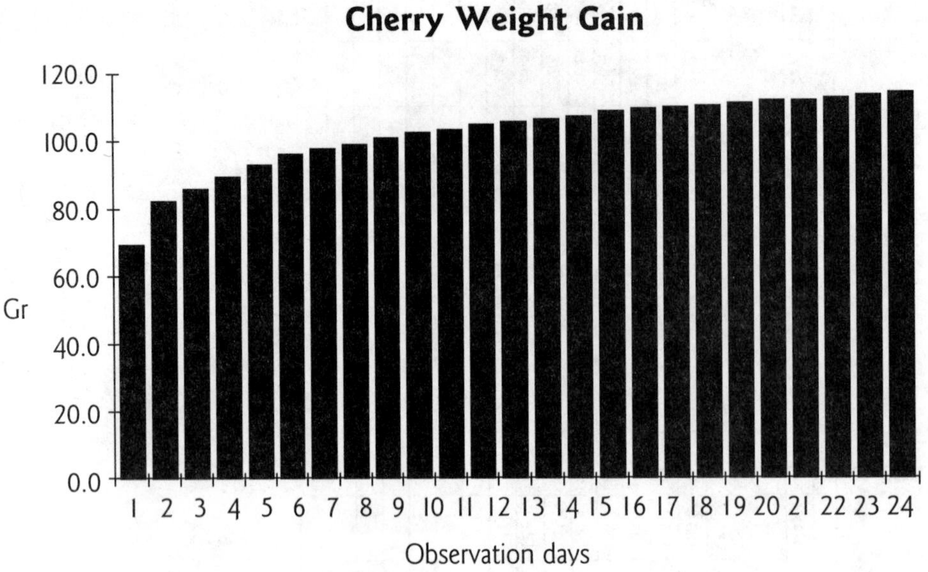

4-16 *Water Absorption in Nine Selected Woods—Graphs of wood type (cherry).*

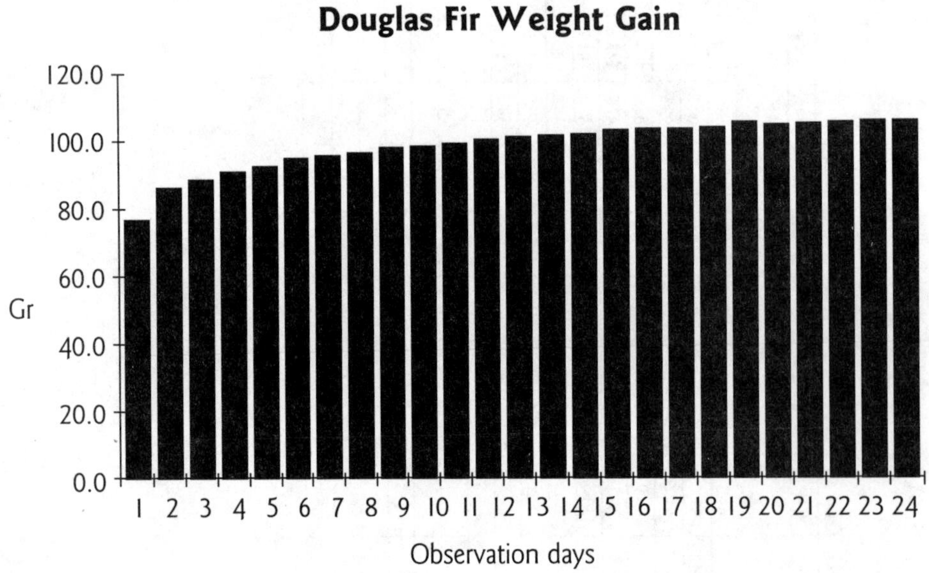

4-17 *Water Absorption in Nine Selected Woods—Graphs of wood type (Douglas fir).*

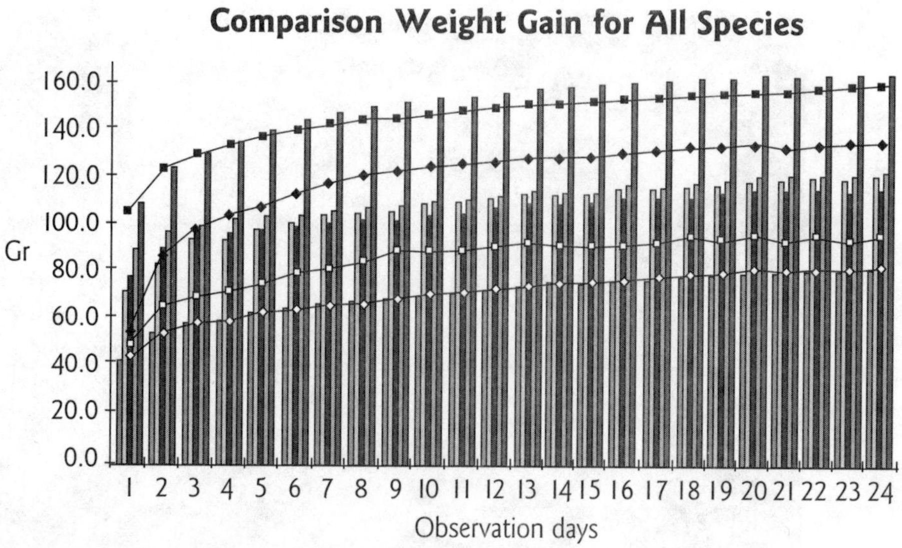

4-18 *Water Absorption in Nine Selected Woods—Graphs—Comparative weight gain.*

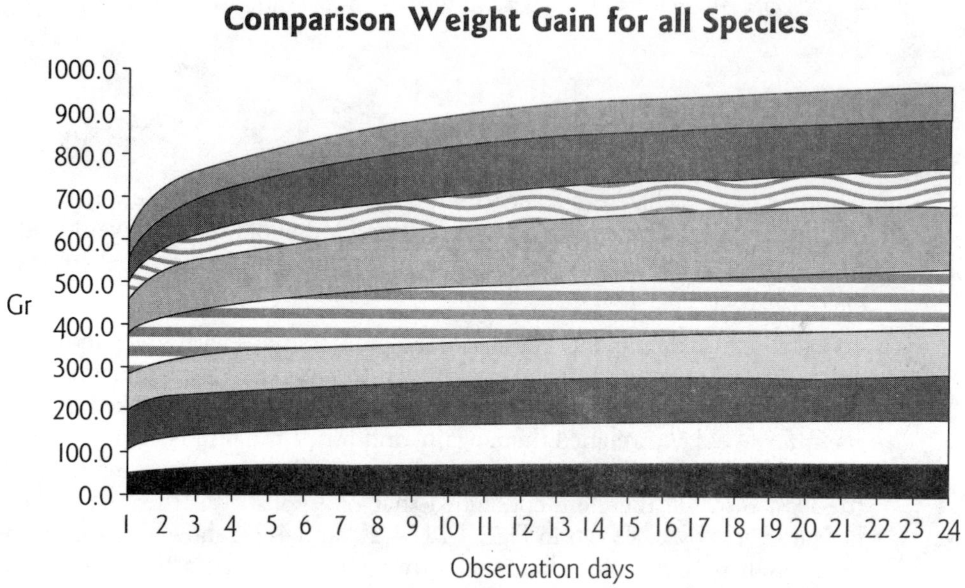

4-19 *Water Absorption in Nine Selected Woods—Graphs—Comparative weight gain.*

Justin produced his notebook with Word for Windows, and he made his graphs based on the data entered in Excel. For his display, Justin included photos of the project on his backboard, as well as the container used to soak the woods. The project display is shown in Fig. 4-20.

4-20 *Water Absorption in Nine Selected Woods—Backboard.*

Rusty nails

Another project that uses some common household items is LeMar Slater's chemistry experiment, entitled "Will Certain Household Items Prevent Rust?" This project tested four common household products for their sealant, rust-preventative properties.

To execute his experiment, LeMar coated ordinary nails with four substances: nail polish, glue, motor oil, and cooking oil, leaving a fifth group uncoated as the control group. He weighed each of the five groups of nails, soaked them in water for five days, weighed them again, and noted the results. The nails that were lightest in weight, the group coated in nail polish, was the group that had the least rust. He therefore concluded that nail polish was the best sealant. LeMar's backboard, shown in Figs. 4-21, 4-22, and 4-23, showed not only the question, hypothesis, procedures, and other written materials, but also had the rusted nails mounted on the panels.

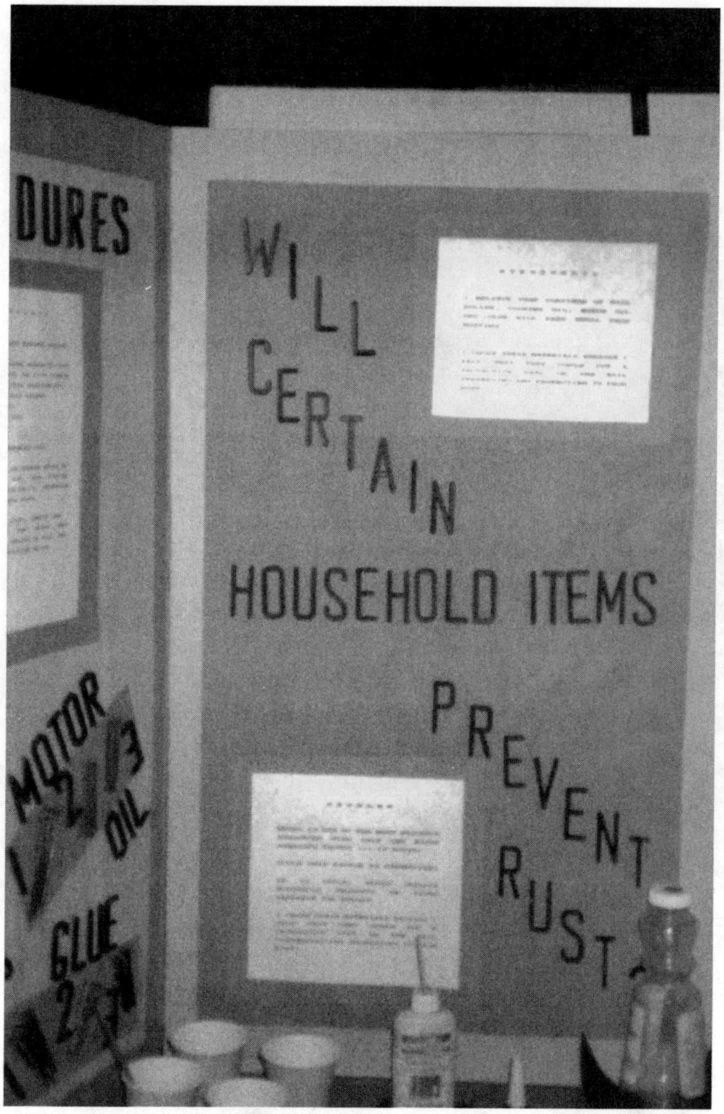

4-21 *Will Certain Household Items Prevent Rust?—Backboard.*

4-22
Will Certain Household Items Prevent Rust?—Backboard.

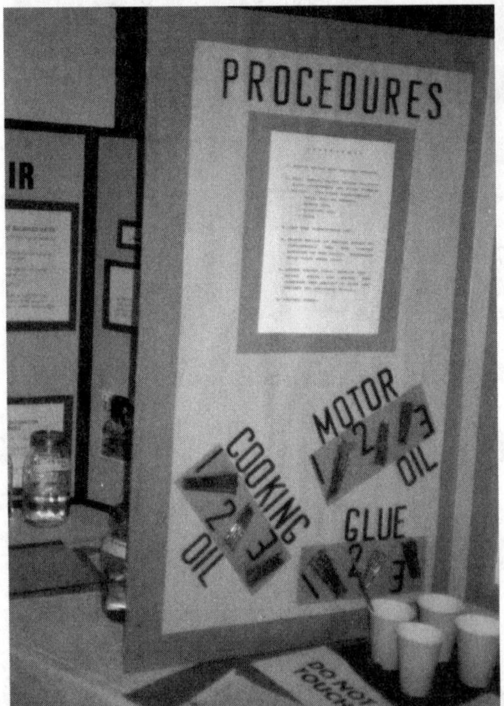

4-23
Will Certain Household Items Prevent Rust?—Backboard.

5
Family ties

These days everyone talks about family values and what it takes to keep families together. There's no doubt that doing a science project can certainly bring family members together when they work as a team. The next two projects show that families can participate in many different ways.

It's no accident

One place to get ideas is from your family, and Elizabeth Eubanks did that with great success. Faced with needing to do a science project, she looked at her family, and found not only a science project, but also her main supporter and mentor in her dad.

Elizabeth's father reconstructs traffic accidents; he determines, after the fact, what really happened after the people involved have told their stories and the police have made their reports. One of the greatest contributing factors appeared to be that cars followed each other too closely, so Elizabeth decided to statistically determine if this was so.

Although her dad was a great wealth of information (and, in fact, got her started by bringing some books from the DMV and excerpts from the vehicle code), she found that she needed to consult some outside sources in order to complete her background research paper. Elizabeth visited just about every library in San Diego, including all the university libraries, to get the information that she needed. In fact, this seems to be true of many students that I talked to. The available research does not exist in just one place. Most students need to cast their nets farther afield than their neighborhood library to find what they need.

The question, Do Cars Follow Too Closely? (which also became the title of the project), naturally flowed into her hypothesis, shown in Fig. 5-1. The procedures for the project were fairly straightforward. Elizabeth planned to time cars to find their following distances at different speeds. To make life easier, she prepared a table on her computer, using a Lotus 1-2-3 spreadsheet. This gave her

Hypothesis

Cars do not appear to follow at a safe following distance for their speed. If a car follows at 90 feet, which is the safe following distance at 25 mph, then that would not be a safe following distance at a higher speed. Cars need to adjust their following distance to fit the speed they are traveling.

5-1 *Do You Follow Too Closely?—Hypothesis.*

a way to enter the data as she collected it. Then she got a stopwatch so that she could time cars whenever she was in the car. Timing involved starting the stopwatch when the rear of a lead car passed a given point, and then stopping the timer when the front of the next car passed the same point.

Project activity was not just limited to local trips around town. Elizabeth even timed cars on a family trip to Disneyland. To help her, she also enlisted her dad to time cars for her. To keep track of everything that they did, Elizabeth maintained a daily log (which she eventually entered in WordPerfect 5.1 to include in her notebook.) A page from the daily log is included in Fig. 5-2.

Every few days, she entered the data on the Lotus 1-2-3 spreadsheet. "I didn't really want to get on the computer every day," she explained, "but I didn't want to leave it all for the last minute either."

"It really got to be fun," said Elizabeth. She reported that she got much more proficient at starting and stopping the stopwatch as the project went on. The project was done between October and January, and a total of 5,713 samples were collected.

When Elizabeth was finished gathering and entering her data, she compiled her results. Because the data was already on the computer, she used the spreadsheet to tabulate, arrange, and graph the information, as shown in Figs. 5-3 through 5-6. Then Elizabeth drew her conclusions, based on her observations and results, as shown in Figs. 5-7 through 5-9.

To create the science fair notebook, Elizabeth formatted and printed the written material from WordPerfect and the tables and graphs from Lotus 1-2-3. The backboard, constructed from blue foam core, contained photos that she took during the project, and an accident photo from her father's files. She also included some of her father's files. A portion of the backboard is shown in Fig. 5-10.

At the science fair, Elizabeth received a second-place award in physics. Because she viewed this experiment not only as a science project but also as a public service, she left DMV cards at her project display, shown in Figs. 5-11 and 5-12, explaining safe stopping distances.

Daily Log

October 13, 1994
I got my project approved. I started on my project. Dad had some DMV driver handbooks and the Vehicle Code. So I got some information from that.

October 14, 1994
I went through some of Dad's books, and found a book on the 3 second rule.

October 15, 1994
I found more books on my topic. This topic is a very good topic. It has a lot of information on it. I started timing the cars today.

October 21, 1994
Turned in topic idea.

October 22, 1994
I went to the library today to find books. I found 5 books but I had to have them shipped to the library near my house.

October 25, 1994
I timed cars. I read through some of the books that came from my library, near my house.

October 28, 1994
Timed cars while driving.

November 8, 1994
Turned in Bibliography.

November 10, 1994
I timed cars. I went to UCSD to find some books on my topic. Then after going to UCSD, I went to the DMV.

I found approximately 5–10 books and pamphlets. I went home and started reading the books and pamphlets.

November 11, 1994
I timed cars. I went to SDSU to find more books on my subject I only found a couple.

After going to SDSU I went to the Auto Club and got some pamphlets. I did read them.

November 12, 1994
I timed cars and read some of the books.

November 15, 1994
I timed cars.

5-2 *Do You Follow Too Closely?—Daily log.*

Results

During my observations, we timed 5,731 vehicles at speeds ranging from 25–65 mph. The minimum time was someone following at 0.10 seconds, and maximum time of 4.3 seconds both times at 65 mph. The gathering of all data was done in good weather conditions.

The data gathered for this experiment is found in Table 1. The minimum time represents the shortest distance between two vehicles at that speed. The maximum time represents the longest time between two vehicles. The average is the numerical result obtained by dividing the sum of the gathered times by the number of quantities.

Speeds	**25**	**30**	**35**	**40**	**45**	**50**	**55**	**60**	**65**
Total	**2772**	**Observer One**							
Count	99	108	201	125	190	60	88	180	1721
Average	1.34	1.41	1.40	1.30	1.33	1.09	1.11	1.24	1.22
Minimum	0.36	0.31	0.21	0.30	0.18	0.24	0.30	0.20	0.10
Maximum	4.09	3.31	4.20	3.32	4.00	3.62	3.46	3.94	4.30
Total	**2959**	**Observer Two**							
Count	112	152	128	137	147	86	221	912	1064
Average	1.58	1.44	1.53	1.5	1.5	1.2	1.09	1.06	1.04
Minimum	0.27	0.11	0.24	0.11	0.22	0.21	0.12	0.15	0.10
Maximum	3.91	3.46	3.14	3.79	3.49	3.24	3.55	3.99	3.83
Total	**5731**	**Combined**							
Count	211	260	329	262	337	146	309	1092	2785
Average	1.47	1.43	1.46	1.41	1.41	1.16	1.10	1.09	1.16
Minimum	0.30	0.10	0.20	0.10	0.20	0.20	0.10	0.21	0.10
Maximum	4.10	3.50	4.20	3.80	4.00	3.60	3.60	4.00	4.30

Table 1

As you can see in Table 1, there is not much difference between the observers' data and the average of the two. The greatest difference between the times found between the two observers is 0.24 sec. The smallest difference between the two is 0.02 sec.

5-3 *Do You Follow Too Closely?—Results.*

Average Times

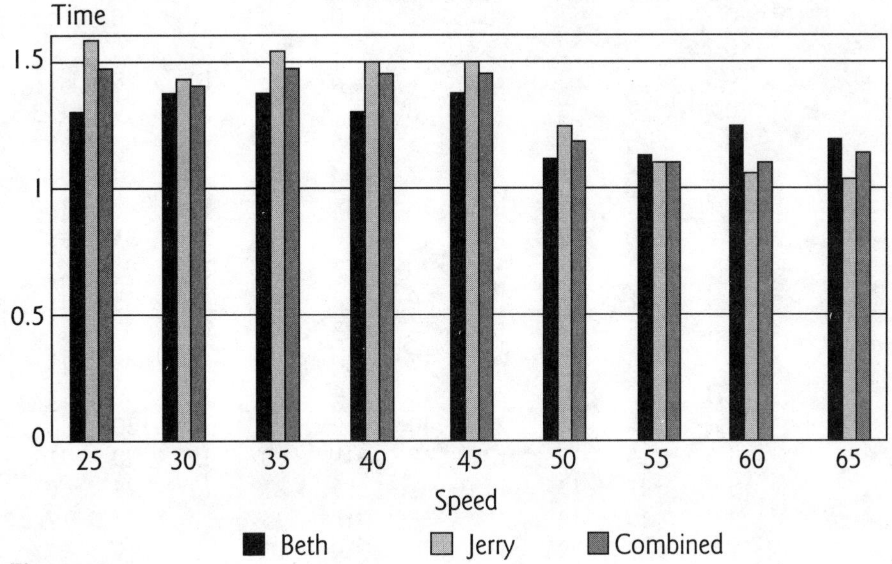

Figure 1

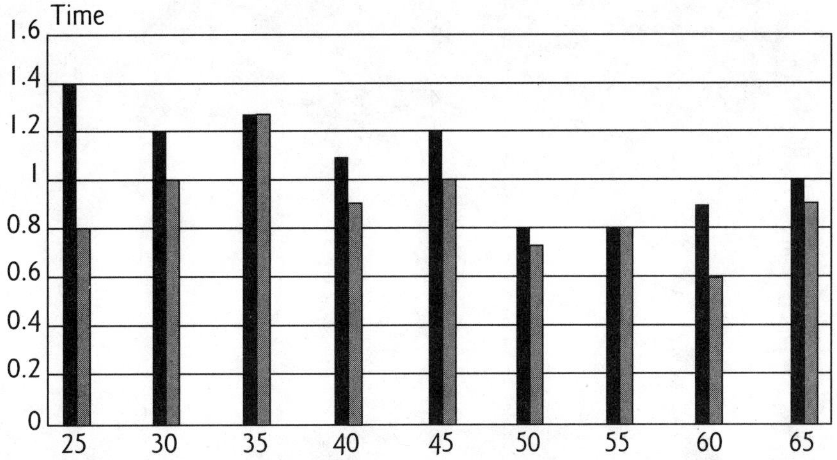

	25	30	35	40	45	50	55	60	65
Median	1.4	1.2	1.3	1.1	1.2	0.8	0.8	0.9	1
Mode	0.8	1	1.3	0.9	1	0.7	0.8	0.6	0.9

Speed

■ Median ■ Mode

Figure 2

5-4 *Do You Follow Too Closely?—Results.*

	Speed (mph)								
Time	25	30	35	40	45	50	55	60	65
0.1	0	1	0	1	0	0	1	0	13
0.2	0	2	3	4	4	2	4	20	61
0.3	1	3	3	7	4	6	14	28	117
0.4	2	4	7	8	7	5	17	59	173
0.5	4	13	10	13	15	4	24	96	187
0.6	6	12	12	7	14	14	27	111	171
0.7	12	11	19	18	11	19	19	97	186
0.8	20	12	16	10	20	7	35	85	193
0.9	13	15	21	20	23	14	15	91	211
1	11	21	17	9	22	10	18	63	161
1.1	5	14	14	18	23	10	12	73	170
1.2	15	11	20	17	20	7	17	43	135
1.3	10	14	24	15	19	2	16	36	122
1.4	12	11	21	10	19	3	11	30	105
1.5	15	13	12	8	11	8	11	40	116
1.6	11	13	17	8	15	3	10	28	71
1.7	10	13	11	6	11	5	14	23	76
1.8	9	9	16	10	9	3	6	19	77
1.9	12	14	12	6	12	4	8	23	64
2	6	7	13	9	17	2	4	17	43
2.1	6	7	4	5	12	4	3	11	53
2.2	9	4	9	7	8	3	1	17	43
2.3	2	4	13	6	3	3	6	14	24
2.4	1	3	6	6	12	1	2	11	32
2.5	2	5	4	8	3	0	2	10	32
2.6	2	7	1	6	1	0	3	6	25
2.7	5	4	4	4	2	1	1	11	18
2.8	3	4	1	5	4	1	2	9	27
2.9	2	3	5	4	3	1	2	1	18
3	1	1	4	1	2	1	1	4	13
3.1	0	0	4	2	4	1	1	3	10
3.2	0	2	0	0	0	0	1	3	9
3.3	0	2	1	2	2	1	1	0	8
3.4	1	0	1	0	2	0	0	3	5
3.5	0	1	0	1	2	0	0	1	7
3.6	1	0	0	0	0	0	0	1	2
3.7	0	0	0	0	0	1	0	0	1
3.8	0	0	0	1	0	0	0	3	3
3.9	1	0	2	0	0	0	0	1	2
4	0	0	0	0	1	0	0	1	0
4.1	1	0	1	0	0	0	0	0	0
4.2	0	0	0	0	0	0	0	0	0
4.3	0	0	1	0	0	0	0	0	1

Table 2

5-5 *Do You Follow Too Closely?—Results.*

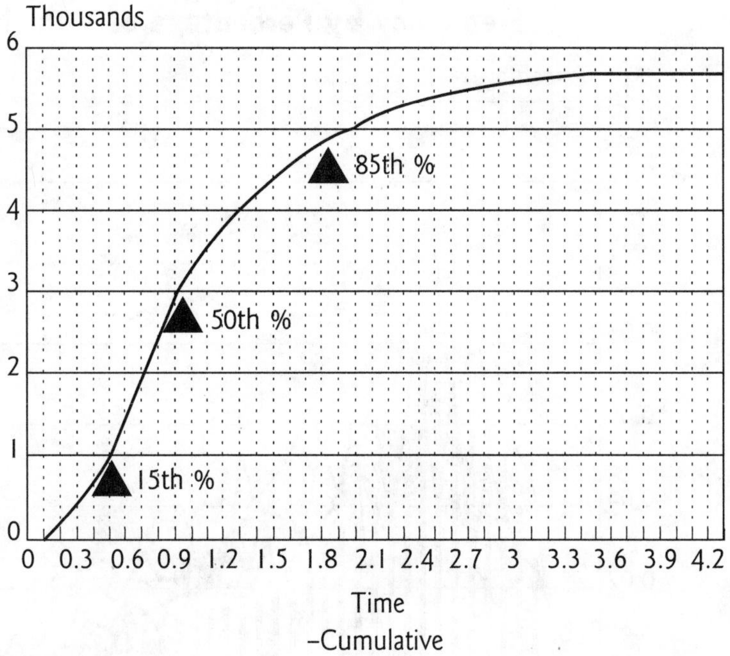

Figure 3

From a review of the data found in this research, it can be determined that 50 percent of the drivers observed followed the car ahead of them at one second or under. More than 86% of the drivers tested follow at two or less seconds, while 98.1% of the drivers follow at 3 seconds or less. This can be seen in figure 3.

5-6 *Do You Follow Too Closely?—Results.*

Conclusions

People do follow too closely. I saw people literally riding on the tail of the car in front of them. I also saw people cut in between two cars that already had no adequate space between them. The survey data clearly shows that most drivers follow the car in front of them too closely for the speed they're travelling.

Assume the 3–4 second rule is correct, my study shows that people need to expand their following distance. For bad conditions such as rain, ice or fog people need to drive even farther apart then in good conditions. Most people are following at an unsafe distance for all speeds.

5-7 *Do You Follow Too Closely?—Conclusion.*

Frequency by Percentage of Vehicles

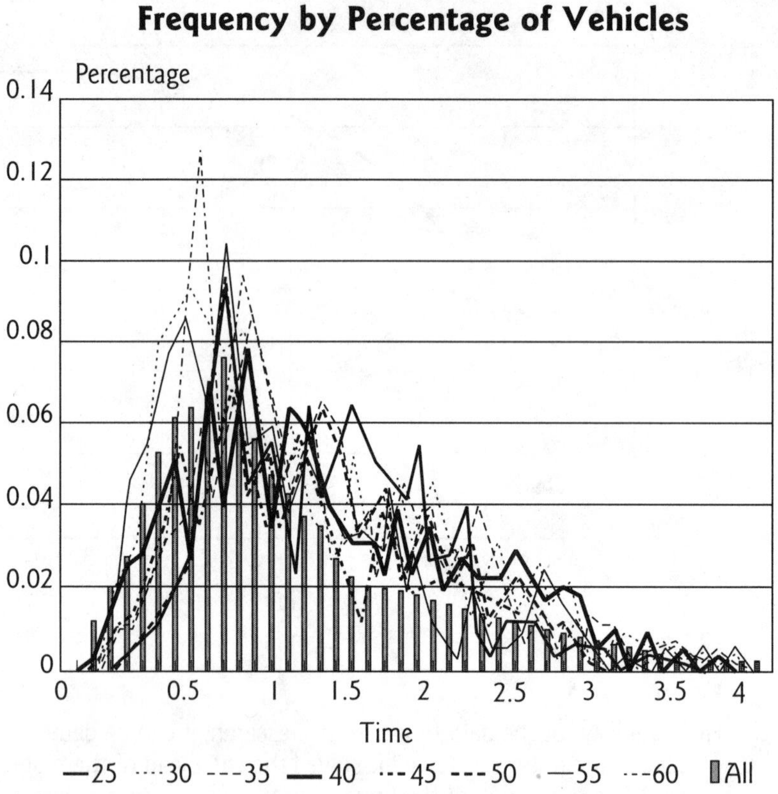

5-8 *Do You Follow Too Closely?—Conclusion.*

25	30	35	40	45	50	55	60	65
Avg dist	54	63	75	83	93	85	89	96	110
20' per 10 mph	50	60	70	80	90	100	110	120	130
2 sec rule	73	88	103	117	132	147	161	176	191
3 sec rule	110	132	154	176	198	220	242	264	286
4 sec rule	147	176	205	235	264	293	323	352	381
percentage	0.49	0.48	0.49	0.47	0.47	0.39	0.37	0.36	0.38

* Avg dist —20' per 10 mph —2 sec rule
—3 sec rule —4 sec rule ◆Percentage

5-9 *Do You Follow Too Closely?—Conclusion.*

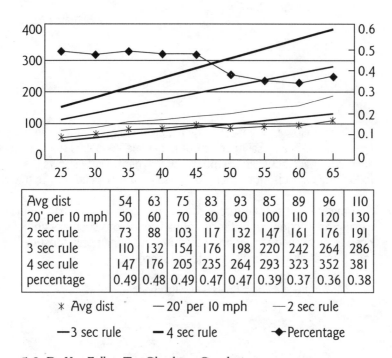

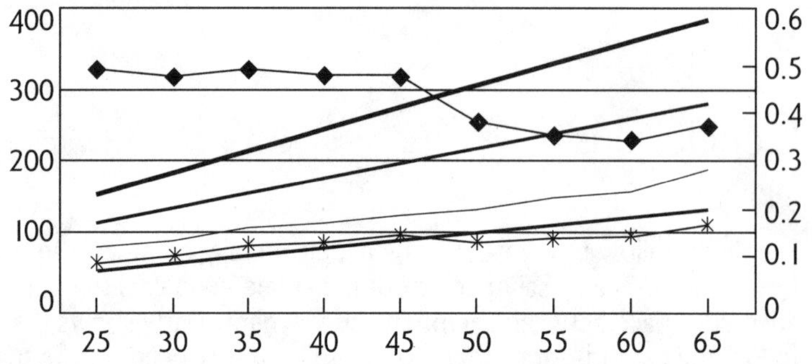

5-10 *Do You Follow Too Closely?—Backboard.*

Stopping Distance Chart

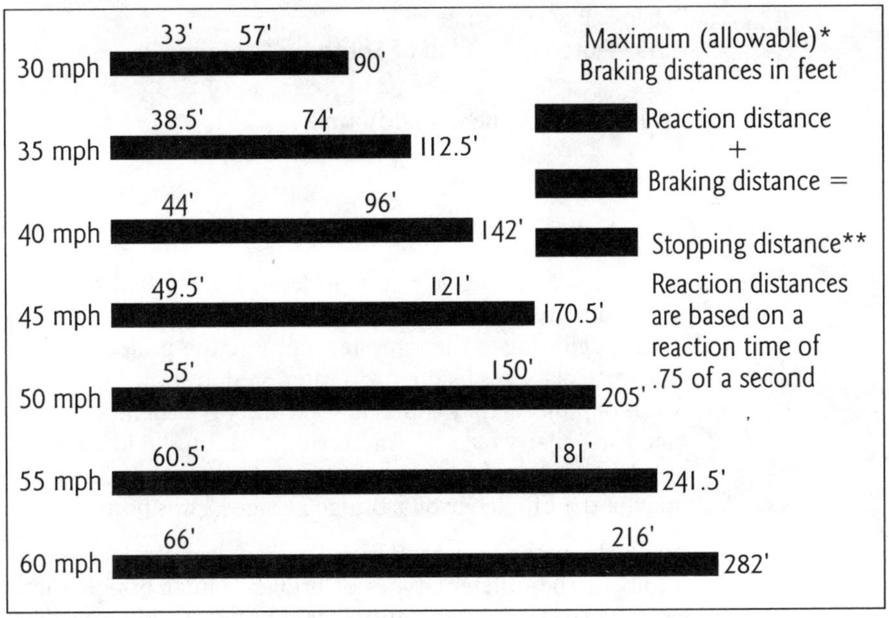

* Federal Motor Vehicle Safety Standard (FMVSS) #105-76 requires all new passenger cars to brake to a stop in no more than the distances above from these speeds.

** Total Stopping Distance is made up of Perception Distance + Reaction Distance + Braking Distance. (These terms are explained on reverse side.)

5-11 *Do You Follow Too Closely?—DMV card.*

The Three-Second Rule for Stopping Distance Safety

Total stopping distance is how far it takes you to brake to a stop. These elements are involved:

1) Driver sees something to stop for (perception distance)
2) Driver reacts by applying brakes (reaction distance)
3) Driver slows to a stop by braking (braking distance)

The best rule to determine a safe following distance is the THREE-SECOND RULE.

Here's what you do. When the vehicle ahead passes a point you have chosen on the road ahead, count how long it takes you to reach there. If you are three seconds back, you should be able to count "one thousand and one, one thousand and two, one thousand and three." In order to see, decide and react to a vehicle slowing ahead, you need three seconds: time to recognize what's happening and then time to react.

Using this rule should provide sufficient following distance to avoid a collision in most situations. However, a tired, inattentive or impaired driver takes longer to perceive, decide and react. Vehicles with poor brakes and those carrying or pulling extra weight also stop more slowly. And braking distances are greater on slippery roads or uneven surfaces. Under any of these conditions, you will need more time and space and should use a FOUR-SECOND or longer RULE. So, the THREE-SECOND RULE is really the three-second MINIMUM rule.

60376 8-91

Public Safety Department

5-12 *Do You Follow Too Closely?—DMV card.*

Building bridges

When Ben Stein was trying to get a project idea, he had no idea what he wanted to do, so he reviewed the list of possible projects that his teacher distributed at the beginning of the semester. Because the project was required for his honors science class, his teacher was interested in showing her students the different kinds of projects they could do. Ben and his father looked over the list to find something that would be interesting and fun. "Although my Dad's a doctor," he said, "we thought it would be fun to build bridges." And so the project, "A Study of the Efficiency of 5 Bridge Designs," was born.

Before actually doing the project, Ben did a good deal of background research, finding out about the different types of bridges, girder bridges, arch bridges, truss bridges, suspension bridges, cantilevered bridges, cable-stayed bridges and drawbridges. He also described the different types of force exerted on bridges, as shown in Figs. 5-13 through 5-16.

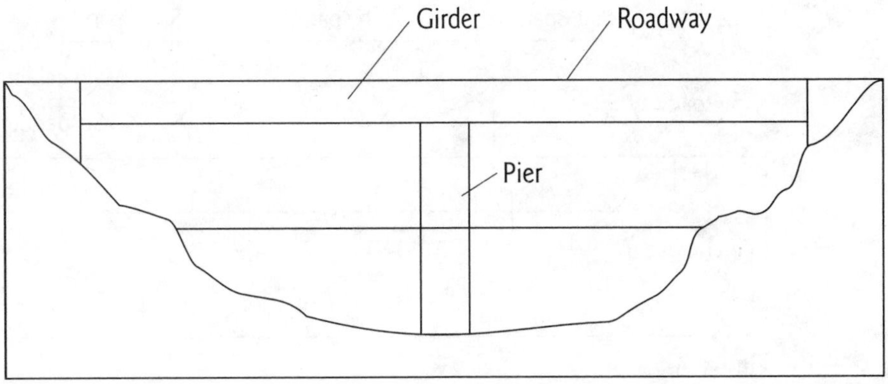

Figure 1

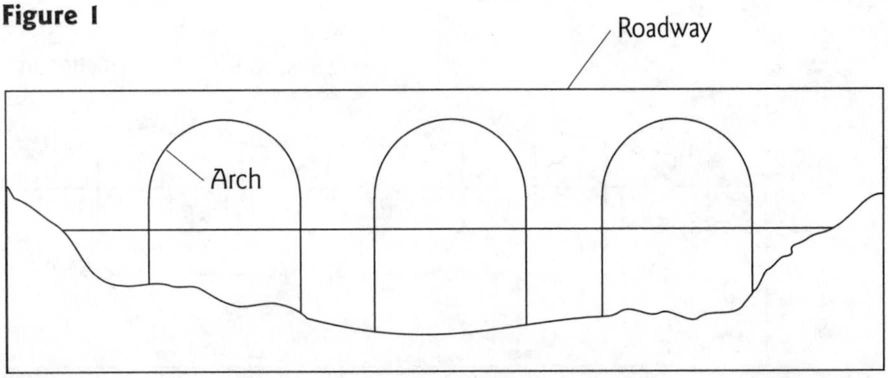

Figure 2

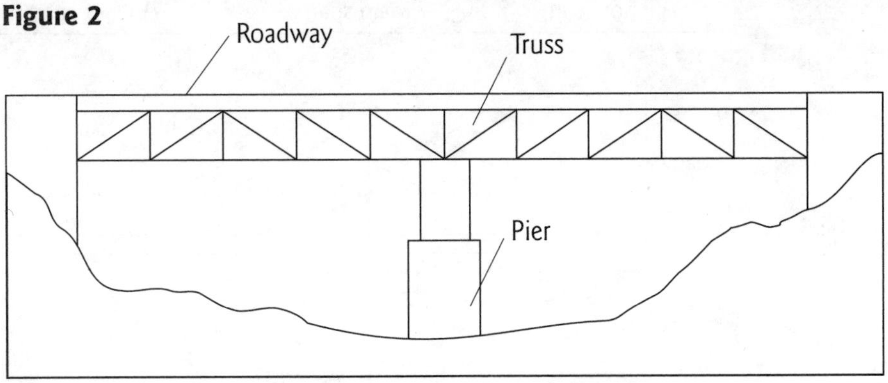

Figure 3

5-13 *A Study of the Efficiency of 5 Bridge Designs—Force exerted on bridges.*

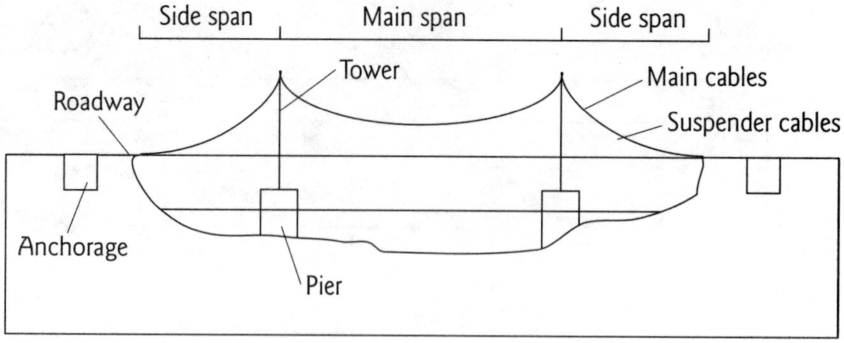

Figure 4

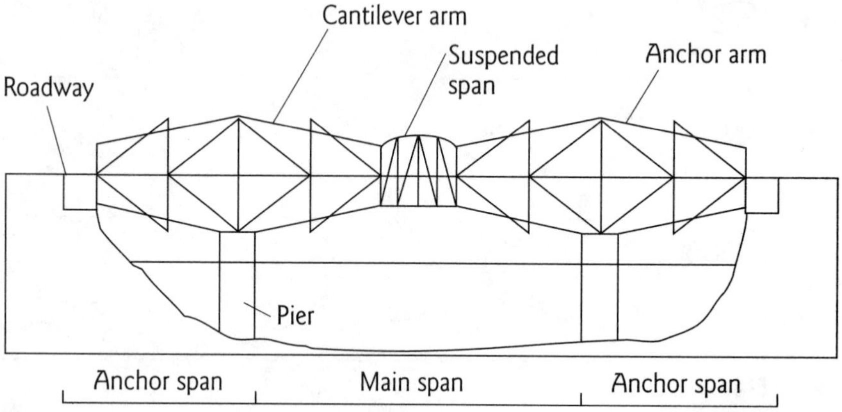

Figure 5

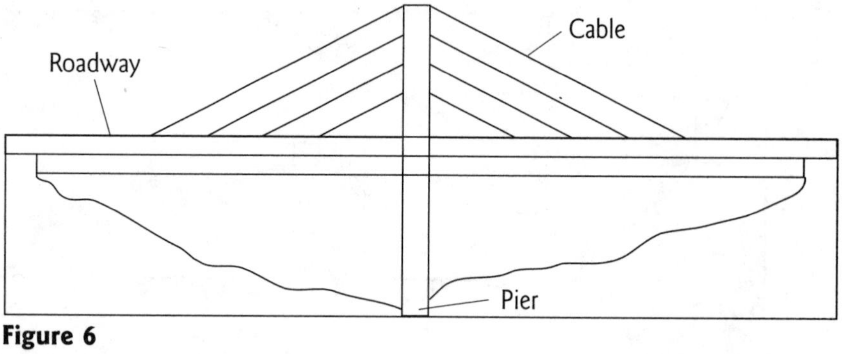

Figure 6

***5-14** A Study of the Efficiency of 5 Bridge Designs—Force exerted on bridges.*

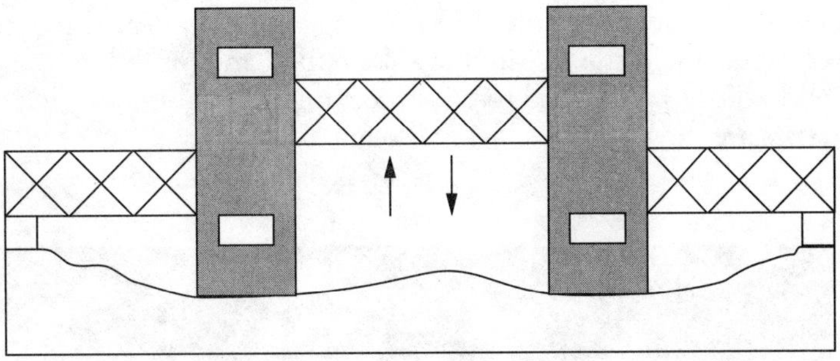

Figure 7

↓ = Direction of force

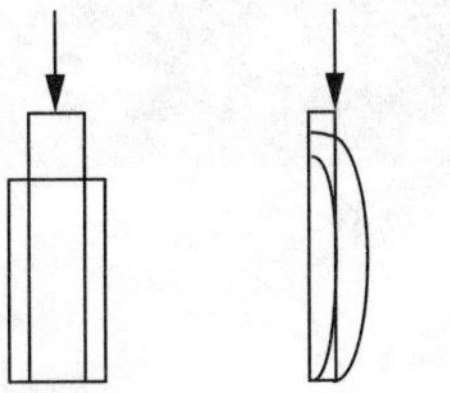

Figure 8

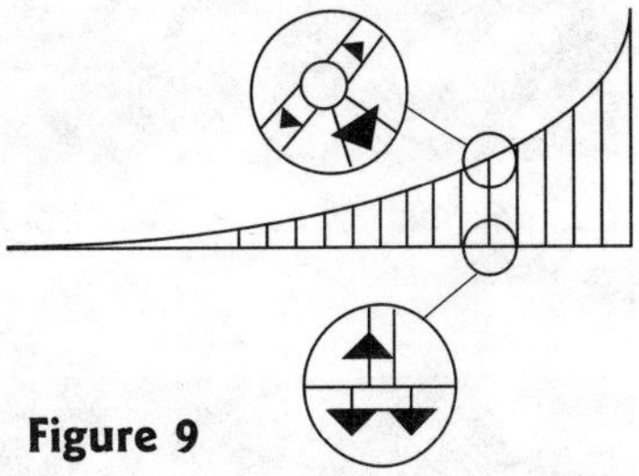

Figure 9

5-15 *A Study of the Efficiency of 5 Bridge Designs—Force exerted on bridges.*

= Force

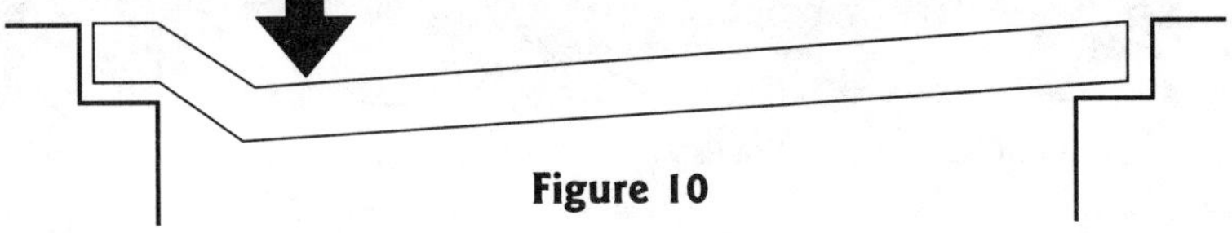

Figure 10

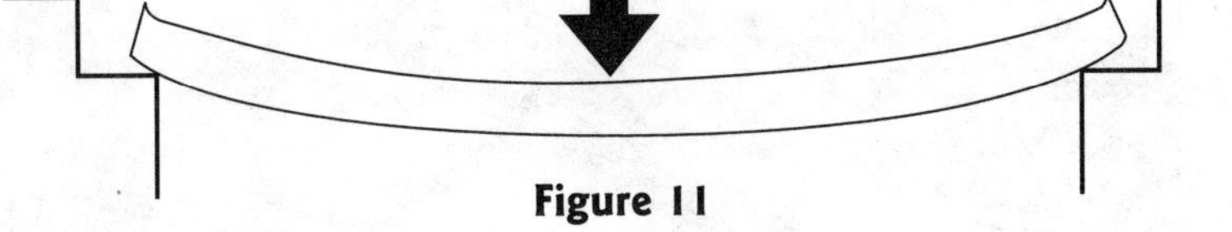

Figure 11

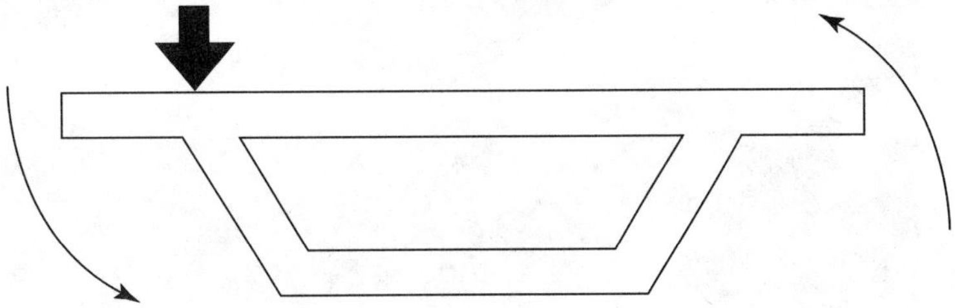

Figure 12

5-16 *A Study of the Efficiency of 5 Bridge Designs—Force exerted on bridges.*

His report gave examples of each type, and the advantages and disadvantages of each. When the research was done, Ben and his father designed each bridge and bought balsa wood to construct three of each model. The different bridge types are shown in Figs. 5-17 through 5-20.

5-17 *A Study of the Efficiency of 5 Bridge Designs.*

5-18 *A Study of the Efficiency of 5 Bridge Designs.*

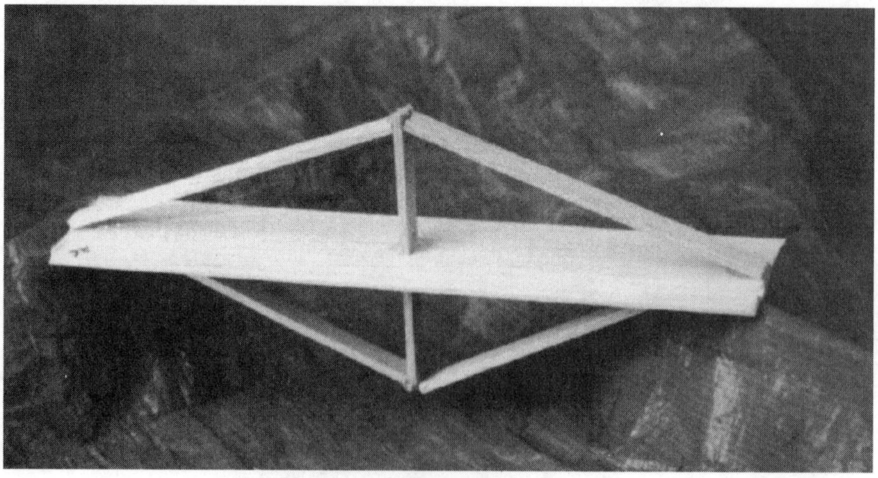

5-19 *A Study of the Efficiency of 5 Bridge Designs.*

5-20 *A Study of the Efficiency of 5 Bridge Designs.*

"Building the bridges was the most fun," said Ben. "Even though the balsa wood is fragile, it was easy to cut and measure." They calculated the cost of each bridge and then began the experiment, designed to measure the weight bearing capacity (WBC) relative to cost. To determine how much weight the bridge could bear, they then applied water to each bridge until it broke. "The project took longer than I thought it would," said Ben, "because the wood was more absorbent than I anticipated." He charted the weight-bearing capacity and cost of each bridge, excluding breakage due to faulty design, as shown in Figs. 5-21 and 5-22, and he graphed the correlation of WBC and cost, as shown in Fig. 5-23.

Based on these results, Ben concluded that the designs with more complex supports were more cost-effective. In the future, labor, or time needed to build the bridge is another factor that could influence the conclusion.

In his display, Ben used actual models of the five bridges, as shown in Fig. 5-24. This project won a first place in engineering, and an award from the Society of Civil Engineers. "I think the project was successful because I enjoyed doing it," said Ben.

Findings

Weight Bearing Capacity and Cost of Model Bridges

	Model Design				
	1	**2**	**3**	**4**	**5**
A	3415 gm	*	5650 gm	*	1100 gm
B	2300	3675 gm	*	*	1330
C	3450	2750	*	7345 gm	1150
Mean	3055 gm	3213 gm	5650 gm	7345 gm	1193 gm
Cost	$0.65	$0.53	$0.89	$1.17	$0.19

* = Premature braking due to imperfections in building.

This table provides the data for each model bridge. In the original experimental design, three models for each bridge design were built. Due to unavoidable error in the construction of support beams in some of the model bridges, the bridges cracked in an early stage of the weight-bearing procedure. Because the cracks in some models occurred so early in the weight-bearing procedure, these results were excluded in the analysis. An example of the faulty construction is illustrated on the following page.

5-21 *A Study of the Efficiency of 5 Bridge Designs—Weight-bearing capacity and cost.*

Examples of Correct and Incorrect Construction of Support Beams

(see preceding page)

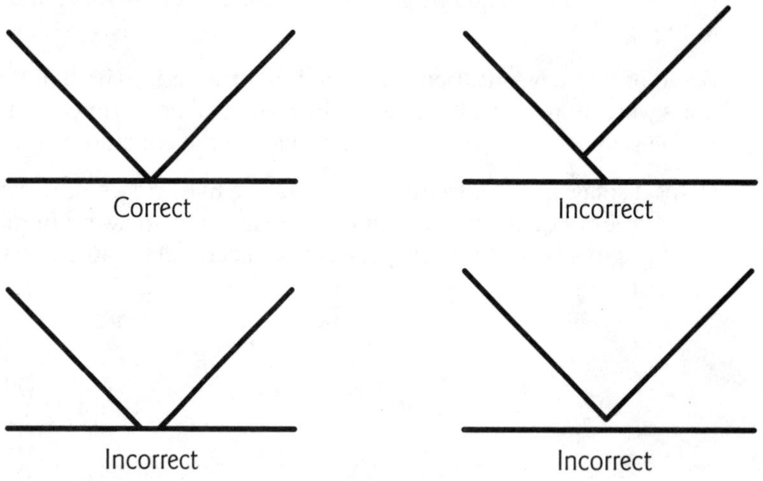

5-22 *A Study of the Efficiency of 5 Bridge Designs.*

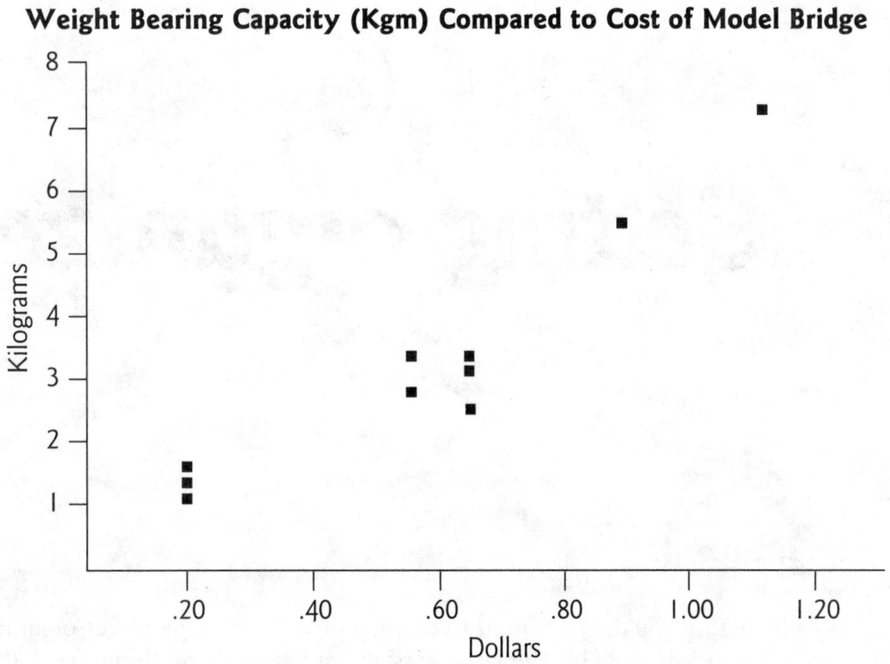

This graph illustrates the linear correlation between the cost of bridge construction and the weight bearing capacity of each model.

5-23 *A Study of the Efficiency of 5 Bridge Designs—Weight-bearing capacity versus cost.*

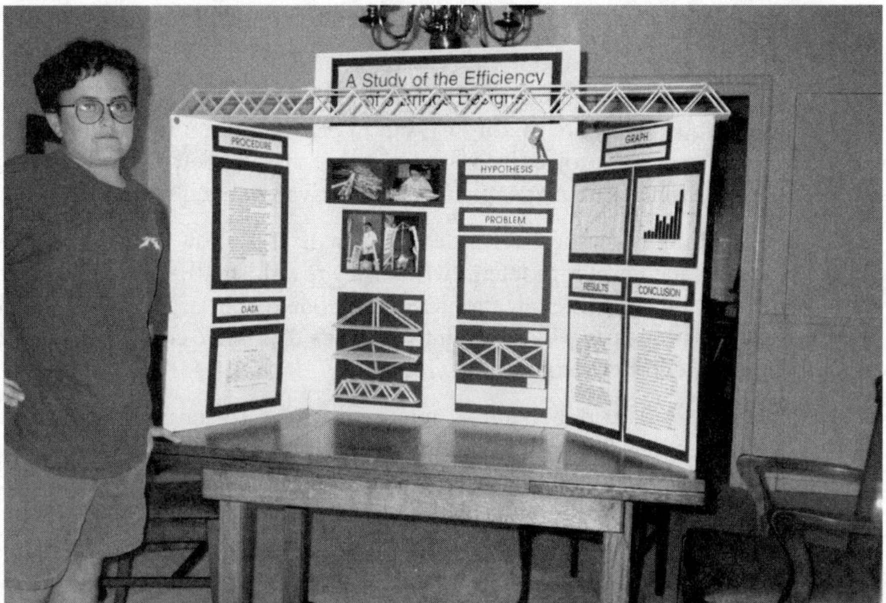

5-24 *A Study of the Efficiency of 5 Bridge Designs—Backboard.*

6

Getting organized

Now that you're committed to doing a project, it's time to get organized. Because this is probably the largest assignment you've ever done, good, thorough planning and organization are crucial to your success.

One of the hardest things about doing a large assignment is the tendency to leave things until the last minute. It's hard to feel pressure to work on something when the deadline is about five months away (and that, incidentally, is as true for many adults as for students working on their first science project.) It is, after all, hard to spend an October afternoon in the library when it would be so easy to go rollerblading, and the project's not due until after New Year's.

If this project is required, your teacher might have set some intermediate deadlines. You might hate this at first, but in the long run it will help you by forcing you to break the project into "bite-sized" segments. Setting and reaching short-term goals helps many people to keep motivated, even with a long road ahead.

A schedule with short-term deadlines will also allow your teacher help you identify and correct problems while they're still small, before they become insurmountable hurdles. If problems turn out to be larger than you expected, finding them early will give you the chance to change course while there is still time to get other resources.

If this project is not required, you might have to set up your own deadlines and schedules. Regardless of who sets the deadlines, you might want to make your own project calendar and hang it on your wall, where it will be a constant reminder of the tasks ahead. A sample project calendar is shown in Fig. 6-1.

1994			October			1994
Sunday	Monday	Tuesday	Wednesday	Thursday	Friday	Saturday
						1 Go to Branch library
2	3	4	5	6	7	8 Go to downtown library
9 Go to downtown library	10 Research paper	11 Research paper	12 Research paper	13 Research paper	14 Research paper	15 Research paper
16 Research paper	17 **Research paper due**	18	19	20	21	22
23 Buy Radish seeds	24	25	26	27	28	29
30	31					

6-1 *Project calendar.*

Besides your schedule, maintain a project log showing what you did and when you did it. This project log is an informal record of the entire project, which will help you to keep organized and "on track." The project log should include:

- Finding a topic
- Conducting research
- Writing the research paper
- Finding and buying supplies
- Building equipment, if necessary
- Setting up the experiment
- Performing the experiment, including testing and observation
- Results and conclusions
- Finishing the project notebook
- Building the backboard

The easiest way is to use a simple planner to keep track of your time. You can use a date book from the office supply store, the calendar or scheduler on your computer, or you can make your own.

Even if this is not required, good records might prove useful later on, especially if your project is late due to factors beyond your control. For example, one participant who needed data on solar activity contacted a division of the government agency, NOAA, who referred him to several U.S. and private agencies. One of these sources turned out to be a research institute library right in his own city! However, having the entire list might have been useful in case that resource did not turn out to be productive.

Documenting your activities could also be useful if you do not receive the responses you requested, or if delivery is late or nonexistent on materials you ordered. This means not only making an entry in your log whenever you call or speak to anyone, but also keeping copies of any letters you send or receive during your project. It will be easier to explain why you missed your deadline when you have documented evidence that you really did order your fruit flies back on November 1st, and called to inquire every Tuesday since then!

Now let's get down to specifics. As you have seen, the first and often the hardest step is to come up with an idea. You might start with some of your interests or hobbies, an item you've heard or read about, or something you're studying in class. However, one of the best ways to get going is to brainstorm, either alone, with your family, with friends, or with your teacher. Just think of as many things as you can, and write them down. To keep track of your project ideas, use the "handy-dandy" list shown in Fig. 6-2.

Next, select the idea you think is the most promising, and do a little reality checking by reviewing the project idea checklist in Fig. 6-3. If, for any reason, you think that your first choice just isn't "doable," go to your next favorite idea, and run through the checklist again. Even after you think you've found the perfect project, discuss it with your teacher. He or she might know something you don't: That it's too easy, too complex, might be disqualified, or that half the city used that topic last year!

Another thing you might want to do before making a final decision on an idea is to see what resources are available, both for your background research paper, and for any help you might need while doing the project. Daryl Smith, whose project is seen in chapter 16, used this as a crucial step before making his decision on a project idea. Figure 6-4 will help you check out the possible sources of information and help.

Now that you've decided and perhaps done some background research, you'll want to get down to the details. Use Fig. 6-5 to state your question and hypothesis. Be as specific as possible when stating your hypothesis because this is what your project must prove or disprove.

Figures 6-6 and 6-7 will help you outline your variables, controls, and your experimental and control groups, if those elements are part of your project. As you will see in chapter 11, not all projects will use variables, controls, experimental groups, or control groups. You might also want to use the table in Fig. 6-8 to outline your sample size or the number of trials you will do.

With any project, it's important to have everything you need before you start. Use the table in Fig. 6-9 to make up your project "shopping list," and perhaps your project budget as well.

PROJECT IDEAS

- ☺
- ☺
- ☺
- ☺
- ☺
- ☺
- ☺
- ☺
- ☺
- ☺
- ☺
- ☺
- ☺
- ☺
- ☺

6-2 *Form for project ideas.*

To keep on track once you actually begin your experiment or program, you'll want to know exactly what you'll be doing and in what sequence. Use the table shown in Fig. 6-10 to carefully and specifically list your procedures.

Incidentally, don't leave out any steps; something that might seem minor could be an important part of your procedures. Include anything that is part of the start-up procedure before the actual testing. For example, Jennifer Ade had to label and punch holes in 120 cups and plant the radish seeds before she could begin the experiment.

Your experimental log, however, might take many forms, depending on the nature of your experiment. Brian Berning and Nguyen Vy had to record daily findings in order to have accurate results, while Yolanda Lockhard recorded results as she tested. In any event, if you look through the projects shown throughout this book, you'll see that each log is very individual, depending on the nature of the project.

√ Is the information I need readily available to me?

√ Where can I find the information?

√ If the information is not available locally, where is it? How long will it take to get?

√ Will I need to pay for the information (for example, government pamphlets)?

√ If I need special books, can I check them out of the library or will I need to use them there?

√ Will I need professional advice? From whom? Are they willing to help?

√ What materials will I need? What will they cost?

√ Can I borrow some of the supplies and equipment I need?

√ Can I build some of the things I need? Do I need help?

√ Can I finish this project in the time available? If not, can I take a small portion of it to work on.

√ Is there anything about this project my family will object to?

6-3 *Project idea checklist.*

Once you've drawn up a plan and a schedule, make sure that you use it as a tool to help you manage the project, and don't allow the schedule to be something that rules you. Do not allow small annoyances to become large frustrations, which prevent you from keeping accurate records. Somewhere during the course of the project, if things aren't going the way you planned, show your teacher your records and explain the reasons you think the plan needs to be changed. He or she will be glad to help you work out the problem and advise you, but the task will be much easier if your documentation is good.

Remember that the purpose of organizing the project is to help you be successful, and not to restrict you to plans or procedures that are not working. Again, these forms are here to help you, not to restrict or limit you. If you find that the form you developed doesn't suit your needs—for example, not allowing enough room to write all your notes—change it! The forms are only a way to remind you of some of the elements of a science project, not to run the project for you. In fact, if your project (or your individual working style) does not lend itself to this type of structure, feel free to completely ignore the forms, and take off on your own!

- Libraries
  - ☺
  - ☺
  - ☺
- Research facilities
  - ☺
  - ☺
  - ☺
- Universities
  - ☺
  - ☺
  - ☺
- Government publications
  - ☺
  - ☺
  - ☺
- Businesses
  - ☺
  - ☺
  - ☺
- Interviews
  - ☺
  - ☺
  - ☺

6-4 *Sources of information and help.*

QUESTION	HYPOTHESIS

6-5 Question and hypothesis form.

VARIABLES	CONTROLS
Experimental	1.
1.	2.
2.	3.
3.	4.
4.	5.
5.	
Measured	
1.	
2.	
3.	
4.	
5.	

6-6 Variables and controls form.

EXPERIMENTAL GROUPS	CONTROL GROUP
1.	
2.	
3.	
4.	
5.	

6-7 Experimental and control groups form.

SAMPLE SIZE	NUMBER OF TRIALS

6-8 *Samples and trials.*

Material	*Source*	*Cost*

6-9 *Supplies and equipment.*

PROCEDURES
1.
2.
3.
4.
5.
6.
7.
8.
9.
10.
11.
12.
13.
14.
15.
16.
17.
18.
19.
20.

6-10 *Procedures.*

7
The rules of the game

When you begin to put together a project that you hope will be a winner at ISEF, you'll want to be sure that your work meets all the criteria for participation. ISEF, which is the International Science and Engineering Fair, is run by Science Service, a nonprofit organization based in Washington, DC. The mission of Science Service is to disseminate science information to scientists and nonscientists alike. To accomplish that objective, they publish *Science News*, a weekly news magazine, and they run Science News Books.

Science Service's second objective, the one that you're probably more familiar with, is to encourage and motivate young people to explore the world of science. To further that goal, Science Service manages the prestigious Westinghouse Science Talent Search, trains science communicators through the *Science News* intern program, and maintains a directory of student science programs, the main source of science opportunities for precollege students.

Our main interest here, however, is ISEF's role as the supervising organization for science fairs. Part of that role is to develop a comprehensive set of rules. These rules are designed to satisfy several objectives:

- The educational value of the projects selected.
- The promotion of the use of the scientific method when developing a project.
- Conformance to the same rules and regulations that professional scientists must follow.

This chapter will describe and summarize the ISEF rules for project research. ISEF also has rules and regulations for project displays, which will be discussed in chapter 16. We have also included, in appendix B, a flowchart that illustrates these rules, a matrix showing exactly which certifications are required, and sample copies of all forms required.

However, to be absolutely sure that your project will be in complete compliance with all ISEF rules, check with your school or local science fair committee to see the rules for the current year. Because the ISEF rules are always being updated, don't rely on an old copy. Your project might fall into the very area where the rules have changed.

If there is no copy available, you can order one (for $.75 per copy) from:

Science Service
1719 N Street N.W.
Washington, DC 20036
Tel. (202) 785-2255

If you are serious about participating, this will probably be the best bargain you'll ever see for under $1.00. It might very well keep you from making serious errors that would disqualify you from participation in a science fair.

The first rule is that every student who wants to enter the ISEF must enter from an ISEF-affiliated fair in the area where the student's school is located (or an ISEF-affiliated state science fair). If there is no affiliated (or feeder) fair in your area, contact Science Service, and they might be able to help.

Your project must be entirely your own work. Group projects are not permitted at ISEF. In addition, your project may not be an identical repetition of a previous year's work, although you can enter a project that expands upon or branches out from prior research and experimentation. Such projects are permitted if they show significant progress compared with previous work. Keep in mind, however, that if your project is continuing research, you must include the prior year's abstract, research reports, and certifications as a separate notebook.

All ISEF projects must have an abstract of no more than 250 words, incorporating the purpose, procedure, results, and conclusions. One copy of the abstract must be displayed with the exhibit, and one must be included with the entry forms for preview by the judges.

Finally, you must complete and display the appropriate certifications in order to compete at ISEF. All projects in any ISEF fair must complete Certification #1, a research plan, which has been approved by a teacher-supervisor prior to research and a Scientific Review Committee (SRC) member at an affiliated fair prior to competition. This form must state the problem and hypothesis of the project, including a specific statement of the purpose of the experiment. The methods and procedures section must give a detailed outline of the project plan, including:

- The exact names and quantities of any substances used, including where or how you will obtain each substance.
- The precise methods to be used in your procedures.
- If any substance or process is potentially dangerous, detail the safety practices you will follow.

Once your methods and procedures have been approved, you may make major changes to the plan only with the approval of your supervisor or a qualified scientist. In the research plan, you will also be required to include a bibliography listing all the books, articles and papers that you used preparing the research plan. This form must be signed by a member of the SRC prior to beginning a experimental research involving vertebrate animals, humans, recombinant DNA tissue, pathogenic agents, or controlled substances. If you did some or all of your work at a summer institute, science training program, or scientists' laboratory, you'll also need to have the supervising qualified scientist complete certification #9. This will document the portion of the research that you completed in the program.

These forms, which you need for all projects, are designed to ensure that you follow the correct scientific method and proper safety practices. Also, ISEF is especially concerned with proper practices in several areas.

When conducting a project using live vertebrates, (excluding human subjects), the rules are designed to ensure humane considerations for the laboratory animals. First of all, the ISEF encourages the use of invertebrates wherever possible. If you haven't considered this, now might be the time to give it some thought. There is a large variety of invertebrates that lend themselves to experimentation, often allowing for a larger sample group than with vertebrates. Although some research can only be done using vertebrates, more supervision and training is required to use vertebrate specimens properly. The ISEF rules concerning vertebrate animals can be summarized as follows (please check the ISEF rules for complete details):

- Development of new surgical techniques are not permitted.
- Surgical procedures can be performed only within academic, hospital, clinical, or institutional facilities under direct adult supervision.
- Nonbehavioral studies involving common laboratory animals (such as rats, mice, hamsters, gerbils, guinea pigs, and rabbits) are only permitted in an institutional environment and cannot be done at home.
- Humane treatment (including food and water, cleanliness of quarters, adequate space) must be provided at all times. This includes daily observation to ensure proper care. Be particularly alert to signs of stress or toxicity (weight loss is one significant sign).
- Sacrifice of specimens can only be done under direct supervision of the animal care supervisor, qualified scientist, or designated adult supervisor.
- Do not use pet-store animals for experimentation.
- If using pets or livestock, the animals must be classified as laboratory animals on the first day of research. Therefore, all certifications must be completed prior to beginning research or experimentation.
- Acid rain, insecticide, or herbicide studies involving live vertebrates are strictly prohibited. If your project involves live vertebrates, be sure that certifications 2 and 3 are completed and submitted to the local or affiliated fair SRC before you begin your research.

Although the philosophy behind the rules concerning human subjects is very similar, the details are somewhat different. Work involving human subjects must be approved by an Institutional Review Board (IRB) consisting of a science teacher (not your project supervisor), an administrator, a social scientist, and an M.D. or R.N. Again, be sure that you read the ISEF rules in this area before you begin.

- All research involving human subjects must comply with federal regulations (Title 45 CFR and "Belmont" report). You can get this information from:

Office for Protection from Research Risks
National Institute of Health
Building 31, Room 5B-59
9000 Rockville Pike
Bethesda, MD 20892
Tel. (301) 496-7041

➢ The practice of medicine is illegal. However, as part of a project, a student may observe and collect data in order to analyze new procedures and medication (under proper supervision).

➢ The IRB must evaluate all proposed projects for physical or psychological risk. The ISEF definition of potential risk includes exercise, emotional stress (including questioning or invasion of privacy), members of a risk group (for example, pregnant women, diabetics, or asthmatics), members of a group covered by federal regulations (such as Native Americans, gifted, handicapped), or students under 21 doing experiments with toxic chemicals, radiation, or known carcinogens or pathogens. It is also illegal to identify, either by name or in photographs, the human subjects in an experiment.

If your project involves human subjects, be sure to complete certification 6. Depending on your specific project, or if the IRB requires, you might also need certifications 4, 5, and 7. Remember that these forms must be reviewed and approved by an SRC member before you begin your experiment.

All research involving Recombinant DNA must be carried out in accordance with the revised NIH Guidelines for Research Involving Recombinant DNA Molecules. For information, contact:

Recombinant DNA Activities
National Institutes of Health
Building 31, Room 4B-11
Bethesda, MD 20892
Tel. (301) 496-9838

You may only conduct this type of research in a microbiological laboratory under the supervision of a qualified scientist. Certifications 4 and 5 are required for projects that involve recombinant DNA research.

You must obtain tissue samples from an institution or biomedical scientist, and you must provide proof and certification of your source. In addition, human blood and blood products must be certified free of AIDS and hepatitis before you receive the tissue. If your project uses tissue samples, you must complete certification #8, submit it to the SRC for review, and display it with the project.

If you plan to use pathogenic agents or controlled substances, you must fill out certifications 4 and 5 and submit them to the SRC before research begins. You must perform such research under the direct supervision of an experienced, qualified scientist or designated adult supervisor in an institutional laboratory.

This might seem like a lot of paperwork just to enter a science fair. However, as we stated up front, the ISEF is striving to make the science project as close to professional scientific activity as possible, while maintaining a moral and ethically responsible approach to animal and human research. As such, the rules of the game are designed to promote an appreciation of scientific methods and procedures, to ensure humane treatment of vertebrates in an experimental environment, and to ensure the safety of student scientists.

8 Writing the background research paper

A background research paper is normally a required element of a science project. For some of you, the idea of writing a paper of any kind is more fearsome than doing the experiment. There's no denying that writing a research paper is a rather large undertaking, but by breaking the process down into manageable steps, it can be less intimidating and more fun.

Why do a paper?

Perhaps it will be easier for you to begin this part of the project if you understand why it is necessary and how much effort is required. The size and extent of the research paper will depend on your teacher's requirements. Sometimes a simple review of the literature is all that's needed, while other teachers want a large paper.

In order to conduct any worthwhile experimentation or research, you must first get as much information as possible to help you to understand the past and current theories, research, and discoveries. If your topic is very general and you're having trouble narrowing it down, research might help you to focus your efforts. Your research will also help you formulate your question and hypothesis.

Doing a research paper will also help in your careers as students. As long as you're in school, you'll need to write research papers on a variety of subjects (even some that you have absolutely no interest in)! Some of these papers might be pure research, calling for gathering and organizing factual data. Others will require you to learn the facts and then make an interpretation, showing your understanding or opinion based on the knowledge you've gained. In any event, you need to know how to plan, organize, and write the research paper.

While doing the paper, you'll learn how to do research. Tracking down information is a skill you will use throughout your lives. As working adults, parents, or curious, informed citizens, the ability to find facts is essential. If your parents are helping you with this research, they'll know what I mean!

Once you get started, this phase of your project can be fun. In many ways, it's like playing detective. You might find one source that is not especially useful, but it might direct you to three or four other sources. As with any other mystery, your research might lead you down some blind alleys, which will temporarily throw you off track. However, if you keep at it, you'll eventually find what you need. Along the way, you might learn other fascinating things, perhaps on other subjects leading to new interests (or next year's project).

Finding the facts: A brief guide

The first step in doing research is finding information. A natural place to start is with the sources that are closest to you. These include your textbooks, any encyclopedias or other reference materials you might have at home, and publications in your school library. These references might give you only the most basic information, but they will at least help you to focus on the various aspects of your topic. Also, the bibliographies in these volumes might point out other sources. Along with the old-fashioned 20-volume encyclopedias, you might have access to an encyclopedia on CD-ROM.

The next stop is your public library. Basically, there are two ways to find information there, through either an online or a card-catalog system.

If your library has On-Line Public Access (OPAC) catalogs, you can get a jump start on your research by finding out what is available in your area. These catalogs are used in many colleges, universities, and public libraries. Some library systems might have their entire systems on an OPAC, but others might only have sources later than a certain date on the system; for earlier works, you'll need to use the card catalog.

In an OPAC, besides searching by author and title, you can find information by keyword—for example, "tsunami" if you wanted all information about tidal waves. Actually, you can use both "tsunami" and "tidal wave" to get a wider scope of information. Sometimes, however, you'll get more sources than you actually want to see, so you'll need to narrow the search. If you're only interested in tidal waves in Alaska during the twentieth century, you can enter this information for a more specific list of references. For sources that are in the local library, you can not only get the list, but you'll also find out if the works are actually in the library or currently circulating.

However, if you need to use the card catalog and do not know how, ask the librarian's help. Local branch libraries often have card catalogs that use the Dewey decimal system. (See Fig. 8-1.) Other libraries use the LC, or Library of Congress, method to catalog books. (See Fig. 8-2). Both methods will guide you to the areas of the library where you'll find materials dealing with your subject.

Some libraries use a microfilm catalog in addition to the card catalog. This usually shows everything available in the entire library system. If the resources you need are in other branches, you might be able to have them delivered to your branch library. Otherwise, you'll need to travel to other parts of your city or county. Eventually, your search will probably lead you to your library's main branch to get all the information you need.

Don't get the impression that you have to live in a big city to do research. To begin, of course, you'll have your school and local libraries. Then all you need

000	General Works
200	Philosophy
300	Religion
400	Language
500	Natural Science
600	Useful Arts
700	Fine Arts
800	Literature
900	History, Biography

550	The World Around Us
551.21	Volcanos
551.22	Earthquakes
551.46	Living Sea

8-1 *Dewey decimal system.*

A	General works
B	Philosophy, psychology, religion
C	Auxiliary sciences of history (archaeology, etc.)
D	History, general and old world
E, F	American history
G	Geography, anthropology and recreation
H	Social science
K	Law
L	Education
M	Music and books on music
N	Fine arts
P	Language and literature
Q	Science
R	Medicine
S	Agriculture
T	Technology
U	Military science
V	Naval science
Z	Bibliography, library science

8-2 *Library of Congress system.*

is a computer (or writing materials and a post office) to gather material from all over the world. However, don't limit your horizons to libraries. Publications dealing with just about every conceivable area of science are available from the U.S. government. Private companies are also cooperative and are usually willing to share information. Even foreign governments and international organizations might be willing to send material.

For the moment, however, back to the library. Some books are available for you to borrow, but before you bring the book home, scan it briefly to see that it really meets your needs. Check the copyright date to see if it's sufficiently recent to have the most up-to-date information. In some fields, even information that is a few months old can be obsolete. Also, be sure that the material is on your level. A manuscript written for use by a Ph.D. candidate in nuclear physics might be too difficult if you're a seventh grader attempting your first science project. Looking at the table of contents, index, and appendices might also give you a good idea of whether the book will be useful for you.

Other materials will be classified as reference material, which means you will have to use them at the library. If you need to do that, please remember library etiquette. Keep your materials close at hand and neat, talk in whispers, and no eating or drinking. Be sure you have plenty of paper and pencils, since there's usually no place to buy anything at the library.

Another way of doing research is to make copies of important information to bring home. Most libraries today have photocopiers, which are most helpful. But be prepared and bring plenty of change. These machines gobble up money faster than a video arcade!

While you're there, see if you can buy a copier card. This works something like a bus pass, since you prepay the cost of making a specific number of copies on the library's machine. Although this might not save you any money, it's usually more convenient because you don't have to worry about carrying a pocket full of change.

Do not limit your research to books. There is a lot of valuable information in periodicals. This includes newspapers and popular magazines, such as *Newsweek*, *Time*, and *Readers Digest*. There are also magazines that popularize scientific subjects, such as *Science Digest*, *National Geographic*, *Today's Health*, or *Psychology Today*. Finally, look into specialized, scholarly periodicals that deal specifically with the field you're interested in. To find these types of articles, use a periodical index, such as *The Readers Guide to Periodic Literature*. Some of these indexes are:

- *Abstracts of Popular Culture*
- *Access*
- *Index to Free Periodicals*
- *Magazine Index*

If your library has computerized catalogs, you might scan through them.

Once you have located your sources, you'll find that if you require a recent edition, the library will usually have the actual issue on hand. Older issues will probably be available on microfilm or microfiche. Occasionally, the microfiche reader will have a copier attached (which also takes nickels, dimes and quarters), so that you can make copies of important pages.

Sometimes, you can access the actual articles on the computer and print out the articles (without the pictures). Again, the printouts are not free, so have your coins or copier card handy.

College and university libraries often will have books and periodicals that a public library does not carry, especially if the college is noted for a particular area of science. The people there, who are sometimes student workers, can be very helpful in guiding you to the facilities available.

If a conveniently located university library has a great deal of useful information for you, see if you can get a library card. Many universities issue these cards for a fee. This gives you the same library privileges as the college or university students, enabling you to check out nonreference materials.

Institutes and foundations usually function the same way as university libraries. Without special access, their materials are available for use only on the premises and cannot be taken out of the building. (There are copiers here too!) However, these materials can be extremely good sources of specialized information and might lead you to experts in your field.

One of the most extensive sources of information is the U.S. government, our nation's largest publisher. Government agencies publish a large variety of materials on a vast range of subjects; in Lois Horowitz's book, *Where to Look, the Ultimate Guide to Research*, the chapter on government documents is the longest!

One way to locate helpful government references is to look at the U.S. government departments and agencies, which publish extensively. Figure 8-3 is a list of just a few government agencies that publish scientific documents.

1. Department of Agriculture
2. Department of Commerce
3. Department of Defense
4. Department of Education
5. Department of Energy
6. Department of Health and Human Services
7. Department of the Interior
8. Department of State
9. Department of the Treasury
10. National Aeronautic and Space Administration
11. National Oceanographic and Atmospheric Administration
12. Bureau of Mines
13. Fish and Wildlife Service
14. Public Health Service
15. Atomic Energy Commission

8-3 *List of government sources.*

In your search for relevant government material, don't look only in the obvious places. The Department of Commerce, for example, publishes an annual entitled *United States Earthquakes*, and the Department of the Treasury, which is in charge of Alcohol and Tobacco, has many publications on those subjects.

There are several indexes to help you wade through the large amounts of government material. Several of these are:

- *Monthly Catalog*
- *Cumulative Subject Index*
- *Publications Reference File*
- *Index to U.S. Government Periodicals*

Even small libraries might have at least one of these research tools. The librarians might be able to help you use them. Some of the sources that you find might not be easily available, but you can buy some government publications from the appropriate agency. Allow sufficient time to receive the materials you order. Many a project has faltered waiting for an order to be processed.

Branches of the military service, corporations, and professional associations are also excellent sources of information on a variety of scientific and engineering topics. Often, they publish pamphlets that are yours for the asking! As you look for your sources of information, review the checklist in Fig. 8-4A to be sure you've left no stone unturned!

Places	**Things**
_____ School Library	_____ Encyclopedia
_____ Public Library	_____ Books
_____ University Library	_____ Magazines
_____ Institutes	_____ Scholarly Journals
_____ Industry	_____ Professional Journals
_____ Government	_____ Newspapers
_____ Military	_____ Government publications
_____ Zoos, Seaquariums	_____ Databases
_____ Museums	_____ Local newspaper
_____ Online services	_____ CD ROM

8-4A *Resource checklist.*

Surf's up!

For those of you who've already done some "net surfing," the next few pages won't seem new. You've probably gotten online to play games, exchange e-mail, and chat with new and old friends. However, even you might find something new and exciting. The information superhighway contains many resources that can help you do your science project.

To define our terms, getting online is simply accessing other computers through your own. To do that, you'll be using the telephone lines to connect to other users. You won't need a special telephone line to do this; you can dial a network (or another computer) on your telephone line.

To get on the superhighway, you'll need a modem in order to connect with the Internet "access ramps." There are many ways to go online. First, you might be able to access the Internet through a university or business. This would be particularly easy if you have a friend or family member who works or studies somewhere with Internet access. There are the large commercial services, such as America On-Line, CompuServ, or Prodigy. These services not only allow you access to the Internet, but they also have their own resources, such as news, magazines, games, entertainment reviews, travel services, games, and what you need most at this stage of your science project—research resources. The commercial services almost always have access to one of the better-known encyclopedias and the more renowned newspapers, such as the *New York Times*, the *Washington Post*, and the *Wall Street Journal*. You might also find that you can access government agencies such as the Weather Service, the Centers for Disease Control, or the Department of Agriculture. Other services, such as Netcom or CR labs, are large Internet providers, which means that for a fee, they will connect you to the Internet. Finally, some libraries provide free Internet access to make these facilities available to everyone, including easy-to-follow instructions to help you find what you need. Therefore, if you don't already have access, your library might be your first stop (can't get away from it)!

Once you're connected, you'll want to access the granddaddy of them all, the Internet. What is it? Simply a collection of *inter*connected *net*works. Started by the Department of Defense and the universities doing military research, it became a widely used tool in many universities. And then, as those university graduates went out into the world, the Internet went right along with them.

Basically, the main things you can do on the Internet are find information, send and receive mail, and talk to other net users throughout the world. The Internet can be most helpful while you're planning your experiment and doing research. What there is for you to find are databases, from universities, museums, and government agencies, and scientists and engineers from all over the world. To wade through this wealth of information, there are several ways of effectively navigating the Internet.

The World Wide Web (WWW or the Web) is a navigation system that will help you travel the Internet. With one word, you can start a search that can give you more information than you ever expected. This makes the WWW a great way to get started on your research, especially if you're not quite sure what you're looking for.

The Web is based on hypertext, which maintains links to a range of related text and graphics files. Unlike an outline form, where the connections only go to the next higher or lower level, hypertext links move wider and deeper. Using the Web can be compared to having a camera with a zoom lens for greater detail on one aspect of your subject, and a wide-angle lens to give you a broader look at the entire field. If, for example, you were interested in prehistoric marine mammals, you might travel the paths shown in Fig. 8-4B.

Gopher is another way of finding what you need on the net. Originally developed at the University of Minnesota to simplify Internet searches, Gopher uses a series of interlocking menus. When you first access Gopher, you will see a menu. When you make a selection, another menu will appear. Continue going through the menus and selecting the topics of interest until you finally see the information that you need on the screen. At that point, you can either print the file, mail it to yourself, or bookmark it for later use.

Other methods of accessing the Internet—for example, Archie or WAIS—require a specific command structure to find information. Although these might be harder to use, they have specific advantages. Archie is ideal for locating software, and WAIS is a good way to search available documents by content. In both cases, however, you'll need to know what you're looking for before you can find it.

Another way to use the Internet for your science project is to "talk" to people. You might already have experience with local bulletin boards (BBS). Many of these are focused on special interests, from the academic to fantasy games. Talking about your project on a BBS might introduce you to knowledgeable people in your community.

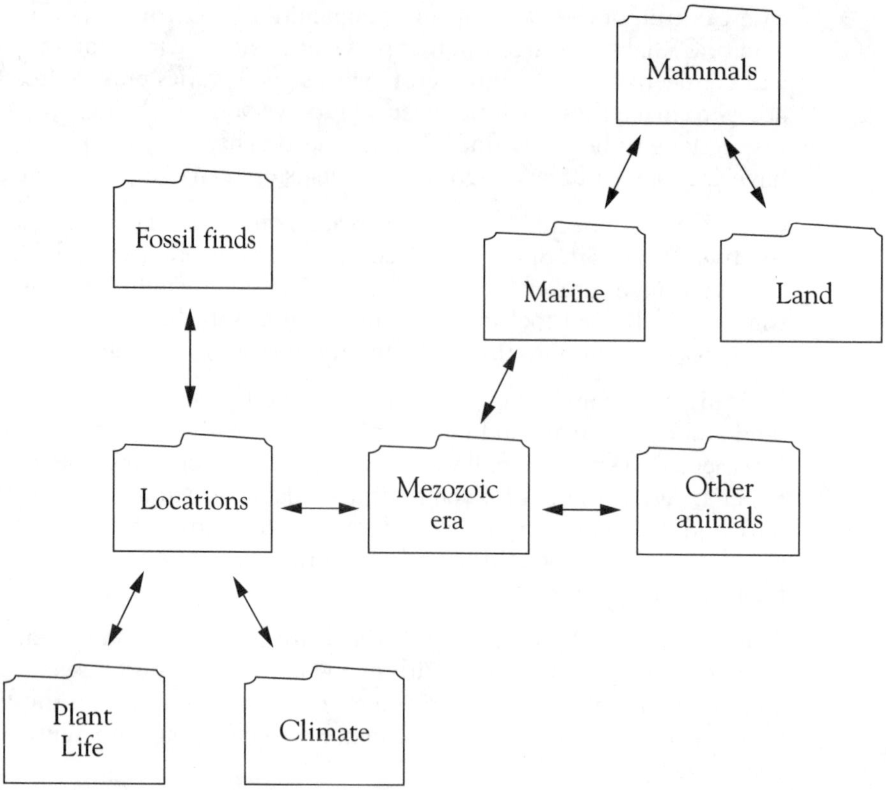

8-4B *Paths for exploring prehistoric marine mammals.*

To look further afield, investigate newsgroups. These are managed by Usenet, which is simply a super-BBS. Newsgroups can be local, regional, national, or global, but each newsgroup contains current files (articles) related to the topic of the newsgroup.

For example, while working on your project, the science and computer newsgroups might contain interesting information for you. At any time, you have no way to know whether there are articles specific to your topic, but because so much information becomes available each day, it's a good idea to check periodically.

Another useful feature of newsgroups is the fact that you can comment or ask questions about an article. If you find an article particularly useful or interesting, you can e-mail the author and perhaps acquire an online mentor. Another way to meet people in your field is to put your ideas or problems "out there," and see who responds. For example, you might go on a BBS or into a newsgroup for people who are interested in fossils in desert areas, and send a message describing your project. Perhaps a geologist who has just conducted research and written a paper on that same subject will read your message. A conversation with that person could give you a look at some information that might affect your project.

If you want to learn more about the Internet, there are several good books, which you can find in any library or computer store. However, like most people who have wandered onto the net for the first time, you'll probably find your way around just fine!

Taking notes

Now that you've found your information, it's time to extract the most meaningful data to use in your background research paper. Since every fact you use will be derived from one of your sources, the first task is to start a working bibliography. Include all the vital information about your source, so you'll have everything you need for the formal bibliography. Examples of items in a working bibliography are as shown in Fig. 8-5.

A. *Encyclopedia International, Vol. 6, Earthquakes*
B. *"Is California Sinking?" Goofy Geography Magazine, 1984*

8-5 *Working bibliography.*

To take notes efficiently and effectively, focus on the most important and relevant facts, analyzing every piece of information to determine whether or not it truly relates to your topic. Take only the information that furthers your understanding of the subject. If you find the same facts in several sources, use the presentation that makes the most sense to you.

Record each fact in your own words. Whether you use index cards, a piece of paper, your word processor, or a database to "write down" the information, it's important to use your own words. This will help you understand and absorb the material. Code each card to show the source of the fact and the page number. If it's important to quote the material word-for-word, be sure to note that it's a direct quotation.

Outlining

Before you begin the actual writing, review all your facts and try to find a few themes or main topics that tie the material together. As you do this, some subtopics should also become apparent.

Write down, in outline form, what you want to say in your background research paper. If you are not well acquainted with using outline form, it is shown in Fig. 8-6. If you're using a word processor, check out its capabilities for automatic numbering. However, whether you're doing it by computer or manually, remember that in outline form, if an item is subdivided, it should contain at least two elements. Otherwise, the information should have been included in the division above.

For example:

IV. Other insects
    A. Tarantulas

should read:

IV. Other insects; tarantulas, etc.

Once you've done the outline, it's easy to arrange your facts. Use the outline to assign all the facts that you've gathered into one of the topics or subtopics.

Don't worry if you have a few cards left over that don't seem to belong anywhere. They might be facts that are irrelevant to your subject, or you might

I. Main Topic I.
- **A. Subtopic A**
- **B. Subtopic B**
  1. Under subtopic B1
  2. Under subtopic B2
     - i. Subtopic B2.1
     - ii. Subtopic B2.2
       - a. Subtopic B2.2a
       - b. Subtopic B2.2b

II. Main Topic II.

8-6
Outline format.

find that you need to include another topic or subtopic in your outline. One helpful hint: Don't send these facts to the circular file just because you don't think they belong in the background research paper. Data you might not need now could be extremely important as you progress in your experiment. Also, if you think you might build on your project next year, these facts that do not fit this year's experiment might be your guiding inspiration next year.

Next, arrange the facts in each topic or subtopic into a logical sequence. These sequenced facts will become the basis of the first draft of your research paper.

Writing the paper

Although your facts are now organized, let's talk about the format of a well-constructed research paper. The first few paragraphs should introduce your paper, stating the topic you're writing about and the experiment you think you will do. Then follow your outline to provide a logical presentation of your background information. The last several paragraphs should summarize the facts you've discussed, and finally, you should predict what you believe your experiment will prove or disprove. In short, tell them what you're going to say, say it, and tell them what you've just said!

If you've recorded your facts using a database or a word processor, use your software to rearrange your facts in the proper sequence. Delete any unrelated facts and store your file under a new name to preserve a copy of your old list "just in case."

If you've recorded all the facts you've found in your own words, it will now be easier to create an original research paper. Remember, however, that a paper is not just a bunch of facts strung together. Your teachers and science fair judges will look for continuity and some creative thought and educated interpretation of the facts. Ultimately, the paper should directly relate to the experiment you're planning to do.

One resource you'll find valuable as you begin to write is Strunk & White's *Elements of Style*. Originally published in 1919, it is the definitive guide to good, clear writing. This small, inexpensive paperback is one you'll need throughout your student career. In fact, your English teacher might require you to use it. The book not only describes rules of correct grammar, but also gives guidelines for writing clearly and concisely and avoiding common, incorrect expressions.

Following even a fraction of the helpful hints in this book will help you create a better research paper.

Credit your sources

At this point, we must discuss an unpleasant little topic called plagiarism, a topic you'll hear discussed throughout your educational career. To put it simply, if you use an author's exact words, be sure to put them in quotes, for example, as Ms. VR says in her book entitled *Atmospheric Conditions in Cyberspace*, "as long as you don't get flamed, you shouldn't find the weather too hot." If you don't use an exact quote but very closely paraphrase the author, you could say: Ms. VR tells us, in *Atmospheric Conditions in Cyberspace*, that the weather's fine as long as you avoid getting flamed.

Another way of crediting the author is by using a footnote. You could state in your paper: As long as you don't get flamed, you shouldn't find the weather too hot,[1] where a footnote, numbered 1, citing Ms. VR's book would appear on the bottom of the page.

As you progress in the academic world, plagiarism is an extremely serious offense because it is taking someone else's original ideas or research and claiming it for your own. Therefore, be sure to get into good habits of crediting your sources right at the start. Just as with the bibliography, footnotes follow a specified format. (See Fig. 8-7.)

For the first footnoted reference to a book:
[1] Robert W. McLuggage, *A History of the American Dental Association*, (Chicago, American Dental Association, 1959), p. 475
For subsequent references:
[4] McLuggage, pp. 14–17
For a periodical:
[7] Psychology Today, October 1990, 47

NOTE: All items referenced in a footnote must also appear in the Bibliography.

8-7 *Footnote format.*

Write and rewrite

Your rough draft is a first attempt at writing your research paper. There are no hard-and-fast rules as to how many drafts you should write, but each draft is an opportunity to correct, revise, rearrange, and reword your material. You might want to type or print your early drafts with triple spacing to give yourself enough room to write in many corrections. If you have a spell checker on your word processor, run it each time you do another draft. Whenever you add new material, you run the risk of introducing more misspelling. Remember, however, that a spell checker will not find everything. "Their are many species of insects" looks fine to a spell checker. That's why it's often helpful to have family members and friends review your work. Although they might not be scientists or writers, they can find spelling errors, awkward grammar, or badly worded sentences that you are too close to spot.

When you are satisfied that your paper is the best that it can be, you are ready to create your final copy. If, until now, your drafts have been handwritten, try to borrow a typewriter or computer. Even if your handwriting is good, your teacher will appreciate seeing typed copy, and it will certainly make a good impression on science fair judges.

Regardless of how it was created, be sure your margins are correct, your text is double-spaced, your name is on the paper, and you have obeyed any formatting rules your teachers have given you. Remember to include your bibliography, in finalized format, at the end of the report. (See Fig. 8-8.)

Now that this phase of the project is complete, make extra copies of everything, including a backup diskette if your paper is on a computer. Be sure that all your files, the notes, bibliography, and footnotes, and the final research paper are included. This is your insurance policy!

Periodical

Patrick Huygne, "Earthquakes, the Solar Connection," Science Digest, XC, (October 1982), 73–75

Interview

Dr. J. Holman III, Orthodontist, Interview, 11/23/89

Books

By single author:

Lauber, Patricia, *Of Man and Mouse*, New York, Viking Press, 1971

By multiple authors:

Anderson, Garron P., S. John Bennett and K. Lawrence DeVries, *Analysis and Testing of Adhesive Bonds*. Long Beach, CA: Foster Publishing Co., 1971 Press, 1971

Encyclopedias

Selection without author:

"Galena," *Encyclopedia International*, 1974

Selection with author:

Roderick, Thomas H., "Gene," *Encyclopedia International*, 1974

Government or other institutional publication:

Science Service, *ABSTRACTS: — 38th International Science and Engineering Fair*, Washington DC, 1987

8-8 Final bibliography format.

9 Using the computer

Back when I wrote my first science project book, very few participants used computers. Facts were recorded on index cards, research papers were typed, graphs were hand-drawn, and stencils or rub-on lettering were the order of the day for backboards. However, while interviewing students for this book, almost everyone I spoke to used computers to help them with their projects. They used computing capabilities for all phases of the project: research, experimentation, record keeping, results, conclusions, and project display. Incidentally, it didn't seem to matter whether they used PCs, Macs, or anything else; they were all happy to be able to make life easier.

Those who had home computers, of course, had it made. All the facilities they needed were at their fingertips. However, it is important to realize that these capabilities are available even for those who do not have a computer at home. Students are often able to use computers at school and keep their information on diskettes for safekeeping. Perhaps there are computers on which you can rent time at a copy center or library. If you find a mentor or are able to work in a college or university lab, you might be able to use a computer there. However, please remember that the science project experience is available to everyone, regardless of the hardware you do or don't have.

If you're fortunate, you already know the software that you can use to help you. You might have a parent, brother, sister, or other relative who can teach you some of the fine points that you'll need to learn. However, several participants that I spoke to started their science projects with very little computer knowledge and found that one of the best "side effects" of the experience was their greatly increased computer literacy.

You certainly won't learn all of the "ins and outs" here, but for those of you who are just getting started with computing, here's a brief summary of the types of software that you can use to help you with your project.

The software most commonly used is the word processor. This software gives you the ability to type your report, format and reformat it to your satisfaction, print it, and save it on disk. Then you can review and edit your report, changing only those parts that need to be revised. Most word processors contain a spell checker to help you make sure that you've spelled everything correctly. However, if you've used a word incorrectly, for example, "Make sure you do not use to much water," the spell checker will not catch it. You will need a grammar checker to find instances of incorrect usage. Your word processor might also have a thesaurus, which can help you find synonyms so that you don't repeat the same word too often in your report.

Another great feature of word processors is the ability to move words, sentences, and paragraphs around. It's not uncommon to find that after a report is written, you find that it makes more sense if you reorganize the material. The capability to execute cut-and-paste commands will allow you to completely reorganize the research paper without retyping. Finally, if you want to incorporate graphs, charts, or other artwork into your paper, you'll find that most word processors let you import pictures into a document. Some of the more popular word processors are WordPerfect, Microsoft Word, and AmiPro. Figure 9-1 shows part of this chapter on an AmiPro screen.

After word processors, the next most commonly used software is the spreadsheet. This software allows you to enter numerical data in a grid or table consisting of columns and rows, and then perform mathematical calculations on the data. Figure 9-2 shows an example of a Lotus 1-2-3 spreadsheet. As you add information—for example, as you conduct your experiment daily—you can add to the spreadsheet and have the program automatically recalculate results for you. Elizabeth Eubanks used a spreadsheet to keep track of distances between cars, which was described in chapter 5.

When the experiment is complete and you want to chart or graph your results, the spreadsheet program will use the data to create tables, charts, and graphs in the format that you designate. Figures 9-3 through 9-7 show some of the graph types created from a spreadsheet. To help you draw your conclusions, you might also want to apply some statistical calculations to your data. Most spreadsheet programs include many commonly used formulas, such as mean, average, standard deviation, variance, and chi-square test.

Some spreadsheet programs, such as Lotus 1-2-3, also have some database capabilities, which allow you to store, sort, and search your data. You might find this feature useful for keeping and rearranging your research information. Some popular spreadsheet programs are Lotus 1-2-3, Quattro, and Excel.

Besides the database feature in your spreadsheet program, you might find use for one of the sophisticated, specialized relational database programs. These programs can tie different pieces of stored information together, usually with programs written in a specific database language. Depending on the complexity of your project, you might find that a large database will require more work to set up than you will save. Some examples of databases are FoxPro, Paradox, or dBase. As described in chapter 3, dBase was used in the "Home-Field Advantage" project.

You might also want to take advantage of a graphics program, especially when you are getting ready to create the project backboard. These programs, such as CorelDraw or Freelance, allow you to use a wide variety of fonts. Most of them also contain a clip-art library, giving you the capacity to add professional drawings to your display. Figure 9-8 shows several clip-art drawings on a CorelDraw screen.

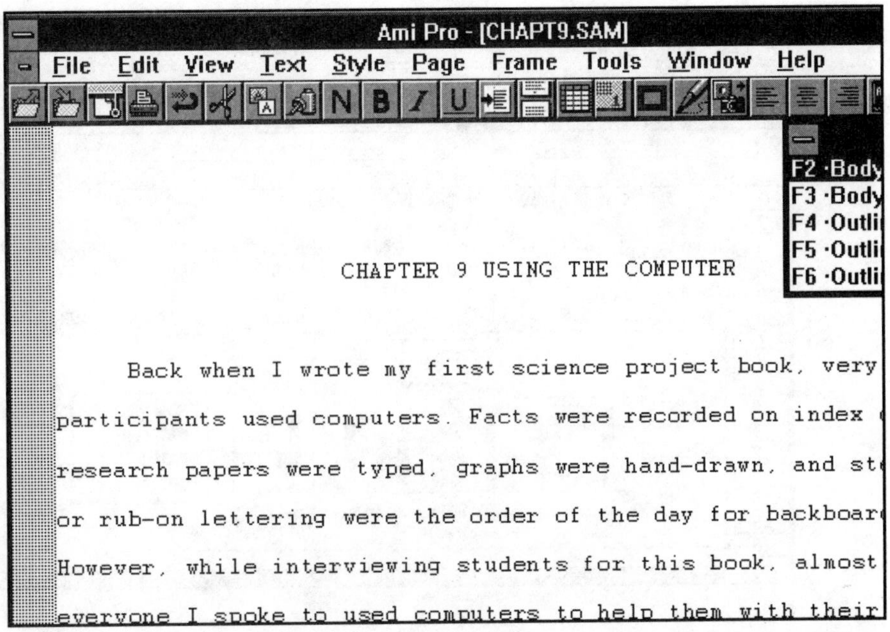

9-1 *AmiPro screen.*

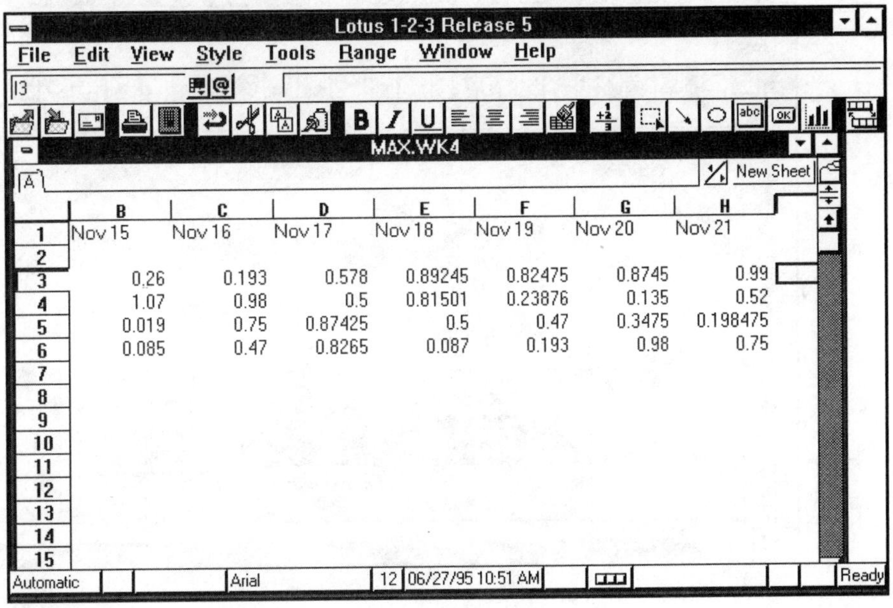

9-2 *Lotus 1-2-3 screen.*

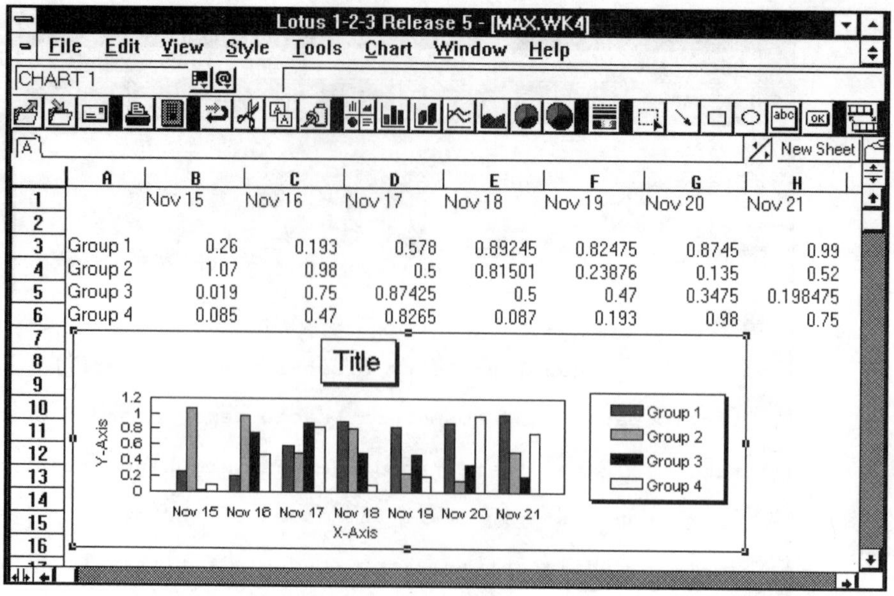

9-3 *Lotus 1-2-3 bar graph.*

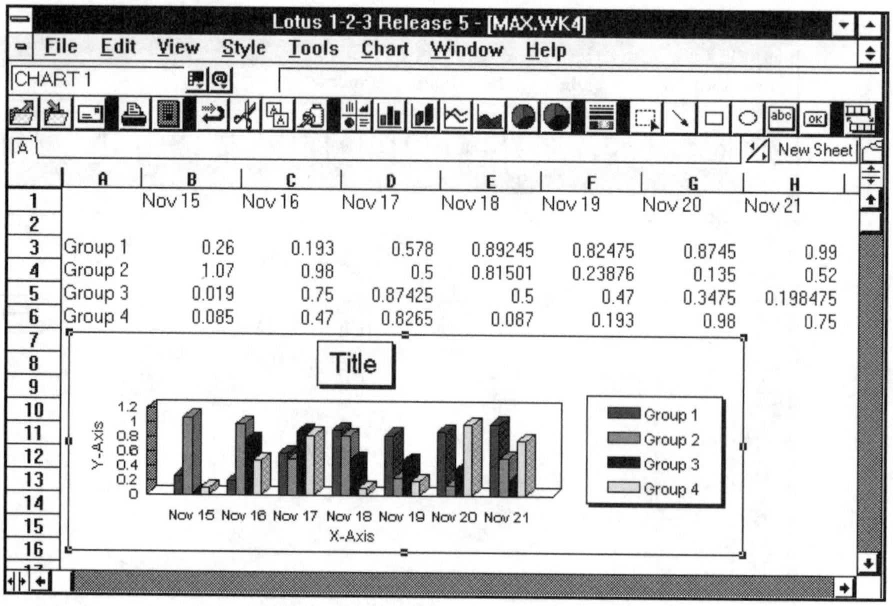

9-4 *Lotus 1-2-3 3D bar graph*

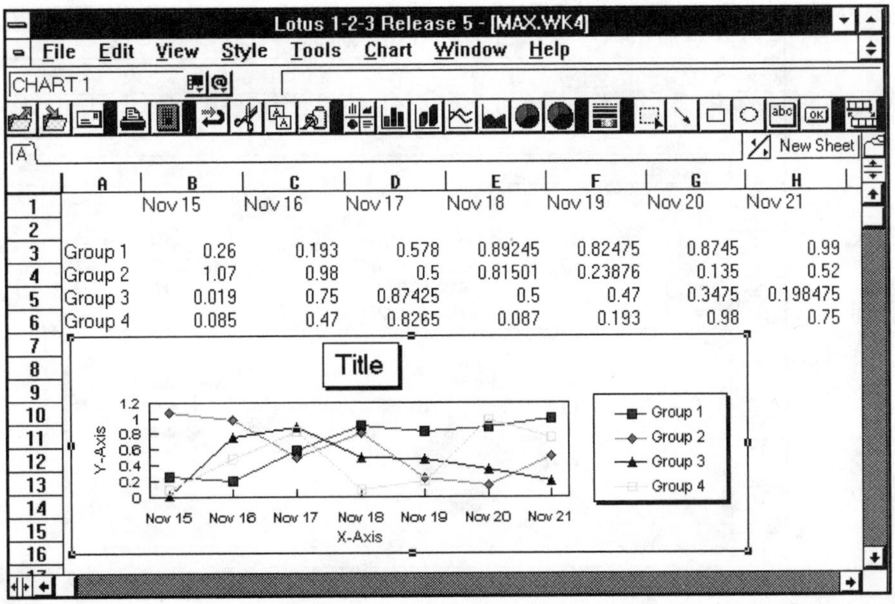

9-5 *Lotus 1-2-3 line graph*

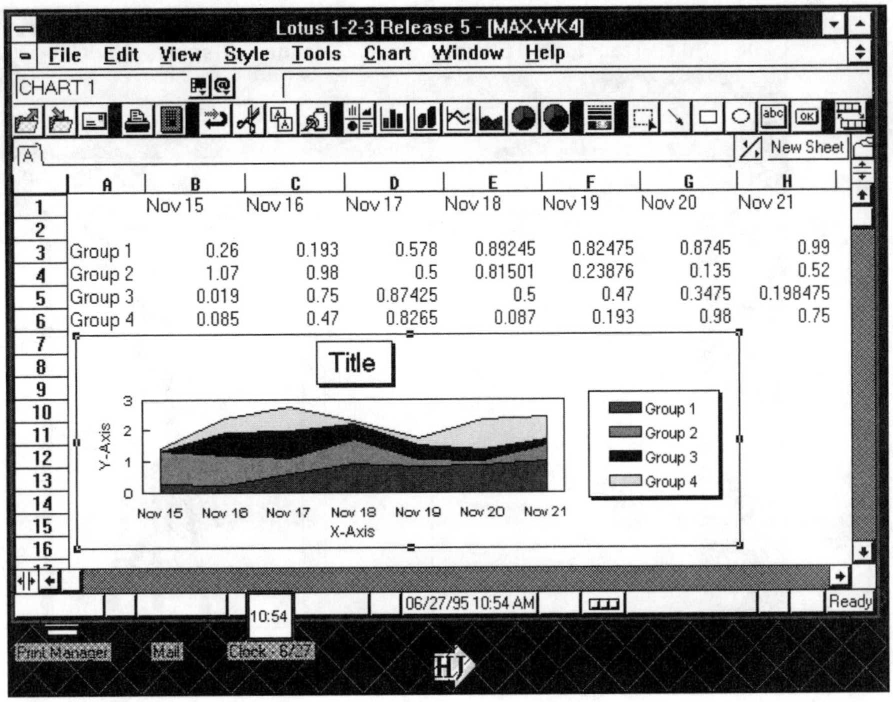

9-6 *Lotus 1-2-3 area graph.*

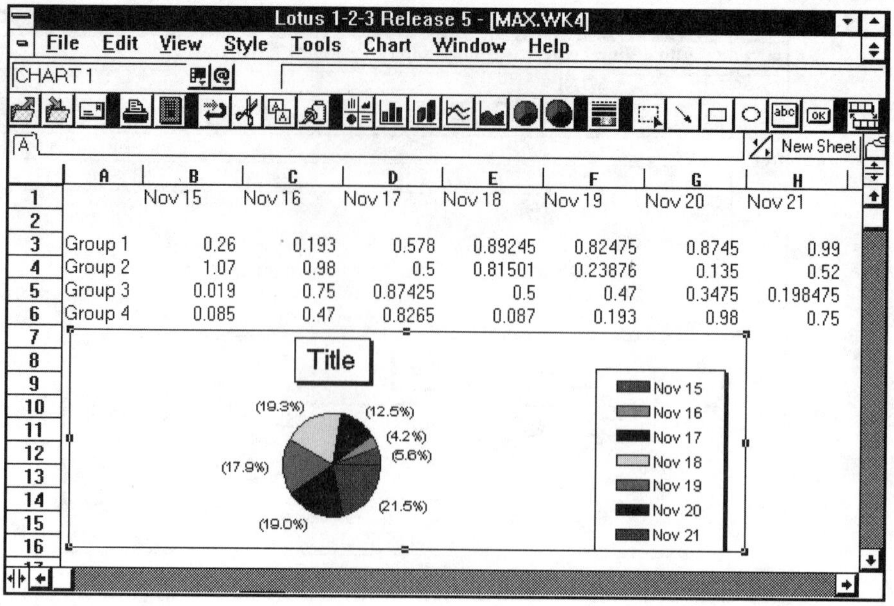

9-7 *Lotus 1-2-3 pie chart.*

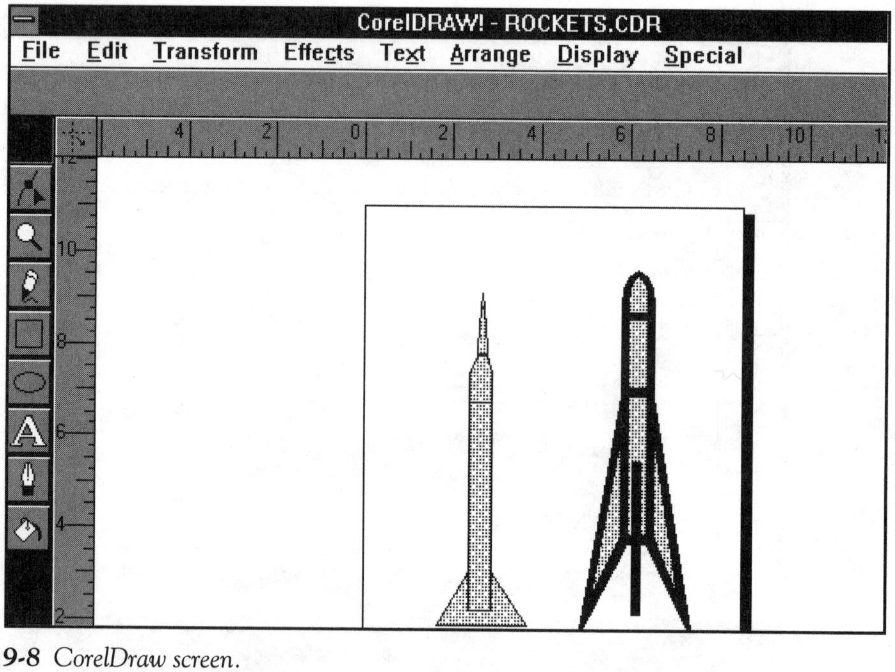

9-8 *CorelDraw screen.*

Desktop publishing programs, such as Ventura and PageMaker, give you the ability to create copy that is ready for a professional printer, often combining word processing, spreadsheet, and graphics data into one file. However, you will probably find that most word processors are adequate for your needs while doing a science project.

As promised in chapter 8, "Writing the research paper," you can also find many resources online to help you with your project. If you belong to services such as America On-Line, CompuServe, or Prodigy, or have access to the Internet, you'll be able to retrieve some reference materials. Another way to use these online services is to look for a forum or bulletin board dealing with the area you're interested in, and see if there's anyone out there who shares your interest and can share some good information. Before venturing online, however, be sure to check with your parents and discuss the amounts of time and money that they're comfortable having you spend online. Whatever computer resources you use to help you, they will not only make your work easier, but they will also give you new and greater insight into this growing, evolving technology.

10
Se habla computer?

Computing is an area all its own. If you're hung up on hardware, passionate about programming, or sensitive to software, a computer science project might be just what you're looking for. A computer science project is quite different from those in botany, chemistry, or medical science. Instead of conducting an experiment, a computer science project generally develops a new product, such as a programming language or a new type of software. Therefore, the entire method of doing a computer science project, from the research to the procedures, follows a different path.

Davis Houlton had no question in his mind that he'd do a computer science project. When the semester began, he was working on a spelling program, and thought he'd do some further work on that. However, a friend of his, whose native language is Spanish, was having a problem with his computer classes because programming requires learning a new language in addition to English. Since computer literacy is important to success in all fields, Davis reasoned that a method of helping non-English speakers to learn programming would be helpful. Besides Spanish, which is important because San Diego is on the Mexican border, Davis chose to translate Tagalog and Vietnamese, which are native languages for many students at his school. He decided not to translate French or German because the ability to program using those languages already exists.

The project plan was to translate Spanish, Tagalog, and Vietnamese into BASIC, the programming language that is taught at his school. The project question and hypothesis are shown in Fig. 10-1.

To do his background research, Davis first consulted several local branch libraries, but he found almost nothing available that related to his topic. He checked the card catalog and found that even the central library had very few current resources. In computer science, which is a rapidly changing field, reference materials become out-of-date very quickly, and new sources of information are published just as fast. However, Point Loma Nazarene College, which was close to his home, had a great deal of material on the BASIC programming language, including how it got started and how it works.

Question	Hypothesis
Can I design and code a system that allows a user to enter a program in his or her native language?	I can use variations of the READ/ WRITE statements in BASIC to develop a system that allows a user to enter a program in his or her native language.

10-1 *XLATE—Question and hypothesis.*

While doing his research, Davis entered each fact and its source and category using Microsoft Windows. When he had accumulated all his information, he used the note-card feature of Windows to sort the facts according to category, format the facts as index cards, and print the cards, which were required as a project milestone in his science class. Then he used the cards as the basis of the background research paper, which he wrote using WordPerfect 5.0.

When developing a complex computer project, it is important to start by designing the system and outlining the steps involved. To develop the system design, Davis created a block diagram, shown in Fig. 10-2, and program information notes, shown in Fig. 10-3. He also produced a pseudocode design, which is an English language outline of a program or system, shown in Figs. 10-4, 10-5, 10-6, and 10-7. The system, named XLATE, consists of three programs. The start-up program allows a user to begin using the XLATE system. Through a menu, shown in Fig. 10-8, the user tells the system the language he or she wants to enter, and whether he or she will use a new or old file. A portion of the start-up program, called MENU.BAS, is shown in Fig. 10-9.

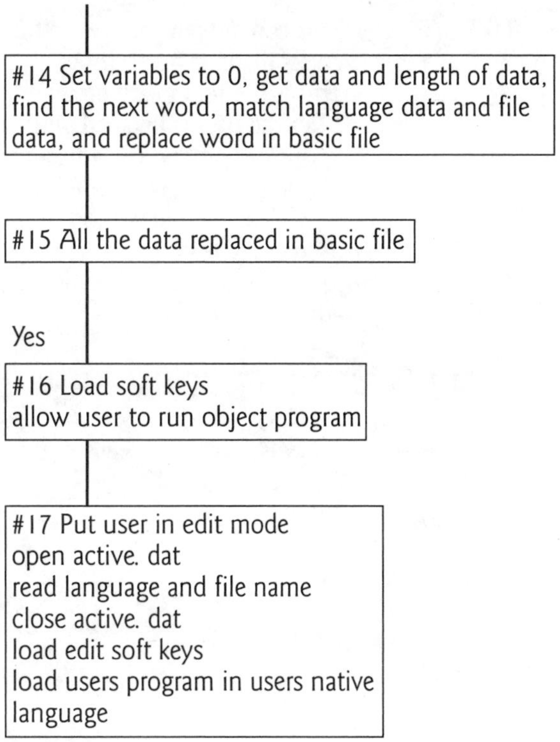

10-2 *XLATE—Block diagram.*

NOTES

PROGRAM INFORMATION:

The three runtime programs are:

MENU.BAS	=	This is the start of the program. It asks the user for speaking language and filename. From here the user has the capability to go to the XLATE program after the user types in his program.
XLATE.BAS	=	This is the main program. This program translates the user's program from foreign to English so BASIC can understand the new program. From here the user can go to the EDIT program.
EDIT.BAS	=	The soft keys are loaded and the user's program is loaded in the user's native language. From here the user can go to XLATE.

There are three data programs. They are:

SPANISH.DAT	=	This program contains all the data needed for translation from Spanish to English.
TAGALOG.DAT	=	This program contains all the data needed for translation from Tagalog to English.
VIET.DAT	=	This program contains all the data needed for translation from Vietnamese to English.

There are four main user programs. They are:

ACTIVE.DAT	=	This contains the active file the user is using and the current language.
T.SRC	=	This is the temporary program to be used by the user. After the user is finished with MENU.BAS and types up his/her program, the user presses the key F3 and the program is saved as T.SRC.
*.OLD	=	This file is the old version of the active file. This is used in file testing.
*.BAS	=	This is what the final edition of the user's program is going to look like.

10-3 *XLATE—Program information notes.*

PROGRAM DESCRIPTION:

Here is the PDL of XLATE:

The first part of XLATE.BAS does the following:
—Opens "ACTIVE.DAT" for input as field #1
—Reads the data in "ACTIVE.DAT"
—Closes "ACTIVE.DAT"

The second part of XLATE.BAS does the following:
—Checks for an error, and if there is one, go to the ERROR handling routine
—Checks to see if there is an OLD FILE. If there is, the OLD FILE is deleted from the disk
—Checks for another error. If there is one, the program goes to the SECOND ERROR handling routine
—Opens the source file, then changes the name of the source file to OLD FILE
—The main file "T.SRC" is named after the source file
—Executes the DATA loading routine
—All files are closed, then the source file is opened in field #1
—The BASIC FILE is opened in field #2
—The dimensions of all subscript variables are assigned
—Data is read into memory. If there is no more data, then executes END

The third part of my program does the following:
—Sets all variables to correct setting
—Gets the length of data
—Grabs a PIECE of the data
—Checks to see if the PIECE is a variable or a reserved word
—Puts the data into the BASIC FILE in field #2
—Gets more data. If there is no more data, then executes END

--- ROUTINES ---
ERROR =
—Returns to where the SOURCE FILE is being opened

SECOND ERROR =
—Returns to where the SOURCE FILE is being named

DATA =
—Loads the correct data set according to language
—Returns to point left off

END =
—Sets up the special keys
—Prints out what the special keys are
—Loads the BASIC FILE
—End of XLATE

10-4 *XLATE—Pseudocode.*

Here is the PDL of MENU.BAS:

Here is the first part of MENU.BAS:
—Wait for user to type in the correct number for speaking language
—If an error happens in the next part, execute the SPEECH routine
—Opens and reads ACTIVE.DAT
—If the language the user entered and the language in ACTIVE.DAT are different, then execute the SPEECH routine
—If the language is SPANISH then goto SPANISH FILE routine
—If the language is TAGALOG then goto TAGALOG file routine
—If the language is VIETNAMESE then goto VIETNAMESE FILE routine

ROUTINES—
SPANISH FILE—
—Print out file screen
—Verify that the specs are proper
—If the file name is incorrect then execute SPANISH ACTIVE.DAT routine
—If the file name is correct then execute SPANISH EDIT

SPANISH ACTIVE.DAT—
—Print out active.dat file screen
—Wait until filename is typed and correct
—Write language and filename to ACTIVE.DAT
—Continue to SPANISH EDIT

SPANISH EDIT—
—Print out edit screen
—Wait for numbered input
—If 1 is entered then run XLATE
—If 2 is entered then goto the SPANISH EDIT KEYS routine

SPANISH EDIT KEYS—
—Set soft keys
—Get user ready to program
—End

TAGALOG FILE—
—Print out file screen
—Verify that the specs are proper
—If the file name is incorrect then execute TAGALOG ACTIVE.DAT routine
—If the file name is correct then execute SPANISH EDIT

TAGALOG ACTIVE.DAT—
—Print out active.dat file screen
—Wait until filename is typed and correct
—Write language and filename to ACTIVE.DAT

10-5 *XLATE—Pseudocode.*

—Continue to TAGALOG EDIT

TAGALOG EDIT—
—Print out edit screen
—Wait for numbered input
—If 1 is entered then run XLATE
—If 2 is entered then goto the TAGALOG EDIT KEYS routine

TAGALOG EDIT KEYS—
—Set soft keys
—Get user ready to program
—End

VIETNAMESE FILE—
—Print out file screen
—Verify that the specs are proper
—If the file name is incorrect then execute VIETNAMESE ACTIVE.DAT routine
—If the file name is correct then execute SPANISH EDIT

VIETNAMESE ACTIVE.DAT—
—Print out active.dat file screen
—Wait until filename is typed and correct
—Write language and filename to ACTIVE.DAT
—Continue to VIETNAMESE EDIT

VIETNAMESE EDIT—
—Print out edit screen
—Wait for numbered input
—If 1 is entered then run XLATE
—If 2 is entered then goto the VIETNAMESE EDIT KEYS routine

VIETNAMESE EDIT KEYS—
—Set soft keys
—Get user ready to program
—End

SPEECH—
—If the language is Spanish then goto SPANISH ACTIVE.DAT
—If the language is Tagalog then goto TAGALOG ACTIVE.DAT
—If the language is Vietnamese then goto VIETNAMESE ACTIVE.DAT

10-6 *XLATE—Pseudocode.*

This is the EDIT PDL:

This is what the first part of EDIT.BAS does:
—Opens and reads ACTIVE.DAT
—If the language is Spanish, then executes SPANISH KEYS
—If the language is Tagalog, then executes TAGALOG KEYS
—If the language is Vietnamese, then executes VIETNAMESE KEYS

ROUTINES ==
SPANISH KEYS—
—Load soft keys
—End

TAGALOG KEYS—
—Load soft keys
—End

VIETNAMESE KEYS—
—Load soft keys
—End

10-7 *XLATE—Pseudo code.*

```
1-Espanol
2-Tagalog
3-Vietnamese
```

10-8 *XLATE—Start-up menu.*

Once the program, called the source, is entered into the computer, the parser translation routine finds each word, which is a series of characters between two blanks. "That was the hardest part of the system to program correctly," said Davis. Once the word is found, the program checks it against a master list for the designated language and finds the word's translation. Portions of the master lists are shown in Spanish in Fig. 10-10, Tagalog in Fig. 10-11, and Vietnamese in Fig. 10-12. If a word is not found on the master list, it remains in its original language. To develop the master list, Davis consulted computer programmers who speak Spanish and Vietnamese, and a teacher who speaks Tagalog. For further reference, he also used dictionaries in all three languages. Portions of the XLATE.BAS program are shown in Figs. 10-13 and 10-14.

```
1    REM  MENU.BAS
2    REM  THIS PROGRAM REQUESTS THE LANGUAGE AND THE LANGUAGE SOURCE FILE
3    REM  INPUT:
4            USER PROMPT: LANGUAGE AND FILENAME
5            ACTIVE.DAT: THE PREVIOUS SESSION LANGUAGE AND FILENAME
6    REM  OUTPUT:
7            ACTIVE.DAT: THE CURRENT LANGUAGE AND FILENAME
8            T.SRC: THE SOURCE LANGUAGE PROGRAM TO BE TRANSLATED
9    :
10   CLS
20   WIDTH 80
30   COLOR 9,4,9:CLS
40   KEY OFF
44   :
45   REM #1 - MAIN MENU
50   PRINT:LOCATE 2,36:PRINT"XLATE SPANISH/VIETNAMESE/TAGALOG
60   PRINT:PRINT"===================================================
==============="
64   :
65   REM #1 - 1 = SPANISH SELECTION. 2 = TAGALOG SELECTION 3 = VIETNAMESE
SELECTION
70   PRINT:PRINT"1-Espanol
80   PRINT:PRINT"2-Tagalog
90   PRINT:PRINT"3-Vietnamese
100 A$=INKEY$:IF A$="" THEN GOTO 100
104 :
105 REM #1 - SET SPEECH CODE
110 IF A$=1 THEN LANG$+"SPANISH":SPEECH=1
120 IF A$=2 THEN LANG$+"TAGALOG":SPEECH=2
130 IF A$=3 THEN LANG$+"VIETNAMESE":SPEECH=3
140 IF A$<>"1" AND A$<>"2" AND A$<>"3" THEN GOTO 100
```

10-9 *XLATE—Portion of MENU.BAS.*

```
7990 REM SPANISH.DATA
7991 REM This file is the Spanish to BASIC reserved word translation
8000 RESTORE:DIM E$(169):DIM F$(169):FOR I TO (169): READ F$(I): READ E$(I):
NEXT I: GOTO 140:
9000 DATA "ABS","ABS"
9010 DATA "YA","AND"
9020 DATA "ASC","ASC"
9030 DATA "ATN","ATN"
9040 DATA "AUTOMATICO","AUTO"
9050 DATA "TONO","BEEP"
9060 DATA "BLOAD","BLOAD"
9070 DATA "BSAVE","BSAVE"
9080 DATA "LLAMA","CALL"
9090 DATA "CDBL","CDBL"
9100 DATA "CADENA","CHAIN"
9110 DATA "CAMDIR","CHDIRL"
9120 DATA "LET$","CHR$"
9130 DATA "CINT","CINT"
9140 DATA "CIRCULO","CIRCLE"
9150 DATA "ACLARA","CLEAR"
9160 DATA "CIERRA","CLOSE"
9170 DATA "BORRAM","CLS"
9180 DATA "COLOR","COLOR"
9190 DATA "COMUN","COMMON"
```

10-10 *XLATE—Portion of Spanish master list.*

```
7990 REM TAGALOG.DATA
7991 REM This file is the Tagalog to BASIC reserved word translation
8000 RESTORE:DIM E$(169):DIM F$(169):FOR I TO (169): READ F$(I): READ E$(I):
NEXT I: GOTO 140:
9000 DATA "TAWAG","CALL"
9010 DATA "BILOG","CIRCLE"
9020 DATA "MALINAW","CLEAR"
9030 DATA "SARADO","CLOSE"
9040 DATA "KULAY","COLOR"
9050 DATA "PUNGKARANIWAN","COMMON"
9060 DATA "PETCHA","DATE$"
9070 DATA "ASLIN","DELETE"
9080 DATA "AT","AND"
9090 DATA "BURAHIN","ERASE"
9100 DATA "BUKIOL","FIELD"
9110 DATA "KUNG","IF"
9120 DATA "PATAYIN","KILL"
9130 DATA "NATILIRA","LEFT$"
9140 DATA "GUHIT","LINE"
9150 DATA "TINGNANOHAMAPIN","LOCATE"
9160 DATA "MAGIISAOMAGSASAME","MERGE"
9170 DATA "PANGALAN","NAME"
9180 DATA "BAGO","NEW"
9190 DATA "SUNSUNOD","NEXT"
```

10-11 *XLATE—Portion of Tagalog master list.*

```
7990 REM VIET.DATA
7991 REM This file is the Vietnamese to BASIC reserved word translation
8000 RESTORE:DIM E$(169):DIM F$(169):FOR I TO (169): READ F$(I): READ E$(I):
NEXT I: GOTO 140:
9000 DATA "TUUETDOI","ABS"
9010 DATA "VA","AND"
9020 DATA "ASC","ASC"
9030 DATA "ATN","ATN"
9040 DATA "AUTO","AUTO"
9050 DATA "BEEP","BEEP"
9060 DATA "BLOAD","BLOAD"
9070 DATA "BSAVE","BSAVE"
9080 DATA "GOI","CALL"
9090 DATA "CDBL","CDBL"
9100 DATA "CHAIN","CHAIN"
9110 DATA "CHDIR","CHDIRL"
9120 DATA "CHU$","CHR$"
9130 DATA "CINT","CINT"
9140 DATA "VONGTRON","CIRCLE"
9150 DATA "XOA","CLEAR"
9160 DATA "DONGLAI","CLOSE"
9170 DATA "XOAMAN","CLS"
9180 DATA "MAU","COLOR"
9190 DATA "COMMON","COMMON"
```

10-12 *Vietnamese master list.*

```
1   REM  XLATE.BAS
2   REM  THIS PROGRAM TRANSLATES THE FOREIGN LANGUAGE BASIC PROGRAM
3   REM  GW-BASIC AND ALLOWS THE USER TO RUN AND DEBUG THE PROGRAM.
4   REM  INPUT:
5            ACTIVE.DAT: LANGUAGE AND FILENAME
6            T.SRC: THE SOURCE LANGUAGE PROGRAM TO BE TRANSLATED
7            USER PROMPT: REQUEST TO EDIT SOURCE LANGUAGE PROGRAM
8   REM  OUTPUT:
9            FILENAME.OLD: PREVIOUS VERSION OF SOURCE LANGUAGE PROGRAM
10           FILENAME.SRC: CURRENT VERSION OF SOURCE LANGUAGE PROGRAM
11           FILENAME.BAS: TRANSLATED PROGRAM IN GW-BASIC
12  :
13  REM #7 - OPEN ACTIVE.DAT, READ LANGUAGE (LANGS) AND THE FILENAME
(FILES) FROM ACTIVE.DAT AND THEN CLOSE ACTIVE.DAT
14  OPEN,"i",#1,"ACTIVE.DAT"
15  INPUT #1,"LANG$,FILE$
16  IF LANG$="SPANISH" THEN NOD=167
17  REM #8 - CHECK FOR OLDFILES (FILE$.OLD).  IF OLDFILE IS NOT LOCATED
CONTINUE TO 5500
18  ON ERROR GOTO 5500
19  IF LANG$="TAGALOG" THEN NOD=73
20  IF LANG$="VIETNAMESE" THEN NOD=169
25  EXE$=".OLD":OFILES=FILES+EXE$
30  CLOSE #3
35  REM #9 - DELETE OLDFILE
40  KILL OFILES
44  :
45  REM #10 - CHECK FOR SOURCE FILE (FILE$.SRC).  IF SOURCE FILE IS NOT
LOCATED, CONTINUE TO 5520
50  ON ERROR, GO TO 5500
```

10-13 *XLATE—Portion of XLATE.BAS.*

```
1565 REM #14 - MATCH DATA FROM SOURCE FILE AGAINST LANGUAGE DATA
1580 IF BS=1 AND TYPE(BS)=1 THEN A$=MID$(B$,START(BS)NUMBER(BS)) ELSE
GOTO 1640:
1600 FOR I=1 TO NOD:IF A$=F$(I) THEN A$=E$(I):GOTO 1740
1601 NEXT I
1602 GOTO 1740
1640 IF BS=1 AND TYPE(BS)=0 THEN A$=MID$(B$,START(BS),NUMBER(BS)):GOTO 1740
1660 IF BS<>1 AND TYPE(BS)=1 THEN WORD$=MID$(B$,START(BS),NUMBER(BS))
ELSE GOTO 1720
1680 FOR I=1 TO NOD:IF WORD$=F$(I) THEN WORD$=E$(I):A$=A$+WORD$:GOTO 1740
1681 NEXT I A$=A$+WORD$:GOTO 1740
1720 IF BS<>1 AND TYPE(BS)=) THEN WORD$=MID$(B$,START(BS),NUMBER(BS))
1740 NEXT BS
1744 :
1760 PRINT#2,A$
1780 GOTO 170
4999 REM #12 - LOAD LANGUAGE DATA AND RETURN TO 140
5010 IF LANG$="SPANISH" THEN CHAIN MERGE "TAGALOG.DAT",8000,ALL
5010 IF LANG$="TAGALOG" THEN CHAIN MERGE "VIET.DAT",8000,ALL
5020 IF LANG$="VIETNAMESE" THEN CHAIN MERGE "VIET.DAT",8000,ALL
5040 GOTO 140
```

10-14 *XLATE—Portion of XLATE.BAS.*

The edit program loads the "soft" keys, listed in Fig. 10-15. Soft keys allow the programmer to use function keys to enter some common commands, instead of typing in the entire command. The program then loads and runs the BASIC program, locating and displaying any errors that it finds. Portions of EDIT.BAS are shown in Fig. 10-16.

To assist users, Davis also developed instructions and menu screens in the three languages. Samples of these menus, translated into Spanish, are shown in Figs. 10-17 through 10-21. Figure 10-17 shows the ready menu, Fig. 10-18 shows the screen that appears when the program is loaded, and Fig. 10-19 lets the user choose whether to edit or run a program. Figure 10-20 lets the user enter a file name, and Fig. 10-21 lets the user verify the file name.

While developing the three programs, Davis used the procedures outlined in Fig. 10-22. However, in his science project notebook, the list of procedures is considerably longer and more detailed.

To test the XLATE system, Davis checked the master lists in Spanish, Tagalog, and Vietnamese, both manually and using DOS (disk operating system) commands. He also developed a demonstration program, which he translated into all three languages and successfully ran.

Overall, he found that he was able to create an effective language translator in all three languages. However, the Tagalog version was somewhat less effective because the language does not contain many technical terms, and several words had to remain untranslated. "XLATE will be most effective in the classroom," says Davis, "where there's a teacher to help the students with the actual BASIC programming." The backboard, which featured the block diagram and portions of the actual BASIC code, and students using the program appear in Fig. 10-23.

The list of editing soft keys are as follows:

F1 = LIST	Lists the program
F2 = RUN XLATE	Runs XLATE
F3 = AUTO	Sets automatic line numbering on
F4 = SAVE T.SRC	Saves the user's program as T.SRC
F5 = LLIST	Prints out the program on the printer
F6 = RENUM	Renumber lines
F7 = DELETE	Delete lines
F8 = EDIT	Edit a line

The runtime soft keys are as follows:

F1 = PRINT	Print out something on the screen
F2 = RUN	Run the program
F3 = SYSTEM	Go to DOS
F4 = RUN EDIT	Run the EDIT.BAS program
F5 = CONT	Continue a STOPped program
F6 = FILES	Lists all the files
F7 = TRON	Trace on
F8 = TROFF	Trace off

10-15 *XLATE—Soft keys.*

```
1    REM  EDTSRC.BAS
2    REM  THIS PROGRAM PROCESSES THE USER SELECTION OF "SRC" FROM THE
3    REM  TRANSLATE PROGRAM.  THE USER CAN EDIT THE SOURCE LANGUAGE
4    REM  PROGRAM.
5    REM  INPUT:
6            ACTIVE.DAT: LANGUAGE AND FILENAME
7            FILENAME.SRC: THE SOURCE LANGUAGE PROGRAM
8            USER PROMPT: REQUEST TO TRANSLATE & RUN SOURCE PROGRAM
9    :
10   CLOSE
11   SCREEN 2 0
15   REM #17 - OPEN ACTIVE.DAT, READ LANGUAGE FILE & FILE NAME FROM
ACTIVE.DAT AND CLOSE ACTIVE.DAT
20   OPEN"I", #1,"ACTIVE.DAT"
40   INPUT#1,"LANG$,FILE$
40   CLOSE
44   :
45   REM #17 - SET USERS FILE NAME
46   EXE$=".SRC":FILE$+EXE$
50   IF LANG$="SPANISH" THEN GOTO 5000
60   IF LANG$="TAGALOG" THEN GOTO 2000
70   IF LANG$="VIETNAMESE" THEN GOTO 3000
1999 :
2000 CLS
2001 REM#17 - LOAD SOFT KEYS
2010 KEY OFF
2020 KEY 3,"AUTO"+CHR$(13)
2030 KEY 1,"LIST"+CHR$(13)
2040 KEY 5,"LLIST"
2050 KEY 6,"RENUM"
2060 KEY 4,"SAVE"+"T.SRC"+"CHR$(34)+",A"+CHR$(13)
2065 KEY2,"RUN"+"XLATE.BAS"+CHR$(13)
2070 KEY 7,"DELETE"
2075 KEY 8,"EDIT"
2080 LOCATE 25,1:PRINT"1-LIST  2-TAKBO  3-AUTO  4-ITABI  5-LLIST  6-RENUM
7-ALISIN  8-EDIT"
2100 PRINT"TAGALOG":PRINT:PRINT:PRINT:PRINT:PRINT:PRINT:PRINT
2105 REM#17 - LOAD FILE.SRC
2110 LOAD FILE$
2999 :
```

10-16 *XLATE—Portion of EDTSRC.BAS.*

```
Listo a Programar



Ok

1-IMPRIME  2-CORRE  3-SYSTEMA  4-SRC  5-CONT  6-ARCHIVOS  7-TRON  8-TROFF
```

10-17 *XLATE—Spanish menu—Ready.*

```



DAVIS.BAS LOADED->
Ok

1-IMPRIME  2-CORRE  3-SYSTEMA  4-SRC  5-CONT  6-ARCHIVOS  7-TRON  8-TROFF
```

10-18 *XLATE—Spanish menu—Program loaded.*

```
REDACTAR / CORRE

1 - REDACTAR
2 - CORRE

FILE:DAVIS.SRC
```

10-19 *XLATE—Spanish menu—Edit or run.*

```
CREAR ACTIVE.DAT

Registrar el nombre de la ficha
```

10-20 *XLATE—Spanish menu—Requesting file name.*

```
     NOMBRE DE LA FICHA:  DAVIS

1 - Es correcto el nombre de la ficha
2 - Es incorrecto el nombre de la ficha
```

10-21 *XLATE-Spanish menu—Verifying file name.*

Procedures
1. Compiled list of BASIC reserved words
2. Acquired translation of BASIC reserved words in Spanish, Tagalog, and Vietnamese
3. Created flowchart for the XLATE system
4. Designed program requirements for the programs, based on the BASIC handbook
5. Designed data files (master lists) in three languages
6. Converted master lists to ASCII, then used DOS commands to check for accuracy and completeness
7. Coded three programs, MENU.BAS, XLATE.BAS, and EDTSRC.BAS
8. Coded a sample program used to test XLATE system

10-22 *XLATE—Procedures.*

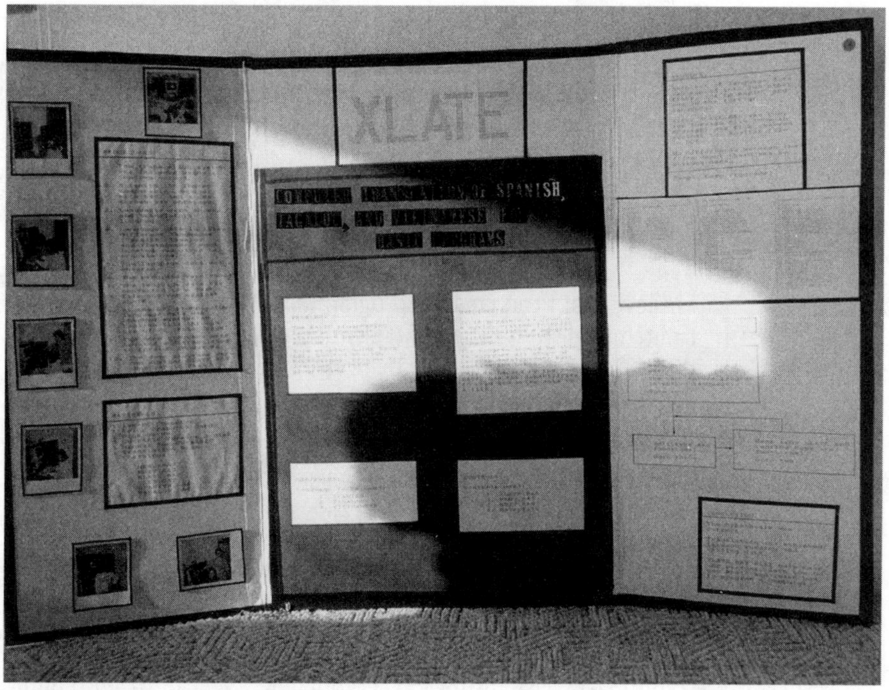

***10-23** XLATE—Backboard.*

When XLATE was complete, Davis identified several enhancements for the program. The most time-consuming part of the system's execution was searching the master list for the translation of each word. The program began at the first word in the list for the selected language. XLATE might have needed to check the entire list of 189 items before it found a match or determined that no match existed. However, in any future version, Davis wanted to use an indexing procedure. This would speed up the search, since not every word must be checked each time.

He also felt that one weakness, which he was unable to correct in the amount of time available, was the lack of documentation in languages other than English for BASIC, DOS, or the PC computer itself. A general system improvement would be to translate some DOS commands, and portions of the BASIC manual, to make it an even more effective tool.

A year later, Davis expanded and embellished on his project, earning him a ticket to the ISEF in Orlando, Florida. The second year, he had four objectives for expanding on his work:

- Speed up the translation portion of XLATE.
- Provide error messages in the user's selected language.
- Provide a DOS interface in the user's selected language.
- Provide the capability to add additional languages to the XL system.

To develop his new system, XL, he developed the hypothesis shown in Fig. 10-24. The equipment he used is enumerated in the materials list, shown in Fig. 10-25. The variables and controls for the project are shown in Fig. 10-26, and the procedures are listed in Fig. 10-27.

Hypothesis

I believe that I can create a programming environment so that Limited English Proficiency (LEP) users can create programs in their native languages. The demonstration languages used were Spanish, Tagalog, and Vietnamese.

10-24 *XL: An English Independent Language—Hypothesis.*

Materials

1. 1 Zenith Data Systems IBM PC compatible ZW-158-42 with 640 Kb memory (or an IBM-PC compatible with 640 Kb memory) with an 8 bit processor (8086), and a MicroDex MHz Turbo 386
2. 1 Hercules CGA, EGA, MCGA, or VGA compatible graphics card
3. 1 5½" (a:l)
4. 1 GW-BASIC version 1 floppy disk
5. 1 GW-BASIC manual
6. 1 Zenith Data Systems computer monitor (or an IBM-PC compatible monitor)
7. 1 120/140 volt power source
8. Two blank, formatted diskettes, or 1 10 Mb hard disk
9. 1 Zenith Data Systems keyboard (or IBM-PC compatible keyboard)
10. 7 program listings
11. 9 data listings
12. 1 mouse
13. 1 Turbo Pascal 5.5 package
14. 1mouse unit
15. 1 Terminate Stay Resident unit
16. 1 self-made window unit

10-25 *XL: An English Independent Language—Materials.*

Variables and Controls

Variables
A) Type of language
B) Speed of XLATE translate process

Variables to be measured
A) Speed of XLATE translation process, in seconds

Controls
A) The base program (XLATE)
B) The variables in the test program
C) Numeric values (0,1,2,3,4,5,6,7,8,9)
D) Special values [ASCII !@#$%^&*():;"' < > ,.?/\|]
E) All project materials

10-26 *XL: An English Independent Language—Variables and controls.*

Procedures

1. Design the programming environment, XL, using top down methodology and PDL.
2. Design XLMETA, the program to process language data.
3. Design XLATE II, including native language BASIC commands, error processing and indexed translation.
4. Design XLDOS to allow English-independent access to key DOS commands.
5. Code XLMETA and XLDOS in PASCAL.
6. Implement XLATE features in BASIC.
7. Obtain translations and implement them in XLMETA.
8. Code sample programs in Spanish, Tagalog and Vietnamese.
9. Test sample programs until they work correctly.

10-27 *XL: An English Independent Language—Procedures.*

The new system consists of three subsystems—XLDOS, XLATE II, and XL-META—as shown in the opening screen displays in Figs. 10-28, 10-29, and 10-30. XLDOS provides a DOS shell in the user's selected language, and XLATE allows a user to create, edit, run, and debug a program in his or her selected language. XLMETA enables the user to generate XLATE and XLDOS main language files in a new language, giving the system greater flexibility.

XL

© Copyright Davis Houlton 1991, All rights reserved
© Copyright Davis Houlton 1991, All rights reserved

Enter your name
Enter your name

Xin cho biet ten
Xin cho biet ten

Isulat ang iyong pangala
Isulat ang iyong pangala

Anotar su nombre
Anotar su nombre

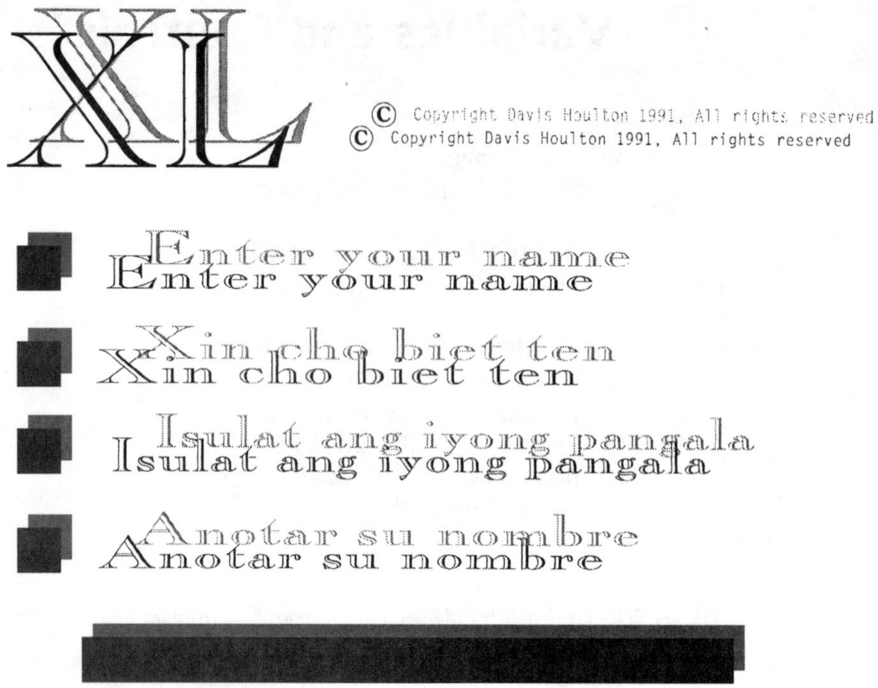

10-28 XL: An English Independent Language—Opening screen.

XLMETA

English only
English only

Environment Manager Only
Environment Manager Only

Press Q to quit, any other key to continue...

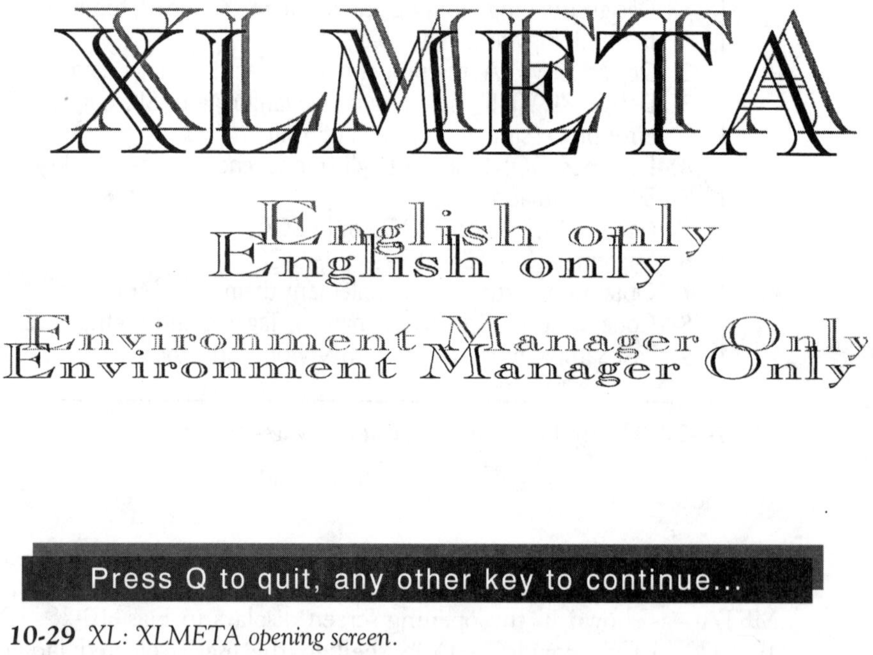

10-29 XL: XLMETA opening screen.

10-30 *XL: An English Independent Language—XLATE II opening screen.*

The following programs, written in PASCAL, make up the new XL system:

- XLDOS.
- STARTUP2. This program starts up the XL environment and transfers to XLDOS via a batch file.
- XLDOS. The main DOS processing program under XL executes whichever DOS function the user selects.
- XLMETA. This program allows the user to select the option that he or she requires (edit XLDOS, menu or language files, or error processing functions).
- XLATE.
    - MENU. The XLATE start-up program.
    - XLATE. The translation program.
    - EDTSRC. The edit source code processing program.
    - EDTERR. The error code processing program.
    - STARTUP4. The start-up screen.
    - XLATE uses the following data files while processing:
      ~(language name.DAT). The reserved word list.
      ~ACTIVE.DAT. Contains the active file name and the current language. T.SRC. Temporary hold area for the current file.
      ~*.OLD. Old version of the active file.
      ~*.BAS. Final version of the active file.

Results

From the main XL menu, shown in Fig. 10-31, the user can execute XLDOS, XLMETA, or XLATE. XLMETA, whose menu screens are shown in Figs. 10-32, 10-33, and 10-34, is an English-only subsystem that is used to process a language file, add or delete a language on the system, or modify an existing language file.

```
XLMETA

Edit Language File
Edit XLDOS Data File
Edit Error Data File
Edit XLATE Translations
Exit to XLDOS
```

```
Help
Movement:

Use Up/Down arrow
keys to move highlight
bar up or down.

Selection:

Use Del key to
select the
highlighted item.
```

10-31 *XL: An English Independent Language—XLMETA menu screen.*

```
Help
Movement:

Use Up/Down arrow
keys to move highlight
bar up or down.

Selection:

Use Del key to
select the
highlighted item.
```

```
Edit old XLDOS data file
Create new XLDOS data file
```

10-32 *XL: An English Independent Language—XLMETA menu screen.*

```
Edit Language File - # 1
English

                              Help
                              Movement:
Edit current
Delete current                Use Up/Down arrow
Skip to ...                   keys to move highlight
Continue                      bar up or down.
Exit and save
Exit without save             Selection:

                              Use Del key to
                              select the
                              highlighted item.
```

10-33 *XL: An English Independent Language—XLMETA menu screen.*

```
DATE:  4/9/91      XLDOS      TIME:  17:54

DIRECTORY:  C:\TP

COMMANDS:              0   SELECT FILE/DIRECTORY OR EXIT
                       Ins
XLMETA
DISK ACTIONS           .   SELECT/DO HIGHLIGHTED ITEM
TAG                    Del
XLATE
QUIT
```

10-34 *XL: An English Independent Language—DOS screen menu.*

By selecting XLATE II, the menu shown in Fig. 10-35 allows the user to select a language and then enter and verify a file name, as shown in the sample screen in Fig. 10-36. The Edit/Run menu, displayed in Spanish in Fig. 10-37, lets the user run or edit the selected file. Figure 10-38 displays a Spanish BASIC program, which was loaded through XLATE II, with the function key definitions shown in Spanish. Figure 10-39 illustrates an error message screen in Spanish.

```
Enter speech data file [Max 8 letters]:
```

```
                    XLATE SPANISH/VIETNAMESE/TAGALOG
================================================================

1-Espanol
2-Tagalog
3-Vietnamese
```

10-35 *XL: An English Independent Language—XLATE II initial screen.*

```
                              ESPANOL
================================================================

      NOMBRE DE LA FICHA:  test1spa


1-Es correcto el nombre de la ficha?
2-Es incorrecto el nombre de la ficha?
```

```
CREAR ACTIVE.DAT
================================================================

Registrar el nombre de la ficha
                              ********
```

10-36 *XL: An English Independent Language—XLATE II file verification screen.*

```
REDACTAR / CORRE
=========================================================================


1 - REDACTAR
2 - CORRE
NOMBRE DE LA FICHA:TEST1SPA.SRC






Listo a Programar



Ok
F1-LISTA  F2-CORRE  F3-AUTO  F4-GUARDA  F5-LLISTA  F6-RENUMERA  F7-DELETE  F8-EDITA
```

10-37 *XL: An English Independent Language—XLATE II edit/run menu screen.*

As part of the procedure, Davis verified the design of the XL system by testing all three subsystems until they worked correctly. To accomplish the other objective of making the translation faster, Davis implemented a new method of searching the selected language file. In the old system, the program checked each word in the "dictionary," which meant that the program might have to look at every word in the list until it found a match. In XLATE II, Davis used a search algorithm. This method encodes each word with a value, based on its starting letter. Using the algorithm and an alphabetic translation dictionary, the program only needs to search the words that begin with that letter.

To verify that this index algorithm speeded the translation, Davis performed timed trials using both the old and new methods. Figures 10-40 through 10-42 show the results of the timed trials.

Davis felt that the new and improved XL system fulfilled his objectives. Although he did not win any awards at ISEF, getting there was a major accomplishment for a ninth grader, the youngest group of students invited to ISEF (and getting to visit the theme parks of Orlando wasn't a bad side benefit either). The project display is shown in Fig. 10-43.

Davis has taken XL to other fairs and exhibitions, where it has been well received. He has also copyrighted the system, anticipating wider use (and perhaps commercial success) in the future.

```
XLATE II...
5   COMMENTA TEST1SPAN.BAS - SPANISH TEST
6   :
10  LLAVE APOGADO
20  PANTALLA 1 : BORRAM
30  LINEA(1,198)-(320,198),2
40  LINEA(1,199)-(320,199),2
50  LINEA(1,175)-(40,197),2,B
60  LINEA(45,175)-(85,197),2,B



150  PINTA(Z,Z),10
160  PINTA(Z,Z),0
170  PINTA(Z,Z),0
180  SIQUIENTE Z
190  RUIDO 370,17
200  PARA D=1 A 1000:SIQUIENTE D
210  PARA P=1 A 115 PASO 6
220  Z=198
230  PARA D=1 A 100:SIQUENTE D
240  RUIDO 300+P,10
250  CIRCULO(Z,Z),P,,,,3/12
260  LINEA(180,175)-(220,197),0,B
270  SI P< >31 LUEGO 300
280  LINEA(135,175)-(175,197),0,B
290  LINEA(225,175)-(265,197),0,B
300  SI P< >79 LUEGO 330
310  LINEA(270,175)-(310,197),0,B
320  LINEA(90,175)-(130,197),0,B
330  SIQUIENTE P
340  END

TEST1SPA.BAS LOADED->
Ok

F1-IMPRIME  F2-CORRE  F3-SYSTEMA  F4-SRC  F5-CONT  F6-ARCHIVO  F7-TRON  F8-TROFF
```

10-38 *XL: An English Independent Language—Spanish BASIC program under XLATE II.*

```
+--------------------------------------------------------------------------+
¦ ERROR SINTAXIS                                                           ¦
+--------------------------------------------------------------------------+
¦ 20                                                                       ¦
+--------------------------------------------------------------------------+
```

Listo a Programar

Ok

F1-LISTA F2-CORRE F3-AUTO F4-GUARDA F5-LLISTA F6-RENUMERA F7-DELETE F8-EDITA

10-39 *XL: An English Independent Language—Spanish BASIC error message XLATE II.*

Translation Times for Original Method

Trial Number	*Average Times*	*Total Times*
1	.8378510	11.73
2	.8257143	11.56
3	.8335714	11.67
4	.8300000	11.62
5	.834285714	11.62
6	.834285714	11.61
7	.8342857	11.68
8	.8342857	11.68
9	.8335714	11.67
10	.8264186	11.57
Mean	.8614924095	11.641

10-40 *XL: An English Independent Language—Timed trials, original method.*

Translation Times for Timing Algorithms

Trial Number	Average Times	Total Times
1	.1192857	1.67
2	.1392857	1.95
3	.1300000	1.82
4	.1385714	1.94
5	.1271429	1.78
6	.1228571	1.72
7	.1300000	1.82
8	.1307143	1.83
9	.1257143	1.76
10	.1228571	1.72
Mean	.12864285	1.801

10-41 *XL: An English Independent Language—Timed trials, new algorithm.*

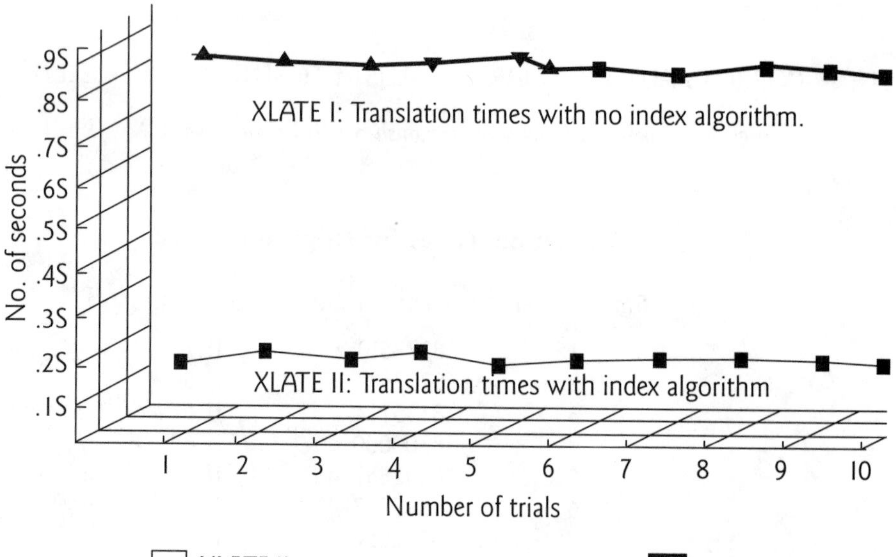

Comparison of translation times before and after indexing.

10-42 *XL: An English Independent Language—Graph, timed trials of translation.*

10-43 *XL: An English Independent Language.*

Helpful hints

- Plan your system before you begin to program. Using block diagrams or pseudocode can help to organize your project and keep you on track.
- Use all the tools that are available on your computer to write your research paper, develop your statistics, or enhance your backboard.

- Computer science projects can be short and simple or long and complex. Before you begin, try to analyze your skills and your desire to be involved with the project. Don't bite off more than you can (comfortably) chew.
- Davis had a few words of wisdom for anyone who makes it to the science fair. "Make sure you know your material," he says, "because if the judges are interested in your project, they'll ask questions."

11
The question and the hypothesis

As discussed previously, the purpose of a project (or any other piece of investigation) is to answer a question or solve a problem. This isn't limited to science; if you ever take journalism, you'll find that the basis of every news story is the five Ws+: who, what, when, where, why, and how. If you think about it, this will be true for your project as well.

When you're deciding on the question (or purpose of the experiment), be sure that it's one that you can answer with the time, resources, skills, and equipment available. If you were thinking of a broad category, narrow it down to a limited aspect of your general topic. Consider exactly how you plan to conduct your experiment and what you need in terms of time, money, space, etc. After careful consideration, you might decide to change your question to make your project more manageable.

Now, however, you have an advantage that you didn't have when you began. The information you gathered for your research paper will help you to focus on the purpose of the project and pose that specific question. Remember, however, that with a few rare exceptions, an effective project cannot be based only on research, but should be one you can solve by experimentation, or development of a concept or a product, followed by analysis of the results. Usually, engineering and computer science projects consist of design, research, and development, rather than an experiment. You'll see the difference in the chapters that follow.

Notice that we've used the words specific, narrow, and focused many times. As we've said before, the biggest mistake beginners make is to define a topic that is too broad.

Notice that the questions in Fig. 11-1 are vague. They don't indicate the substances or quantities to be tested, or how differences will be measured. To be a helpful tool, identify exactly what your experiment will test and the comparisons you intend to make. Examine Fig. 11-2 and notice how the same topics were narrowed down and reworded into specific questions that indicate what will be compared and measured to show similarities or differences. For exam-

1. Does television have a bad effect on test scores?
2. Does sound affect appetite?
3. What plants are flame retardant?
4. What is the effect of irrigating plants with purified water?
5. Do teenagers get overexcited watching Beavis and Butthead?

11-1 *Poorly worded questions.*

1. What is the difference in test scores between fifth graders watching less than 4 hours of television per night and more than 4 hours of television per night?
2. What is the difference between the appetite of goldfish subject to low and high frequency sound, or no sound at all?
3. What is the different rate of combustion of 5 plant types in San Diego county canyons?
4. What is the difference in growth rate of four different types of plants irrigated with tap water or purified water?
5. What is the difference in pulse rate of teenagers watching Beavis and Butthead?

11-2 *Well-worded questions.*

ple, question 3 states what we are attempting to accomplish and also names the types of plants to be used and what is to be measured.

When you carefully read and compare the questions on both lists, you'll see that the best questions are limited in scope. They state the intent of the experiment, list the type and number of subjects to be tested, and describe results to be measured.

Once you have decided on your question, you must develop your hypothesis, which is your theory of the probable answer to your question. You probably have a good guess, or at least an opinion, on what you think will happen during the project. You might have held this theory before doing your research, but after gathering the data, you'll have an educated guess, based on the information you've learned.

Before we go on, let's define our terms. A fact is something that's been proven true, but an opinion is something that you believe is true. *Webster's Ninth New Collegiate Dictionary* defines an opinion as: "a belief stronger than an impression and less strong than positive knowledge." A hypothesis, on the other hand, is stronger than an opinion and weaker than a fact; in other words, it is your prediction of the results, which is an opinion based on the facts.

The purpose of your experiment is to prove your hypothesis. You'll perform a series of tests or trials, which will prove your theory, by applying various substances or using different quantities of something. Then you'll make observations, measure the variations, and record the results. Therefore, your statement must identify what you are testing, how you are testing it, and why you expect the results to prove your hypothesis.

Fig. 11-3 gives examples of well-worded hypotheses, which relate to the specific questions asked in Fig. 11-2. You'll notice that all the hypotheses begin with the words "I believe..." This shows that it is only a theory until the experiment has been done and its results analyzed.

1. I believe that the test scores of sixth graders watching more than 4 hours of television per night will be lower than those watching less than 4 hours of television per night.
2. I believe that the amount of food eaten by goldfish subject to low and high frequency sound will differ from the amount eaten by those subject to no sound.
3. I believe that succulent plants will burn more slowly than nonsucculent plant types in San Diego county canyons.
4. I believe that plants irrigated with tap water will have a higher growth rate than those irrigated with purified water.
5. I believe that teenagers watching Beavis and Butthead will have a higher pulse rate than those watching the Discovery Channel.

11-3 *Hypotheses.*

Sometimes a hypothesis will also state why you're making this assumption. For example, in Andrew Wolf's experiment testing the porosity of various types of Hohokam pottery, he assumed that cooking pottery required a different porosity than storage pottery.

In certain types of projects—particularly engineering, computer science, or mathematics—the hypothesis might be a statement of what the experiment hopes to accomplish. For example, when Davis Houlton developed his XL and XLATE software, he was not attempting to prove a hypothesis, but rather to create a system that would allow students to enter BASIC commands in their native languages.

Although you haven't yet started the experiment, now is the time to decide on the variables and controls you will use. Perhaps you've already incorporated this in your hypothesis. Briefly, a *variable* is something to be changed during the experiment, and a *control* is something to be held constant, against which measurement is made. As shown in the examples, your hypothesis should mention:

- The subject of your experiment
- The variable to be changed
- The variable to be measured
- The results you expect

In the first example, the subjects are sixth-grade students. The measured variable is the test scores, the experimental variable is the amount of television watched, and the result expected is that the students watching more TV will have lower scores. In the third example listed, the subject is brushfire, the variable to be tested is the type of plant, the variable to be measured is the rate of burning, and the expected result is that succulent plants burn more slowly than nonsucculent plants. In the next example, the experimental variable is the type of water, the controls are the type of plant and amount of water, and the measured variable is the amount of growth.

The question and hypothesis are the shortest but most important pieces of writing in your project. They form the foundation of the entire experiment and are therefore the basis on which your results are judged.

12
The experiment

Finally, you're done with your research, your paper, your question, and your hypothesis. You're ready to start doing the project! Because the heart of your science project is the experiment, it must be carefully planned and carried out to be effective and successful. Science fair judges on all levels agree that the most important factor in rating your entire project is that you follow proper scientific practices.

The scientific method is an organized way of doing an experiment, including collecting, measuring, and documenting the data. If applicable, the experiment must include a specified variable and control, and at least one experimental and one control group. For valid results, you must use a large enough number of samples, or perform a sufficient number of tests, to ensure that what happens is not pure coincidence. Before getting down to brass tacks, let's define some important terms.

Subject of the experiment

The objective of an experiment is to test and examine the effect of a change in environment or condition. You must choose a specific subject, one or more variables, and a control. For example, in Teri Vertullo's and Jennifer Ade's projects, described in chapter 14, the plants are the subject of the experiment. In Justin Evenson's project on how wood absorbs water, the subjects are the nine types of wood. In Talina Konotchik's project, the different swimsuit fabrics are the subject of the experiment.

Variables

Almost all experiments use variables. An *experimental* or *independent variable* is the substance or condition that you are altering, or that is being altered by the experiment. For example, in Aaron Barclay's project, "Court Surface Effect on Tennis Balls," the three types of courts are the variables.

Another type of variable is the *measured variable*, which is also known as the *dependent variable*. This represents the substance or condition you are evaluating, such as the amount of growth in a particular specimen. In Nguyen Vy's experiment on popcorn, the measured variable was the number of popped kernels. To illustrate, Fig. 12-1 shows the independent and dependent (or experimental and measured) variables for the projects we discussed in chapter 11.

Subject	Experimental Variable	Measured Variable
Students	Hours of TV watched	Test scores
Goldfish	Type of sound	Appetite
Fire	Type of plant	Rate of combustion
Plants	Type of water	Growth
Teenagers	Type of show watched	Heartrate

12-1 *Subjects and variables.*

Controls

To make sure that your experiment is valid, you'll need to make sure that no unpredictable changes affect the experiment. *Controls*, or *controlled variables* are the factors that cannot be allowed to change. Controls are applied to all subjects being tested (as opposed to control group, which we'll define shortly). If your experiment changes in any way other than the stated variables, it will be impossible to prove what caused the results. For example, if you're testing the effects of caffeine on different groups of goldfish, the amount and type of food given to each group, and the available lighting and size of each tank, must be identical. Otherwise, it would be impossible to prove whether differences in the groups at the end of the experiment were caused by varying amounts of caffeine or the alterations in diet, lighting, etc. Notice that the controls for our famous five projects, shown in Fig. 12-2, will keep all the factors except the independent variable identical throughout the experiment.

Experimental and control groups

In order to draw a conclusion, you must compare the results of your experiment (applying your variable to your subject) with the normal condition of your subject (without applying any changes). To make this comparison, you will need to divide your subjects into at least two groups: the experimental group and the control group.

The *experimental group* contains a number of subjects to which you apply the experimental variable. To make sure that your experiment is valid, apply these guidelines:

If you have multiple independent variables, apply one at a time so that you'll be sure exactly what caused your results. You can also apply multiple variables by using multiple experimental groups. In chapter 15, Pippa Munro's experiment, which measured residual smoke from four cigarette brands, used four experimental groups. Daryl Smith's project on secondhand smoke also had four groups—children of smokers and children of nonsmokers, both equally divided into male and female subjects.

Subjects	Project Controls
Students Goldfish Fire Plants Teenagers	The type of courses they take, the family environment Number of goldfish per tank Native environment Amount of light that each specimen receives Amount of rest that the students get

12-2 *Project controls.*

It is also very important to be sure that all the subjects in the experimental groups are identical. For example, in Yolanda Lockhart's project on peripheral vision, each of the groups contained students with the same type of vision.

To prevent the project from becoming too complex, restrict the number of variables and experimental groups. By limiting the factors you're changing, your project will be easier, from your preparation to your procedures and record keeping, and the project notebook and display.

The *control group* is a collection of subjects that is identical to those in the experimental groups, but with no variables applied. Except for not applying the stated variable, the control group must be exactly like the other group(s) in all other respects, such as type, number, environment, brand, etc. Otherwise, there is no basis for comparison, and this might invalidate the results of your experiment. For example, if you are testing the effect of crushed bone meal added to the soil for tomato plants, your control group would consist of a group of tomato plants that did not have bone meal added to the soil. Figure 12-3 shows experimental and control groups.

Subject	Experimental group	Control group
Students Goldfish Fire Plants Teenagers	Watched more than 5 hours Subject to periods of sound Burning of succulent plants Watered with purified water Watched Beavis & Butthead	Watched less than 5 hours No sound Burning of succulent plants Watered with tap water Watched Discovery channel

12-3 *Experimental and control groups.*

Procedures

The first step in designing your project is to write a detailed list of the exact experimental procedures you will use. It should be a step-by-step, sequential list that anyone could follow in order to duplicate the experiment. Some of these steps will be done only once, such as the steps taken to buy, borrow or build your materials, and setting up your equipment. Others might be repetitive, such as testing your subjects and recording your data. Your procedure might contain several pages because you are breaking the procedure down to such minute detail.

Your adviser or science teacher might want to review your procedures before you begin. He or she will review each item, looking for specific, detailed, sequential steps. If your sample is too small, or you plan to conduct too few tests, he or she might ask you to add steps. If the procedure is too vague, you might need to describe your steps in more detail. Remember that your teacher can't read your mind; if it's not on the list, it might not be obvious to anyone but you.

Study Fig. 12-4. It shows a list of procedures for a well-thought-out experiment involving the correlation between sound and mouse appetite. However, the steps are too vague for anyone who's uninformed on the topic. However, by simply spelling out every step in detail, as shown in Fig. 12-5, the list becomes an effective statement of procedures.

Remember that if you're using live vertebrate specimens, you need to list the steps you'll be taking to ensure the adequate care and humane treatment of your subjects. Also, make sure you've completed the necessary ISEF forms and authorizations, as shown in appendix B. You'll also need your ISEF forms complete if your experiment uses tissues, organs, or human or animal parts.

1. Buy plants
2. Divide plants into 2 groups
3. Each day, water one group with tap water and one group with purified water
4. Measure the plants each day
5. Record the plant measurement in the spreadsheet

12-4 *Poor procedures.*

1. Buy 30 radish seedlings.
2. Divide into two groups (A and B) of 15 seedlings each.
3. Label each seedling and measure each seedling's beginning height (in mm).
4. Each day, water seedlings in Group A with .25 liter distilled water, and water seedlings in group B with .25 liter tap water.
5. Each Friday, measure the seedlings (in mm) and record the size in the spreadsheet.
6. At the end of the project period, calculate the amount and percentage of growth of each seedling in each of the two groups.

12-5 *Good procedures.*

Materials

Before beginning the experiment, you should also list your materials inventory, which lists everything you will use. This list should be precise and specific so that anyone could follow it to set up the experiment, including the brands, sizes, quantities, contents, and temperatures of all products you will use, as shown in Fig. 12-6.

Sometimes, students need to improvise or build their own machines or containers to use in their experiments. Because these materials might be difficult to describe in words, illustrate it by including diagrams or photographs. For example, in Teri Vertullo's project, she and her father built the apparatus to rotate some of the plants and keep others in darkness. Brian Berning and his dad built a rack on which he could conduct and display the experiment. For original equipment, you should also give instructions on how to construct it. Again, the criteria for whether a set of instructions is good is whether anyone could follow them.

Many extraordinary projects can be done using common household materials. However, if you need special equipment or supplies, you might need some help in locating them. Perhaps you can borrow the equipment from your school laboratory, especially if you plan to use it on the weekends or holidays. Make sure, however, that you know what your responsibilities will be if anything breaks.

You might also be able to use university or corporate lab facilities, especially if you're working with a mentor or adviser who works in a laboratory. Often, students have developed excellent working relationships with scientists who have helped them, and have developed friendships that extended far beyond the life of the science project.

However, your only alternative might be to buy your materials. If so, see if you can buy these through your school, or ask your teacher to help you locate the best source. Otherwise, you'll have to contact various supply houses for the specimens, chemicals, or equipment you might need. One place to look is your local Yellow Pages, for chemicals, biological supplies, laboratory equipment, plant nurseries, etc.

Sample size and number of tests

The size of the experimental and control groups will have a great impact on the success of your project. You must work with a large enough group to do adequate testing and collect enough data to provide conclusive information. Your results will be more credible if they happened to five subjects than to two, and

1. Flat of radish seedlings containing at least 30 plants
2. 30 Styrofoam cups filled with *Greengold* potting soil
3. 1 gallon bottle of distilled water
4. 1 gallon bottle filled with ordinary tap water
5. 2 watering cans
6. 1 ruler, marked in millimeters
7. Lotus 1-2-3 spreadsheet, set up to record plant measurements for specified dates

12-6 *Materials list.*

your resources will be just about conclusive if your sample size was ten. At the same time, you'll want to limit the number of elements to those you can adequately manage.

Another reason for having an adequate sample size is to include a number of extras, "just in case." In case what? The dog ate it, the baby knocked it over, someone threw it away, or it just plain disappeared. When dealing with plant life, you'll need an even larger sample size because it might be almost impossible to determine whether the individuals in the group were average or abnormal. If you're dealing with seedlings, start with at least 50, and preferably more, to account for the fact that many will not germinate, or might later die.

When dealing with human responses to a survey or questionnaire, include enough subjects to ensure that your results are representative. For surveys, any sample size less than 100 would be considered inadequate. When planning a survey, it's probably a good idea to distribute many more than you need, to compensate for those who throw away your survey or don't have time to complete it. Review Figs. 12-7 and 12-8 as a guideline on sample sizes and number of tests.

You'll also have to perform a sufficient number of tests or trials to provide conclusive results. Statistically, you can draw no conclusions based on too few trials. You'll need a minimum of five trials to prove a hypothesis, and even five trials would only prove conclusive if they all yielded the same result. To provide for any eventualities, plan for a minimum of ten trials.

Subjects	Suggested number of subjects per group
Plants	10–50
Live vertebrates or invertebrates	10–15
Humans	50–100

12-7 *Sample size.*

Type of Project	Minimum	Suggested
Physics	20	50–100
Animal Behavior	10	25–50
Other	5	20–50

12-8 *Number of trials.*

Doing the experiment

By now you have probably collected all your equipment, defined your procedures, variables, and controls, and can't wait to begin. However, let's take a moment to reemphasize why you're doing this and what you hope to gain.

To be successful, you'll need to follow a few important guidelines. Perform your trials on a regular schedule, and consistently record the necessary data. Understanding and following a proper scientific method will give your project credibility, regardless of whether your experiment has "worked."

Observation and measurement

While you are doing your experiment, precise observation, measurement, and computation is essential. To make sure that your measurements are exact, be sure that any instruments you use are balanced and calibrated. Wherever possible, use metrics when recording your data.

Scientifically, a quantitative analysis of your results, based on true measurements, is more exact than a qualitative analysis, which relies on observation. For example, "Soil sample A weighs twice as much as soil sample B" is considered a qualitative analysis. Catherine Davis's project on acid rain precisely measured the amount of acid in rain samples collected in five San Diego neighborhoods and used qualitative analysis.

"Group A, kept in the dark room, ate between 8 and 10 cc per day, and group B, kept in the lighted room, ate between 4 and 6 cc per day," is an example of quantitative analysis and is based on exact measurement. It is far more accurate than "More food was eaten by the group in the light."

If you are using scales, rulers, vessels, or other items that measure weight, size or volume, choose those that can show the smallest gradations you might require. This will allow you to make precise measurements and therefore account for small variations in the data. "A little less than a millimeter" cannot be precisely compared to a quantity that is "almost a millimeter."

Record keeping

While you are conducting the trials, immediately record your results in writing every time you make an observation. This might well be the most important thing you'll do during the course of the project. If you wait a few minutes, you might forget exactly what you saw or what calculations you made. A few hours later, you might begin to interpret what you observed, changing a quantitative analysis to a qualitative one. Even if you have a photographic memory, your experiment will lose credibility if your record keeping is not current and accurate.

Logs and tables will record everything that happens during your project. Use tables to help you document the raw data you gather. To make it as easy as possible, design a table before you even begin your experiment, as Elizabeth Eubanks did in her project on automobiles following too closely. Then you can concentrate on conducting the procedures, making observations, and measuring your results without having to worry about how to keep track of the information.

Your table form should include a place for the date and time of each entry, and whatever measurements and observations you make at the time. Also, leave a final column for notes or comments. This will come in handy if you have any unusual occurrences to report, which might require a detailed explanation. Such a condition might very well make your observations invalid and might require you to alter the project. If you have a control group and one or more experimental groups, it's a good idea to have a separate table for each group, which will help you to accurately record the information for each group.

While you're doing the experiment and recording the data, don't forget to maintain your project log. This is a good place to show any information that can't be recorded on your table, such as locating a graphing program, or conversations you've had with teachers or advisers. Include any additional research material you've found, or perhaps new discoveries you've made. Sometimes you might have unforeseen problems during the project, which can cause you to change your procedures. Document these changes, either descriptively or by using photographs, illustrations, sketches, charts, or graphs.

If all else fails

For most of you, you're probably in the thick of things, and your experiment is going according to plan. You have measurable observations, which show the results of your testing. If, however, things are going poorly, consider changing your procedures or altering your hypothesis. If you started early enough and budgeted your time, you might even be able to change your topic if that becomes necessary.

Before you take any of these steps, please discuss it with your teacher or adviser. She or he might realize that if you "hang in there" a little longer, the experiment will produce results. On the other hand, the teacher might see that by "not getting any results," you are concretely disproving your hypothesis, which is equally valuable.

However, if you cannot salvage your experiment, your teacher might be able to guide you towards an alternate project that can use some of your background research and the materials you've gathered. In any event, you don't need to go it alone! If you've done your work and tried your best (your research, tables, and logs will give ample evidence of that), there's always plenty of help available to you.

Whatever happens, don't try to "fudge" your observations or measurements. Even if it appears that your experiment is completely disproving your hypothesis, or, worse yet, doing nothing at all, your project is valuable. First of all, let me sympathize. Stuart Allen's experiment on dental adhesives "didn't work," and he was extremely discouraged to find that after all the research and preparation, absolutely nothing happened. Because he "guessed wrong," he felt that the project was unsuccessful and he would receive a poor grade. However, because the experiment was well executed and his records were thorough, the project received a good grade, and Stuart learned some important lessons about science.

Remember that "nothing happening" is a result. Instead of giving the expected effect of the variable on the subject, your experiment might show that the variable has little or no effect on the subject in the quantities you used. Although this did not prove your original hypothesis, your experiment is equally valid. Disproving the hypothesis is as important as proving it.

Rather than entirely disproving your theory, the experiment might prove to be inconclusive. This might indicate that the variable was applied in the wrong quantity, strength, or temperature, or that further testing is required. However, the silver lining behind the cloud is that you now have a built-in science project topic for next year!

Throughout scientific history, and the history of science projects, additional experimentation and research have turned failed projects into successful ones. Even experiments that work are often refined and enhanced to yield even more significant results, as Davis Houlton's work in computer science shows. As you go through the phases of your experiment, remember that how you play is the key to winning the science project game!

13
Earth day

Many of you are concerned about the important issues in the world today. Some of these issues—such as war, poverty, and hunger—might not immediately give you any science project ideas. However, the future of our planet and its resources can inspire some interesting science projects.

Projects that deal with preserving and protecting the earth can fall into almost any category. Engineering projects might find a more efficient way to use energy, chemistry can test methods of purifying our resources, botany might find ways to grow more food, and zoology can determine the effects of various substances on animal life. However, most projects that deal with ecological issues fall into the categories of earth and space sciences or environmental sciences.

If you are interested in these areas, a science project idea is no further away than your radio, television, or newspaper. However, since most of the questions are very broad and often complicated, you will probably need to narrow down the idea to something you can do in a few months.

These next two projects deal with important issues for our time—retaining our soil and preventing the polluting affects of acid rain. In both cases, students took a broad topic and narrowed it down to a small, manageable project that they could handle. Brian Berning's idea to do an experiment on erosion was based on a project he had previously seen. He expanded the sample size to create a more comprehensive experiment. Catherine Davis, on the other hand, could not adequately cover the topic of acid rain in one semester, so she limited her project to San Diego, using rainwater samples from five locations throughout the county.

The good earth

Brian Berning found his idea when he saw a project about erosion at a science fair at another school. He decided that the following year, he would also test soil erosion using several soil types. Over the summer vacation, he and his family visited relatives in other parts of the country. While travelling, he collected samples of Ohio farm soil and Virginia clay and brought them home despite protests from members of his family, who objected to using luggage space for dirt. In September, he also gathered three samples from San Diego: soil, topsoil, and sod. These five samples formed the basis of his science project in the earth and space sciences category.

For his background research, Brian used a branch library and the central library in San Diego. As he did research, Brian took notes on index cards. Then he separated his index cards into several categories, representing the paragraphs in the research paper. Once the material was organized, Brian wrote the paper on the Apple IIe, using Appleworks, and then developed the project question and hypothesis, shown in Fig. 13-1. The experimental variables and controls, and the five experimental groups, are shown in Fig. 13-2.

Question	Hypothesis
Do some soils erode faster than others?	Sandy soil erodes faster than sod.

13-1 *Erosion and Its Effects—Question and hypothesis.*

Experimental Groups
1. California Sod 2. California Soil 3. California Topsoil 4. Ohio Farm Soil 5. Virginia Clay

Variables	Controls
Experimental Soil samples **Measured** Weight of soil samples	Amount and rate of water given for each sample

13-2 *Erosion and Its Effects—Variables and controls; experimental and control group.*

To prepare for the experiment, Brian's father helped him build a rack that he could use to conduct and display the project. This rack, constructed of wood and nails, is shown in Fig. 13-3. The complete materials list for the project is shown in Fig. 13-4.

Once all the materials were assembled, Brian set up the experiment by filling five trays with the soil samples and weighing each one on a kitchen scale. He then arranged the samples, the runoff trays, and the "watering" cans on the rack.

Brian conducted his entire experiment at home, over a period of two weeks. During the experimental period, Brian tested his samples every day. In the morning, he weighed each specimen and recorded the measurements in his

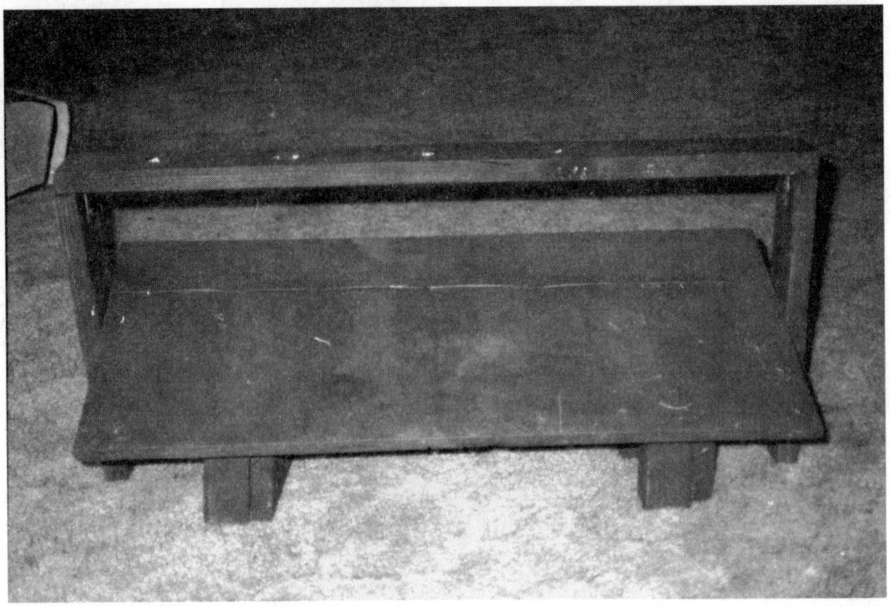

13-3 Erosion and Its Effects—Experiment rack.

Materials
1. Wooden rack
2. Five soil samples, Ohio farm soil, Virginia clay, California soil, California topsoil, and California sod.
3. Five interlocking Rubbermaid storage trays, with small drainage holes hammered in, to hold the soil samples.
4. Five interlocking Rubbermaid storage trays to catch the runoff soil and water.
5. Five peanut cans, with nails hammered into the bottoms of the cans. This allowed gradual watering of the soil samples, rather than having all the water absorbed at once.
6. Kitchen scale.

13-4 Erosion and Its Effects—Materials.

daily log, shown in Fig. 13-5. He then poured 2 cups of water into the cans above each sample, and allowed the water to drip into the soil. Each night, he again watered the soil and allowed it to dry out overnight.

While conducting the experiment, Brian observed that the erosion occurred in different patterns in the various soil samples. For example, the California topsoil showed a pattern of gullied erosion, with a lot of dirt running off. In the Virginia clay and the Ohio farm soil, however, the dirt spread out evenly when it was watered.

Amount of water—4 cups

12-7-89
1. 1 pound 14.5 ounces Ca. Topsoil
2. 2 pounds 4 ounces Ca. Soil
3. 1 pound 14 ounces Virginia Clay
4. 1 pound 14.5 ounces Ohio Soil
5. 2 pounds 6 ounces Ca. Sod

12-8-89
1. 1 pound 14.5 ounces Ca. Topsoil
2. 2 pounds 4.5 ounces Ca. Soil
3. 1 pound 14 ounces Virginia Clay
4. 1 pound 14.5 ounces Ohio Soil
5. 2 pounds 6 ounces Ca. Sod

12-9-89
1. 1 pound 14.5 ounces Ca. Topsoil
2. 2 pounds 4 ounces Ca. Soil
3. 1 pound 14 ounces Virginia Clay
4. 1 pound 14.5 ounces Ohio Soil
5. 2 pounds 6 ounces Ca. Sod

13-5
Erosion and Its Effects—Experimental log.

The daily experimental procedures are summarized in Fig. 13-6. At the end of the two-week period, Brian summarized the recorded data, as shown in Fig. 13-7. He also used this data to graph the weights of each soil sample. Figure 13-8 shows the graph for California topsoil, Fig. 13-9 shows the graph for California soil, Fig. 13-10 shows the graph for California sod, Fig. 13-11 shows the graph for Ohio farm soil, and Fig. 13-12 shows the graph for Virginia clay.

The results showed that California topsoil, which is sandy soil, eroded the most, and California sod eroded the least. Therefore the results of Brian's experiment proved his hypothesis.

When assembling his backboard, Brian used Print Shop on the Apple IIe to create the titles and other printed materials. In front of the backboard, Brian displayed the actual rack, together with the experimental samples. The complete display for the project, entitled "Erosion and Its Effects," is shown in Fig. 13-13. Brian felt satisfied with his project, so much so that next time, he will try a completely different topic.

Procedures
1. Every morning, weighed each soil sample on the kitchen scale and recorded the measurements in the project log.
2. Every morning and evening, poured two cups of water into the cans above each soil sample, and allowed the water to drip into the soil.
3. Each night, allowed samples to dry out.

13-6 *Erosion and Its Effects—Procedures.*

	11/25	11/26	11/27	11/28	11/29	11/30	12/1	12/2	12/3	12/4	12/5	12/6	12/7	12/8	12/9
CA Topsoil	31.0	36.0	36.0	33.5	37.0	32.0	31.5	31.0	31.0	31.0	31.5	31.0	30.5	30.5	30.5
CA Soil	30.0	36.5	36.5	36.5	36.0	36.0	36.0	36.5	36.0	36.0	36.5	36.0	36.0	36.5	36.0
VA Clay	28.5	30.5	30.5	29.5	30.0	30.0	30.0	29.5	29.5	29.5	30.5	30.0	30.0	30.0	30.0
OH Farm Soil	30.0	30.5	30.5	29.5	30.0	30.0	30.5	30.5	30.0	30.5	31.0	30.5	30.5	30.5	30.5
CA Sod	35.0	36.0	36.0	36.5	36.5	36.5	37.5	37.0	37.0	37.5	37.5	37.5	38.0	38.0	38.0

13-7 *Erosion and Its Effects—Summarized recorded data.*

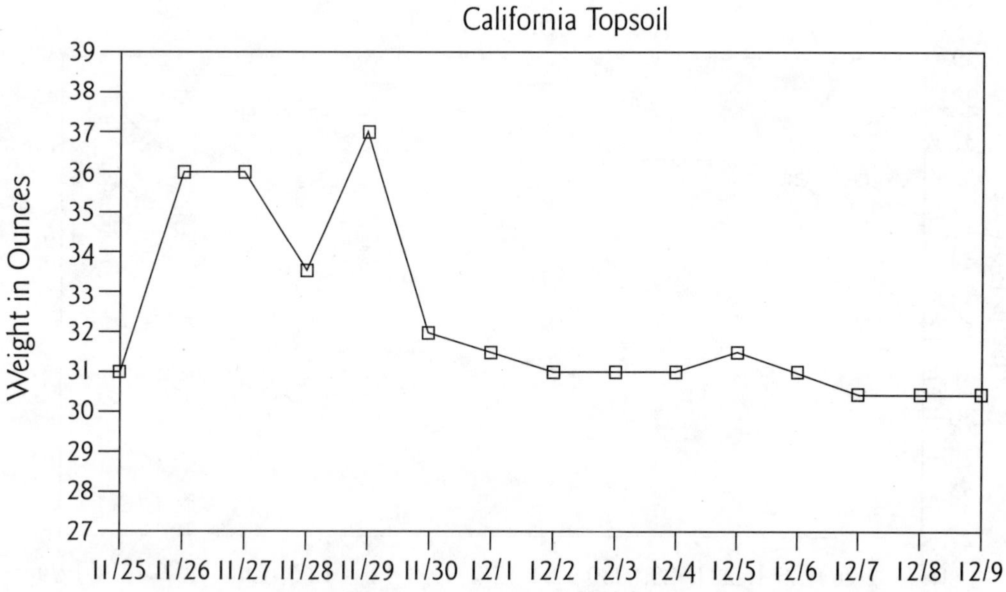

13-8 *Erosion and Its Effects—Graph of California topsoil.*

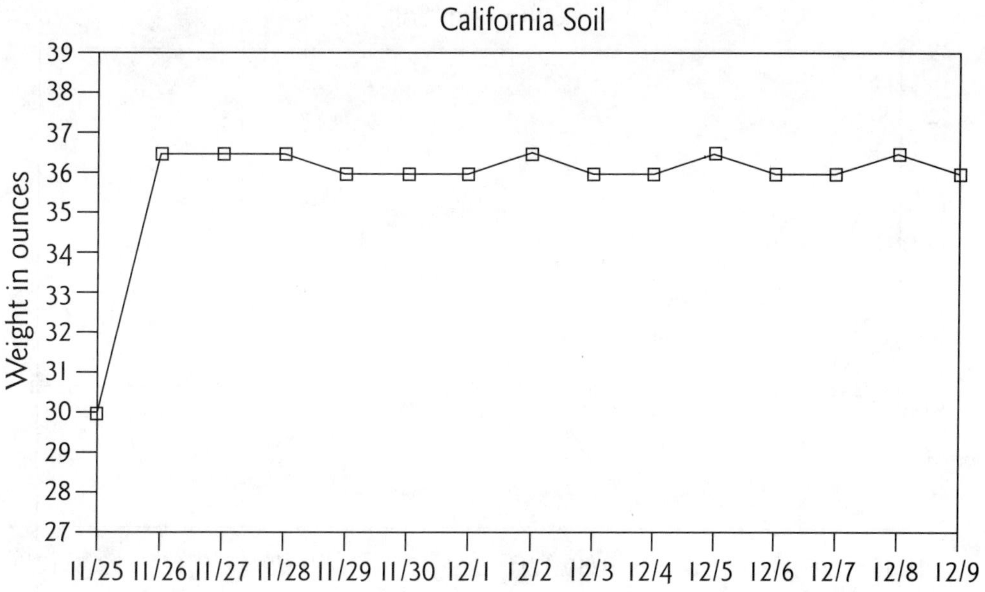

13-9 *Erosion and Its Effects—Graph of California soil.*

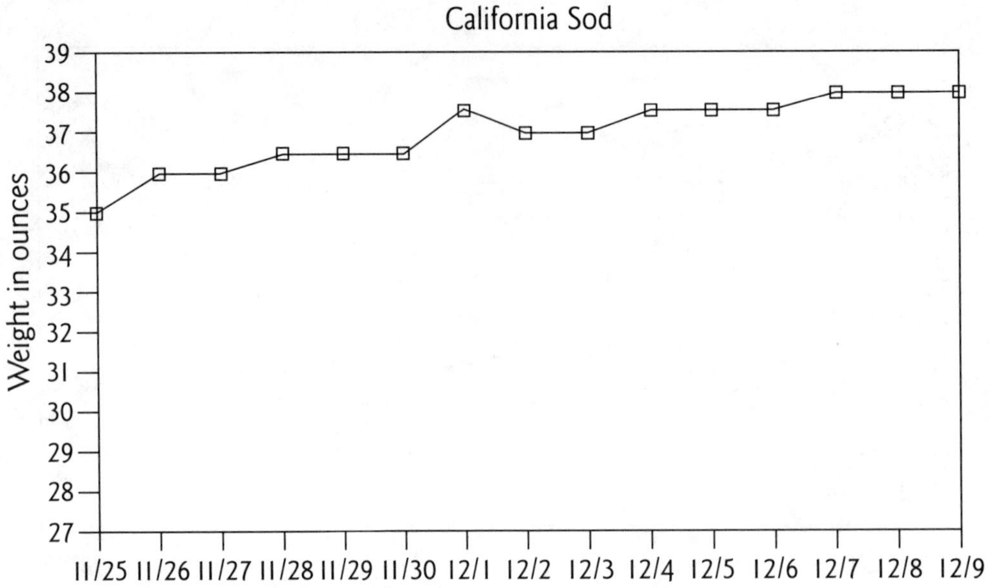

13-10 *Erosion and Its Effects—Graph of California sod.*

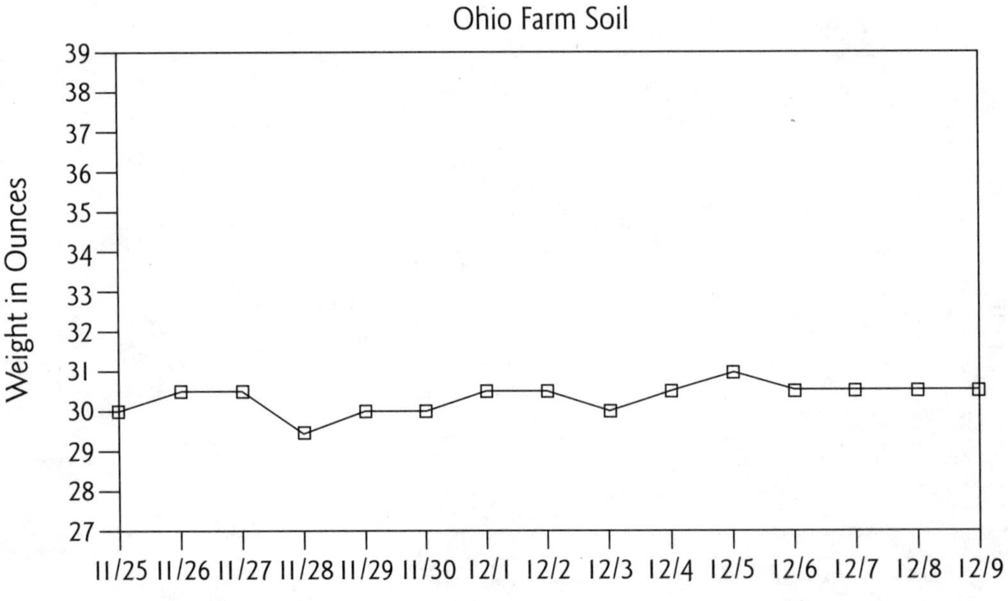

13-11 *Erosion and Its Effects—Graph of Ohio farm soil.*

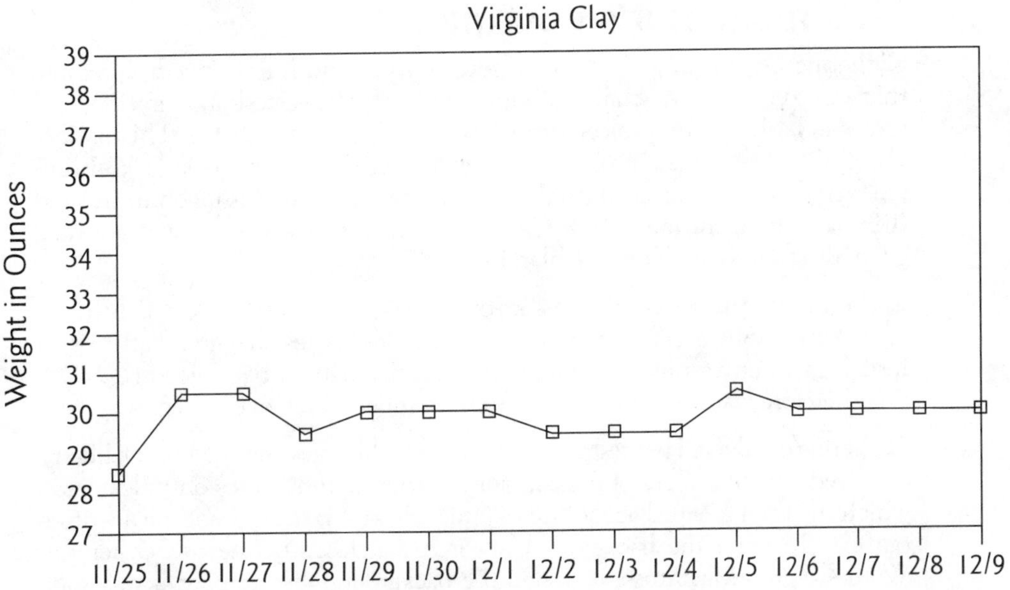

13-12 *Erosion and Its Effects—Graph of Virginia clay.*

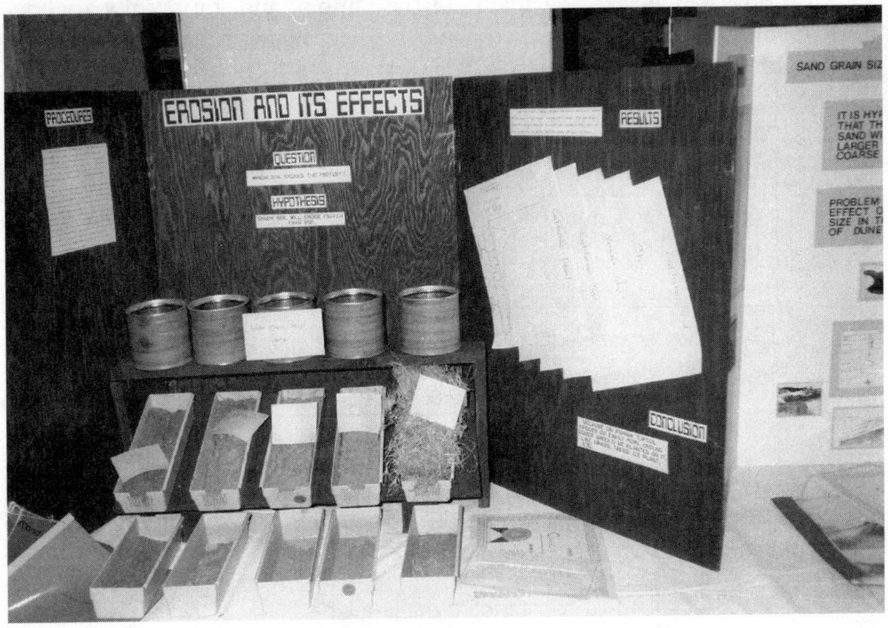

13-13 *Erosion and Its Effects—Backboard.*

"It's raining; it's pouring..."

Catherine Davis's project, "San Diego County's Acid Rain," began as a topic that was too broad and complex. However, with some good organization, and professional help, the project turned out to be quite successful. This project also had to overcome a problem that many students run into—a lack of supplies. In this case, a drought produced a shortage of rain. Although in the end there was sufficient rainfall for Catherine to finish her project, it is always a good idea to have an alternate plan in mind.

Catherine was interested in the issues of ecology and pollution, especially in the area of water. She became involved in these fields because her grandfather is an instructor in environmental studies at the University of San Diego (U.S.D.). She therefore wanted a project in the environmental sciences category.

Catherine conducted her research in four public libraries and the U.S.D. library. She used several sources of information. Catherine took notes on index cards, which she then grouped according to topic. However, she did not use a written outline. To write the background research paper, Catherine used Microsoft Word 4.0 on a Macintosh +. When the background research paper was complete, she developed the project question and hypothesis, shown in Fig. 13-14.

Catherine's experiment involved collecting samples of rainfall from five San Diego county locations: Clairemont, El Cajon, Hillcrest, La Jolla, and Tierra Santa. She tested the acidity of the samples and statistically analyzed the results. To conduct the experiment, she used the materials shown in the list in Fig. 13-15 (which cost less than $15.00).

Question	Hypothesis
Is San Diego County endangered by acid rain?	The acidity of rain in San Diego County is proportional to the distance from the ocean.

13-14 *San Diego County's Acid Rain—Question and hypothesis.*

Materials
1. Markson temperature pH meter
2. Thermolyne Midget Stir Plate
3. 2 dozen one pint Ball canning jars and lids
4. 1 set standard mailing labels
5. 10 plastic grocery bags
6. 4.01 and 6.68 pH buffer solution
7. Small squirt bottle of distilled Water
8. One large Pyrex bowl
9. One test tube
10. Two 8 ounce beakers

13-15 *San Diego County's Acid Rain—Materials.*

At each location, two people volunteered to collect samples for her. Catherine gave each "assistant" a "test kit" consisting of two jars and mailing labels. She also gave each volunteer an instruction sheet, shown in Fig. 13-16.

Directions for collecting rain:

1. Set out a large clean glass bowl when you suspect it will rain.
2. The next morning, take the rain you have collected and pour it into one of the jars.
3. Mark the label with the date and the location in San Diego where the rain was collected.
4. I will arrange to pick up the jars from you as soon as possible.

13-16 *San Diego County's Acid Rain—Collection instructions.*

The samples were collected between November 28, 1989, and January 17, 1990. To make sure that she had enough samples, especially during the holiday season, Catherine sometimes had to remind her volunteers to collect, but everyone seemed eager to help. During November and December, another problem was a lack of rainfall, and Catherine worried that she wouldn't have enough samples to finish the project. However, there were a few storms in January, some lasting several days, which yielded a number of samples.

As soon as possible after each rainfall, Catherine picked up her samples. She originally planned to test the rainwater at the U.S.D. laboratory, but she had problems with the equipment, so she did all the testing at home. The testing consisted of two phases: calibrating the meter and testing the samples.

First Catherine calibrated the pH meter. She mixed buffer material with 4 ounces of distilled water in an 8-ounce beaker, using a Thermolyne Midget Stir plate. Then she cleaned the electrode by spraying it with distilled water. She stirred the needle in the buffer solution, and calibrated it to pH 6.86. She cleaned the electrode again, and then calibrated the meter to a temperature of 4.01.

Once the meter was calibrated, Catherine was ready to test her samples. She again cleaned the electrode and placed it in the jar of rainwater. She gently shook the water until the needle stopped, then she took the reading and recorded it in a daily log. A summary of the experimental procedures is outlined in Fig. 13-17.

When all samples were tested, Catherine entered all her findings into the computer and listed them by location and date, as shown in Figs. 13-18 and 13-19. This data formed the basis of the statistical analysis she needed. Here too, Catherine had the benefit of some expert help, since her mother teaches mathematics and statistics. She computed descriptive statistics for each date and location tested. The statistics by location are shown in Fig. 13-20. By using a t-test, she also compared the results against the average acidity for rainwater, which is between 5.0 and 6.5. The t-tests also showed the statistical difference of each location from the norm, which is 5.60, as illustrated in Fig. 13-21. Each location was tested against the other four locations for statistical significance, as shown in Fig. 13-22. Each date was also tested against the other dates, as shown in Fig. 13-23.

Procedures

1. Calibrated pH meter as follows:
   a. Mixed buffer solution with 4 ounces of distilled water in an 8 ounce beaker, using a Thermolyne Midget Stir Plate.
   b. Cleaned electrode by spraying it with distilled water from squeeze bottle.
   c. Placed electrode in 6.68 buffer solution and calibrated the meter to pH 6.68.

   Note: The meter readings range from 2 through 12. Readings below 7 are acidic, and readings above 7 are alkaline. A reading of 7 is neutral.

   d. Cleaned electrode by spraying it with distilled water from squeeze bottle.
   e. Calibrated electrode using 4.01 buffer solution, and adjusted temperature reading.
2. Tested each sample, as follows:
   a. Cleaned electrode by spraying it with distilled water from squeeze bottle.
   b. Placed electrode in a jar of rain water.
   c. Gently shook water until the needle on the pH meter stabilized, and recorded the reading, to the nearest hundredth, in log.

   Note: If there was insufficient rain water in the jar, poured the sample into the test tube before testing.

13-17 *San Diego County's Acid Rain—Procedures.*

Data

pH Readings by Location

La Jolla	Clairmont	Hillcrest	Tierra Santa	El Cajon
6.00	5.80	4.30	6.25	6.45
5.50	3.90	5.45	5.85	5.65
4.35	3.95	5.75	5.95	5.65
3.80	4.75	5.15	4.90	5.85
5.82	5.65	5.95	5.35	5.85
5.25	5.55	5.65	5.95	6.65
5.95	5.99	5.98	6.25	
4.65	6.05		5.72	
5.85	6.15		6.10	
6.01	6.50		6.60	
6.15	6.35		6.15	
6.25	6.20			
4.65	6.20			
5.70				
5.85				
5.70				
5.65				
6.00				
5.85				

13-18 *San Diego County's Acid Rain—Summarized recordings.*

11/28	12/28	1/2	1/7	1/12–1/13	1/13	1/13–1/14
6.00	5.85	5.65	5.75	5.65	4.65	6.15
5.80	5.95	5.55	5.15	5.95	5.85	5.75
6.25	5.50		5.95	5.99	6.05	6.01
6.45	4.35		4.90	5.55	5.85	5.85
	3.80		5.35		6.25	5.70
	4.30		5.65			
	3.90					
	3.95					
	4.75					
	5.82					

1/14	1/14–1/15	1/15–1/16	1/16–1/17
5.95	6.35	4.65	6.20
6.65	6.25	5.98	6.15
6.15	6.60	5.70	6.20
6.10	5.65		5.65
6.50	5.85		6.00
			5.85

13-19 *San Diego County's Acid Rain—pH data by date.*

Descriptive Statistics by Location

La Jolla		Observations:	19
Minimum:	3.800	Maximum:	6.250
Range:	2.450	Median:	5.820
Mean:	5.525	Standard Error:	0.155
Variance:		0.457	
Standard Deviation:		0.676	

Clairmont		Observations:	13
Minimum:	3.900	Maximum:	6.500
Range:	2.600	Median:	5.990
Mean:	5.618	Standard Error:	0.242
Variance:		0.760	
Standard Deviation:		0.872	

Hillcrest		Observations:	8
Minimum:	4.300	Maximum:	5.980
Range:	1.680	Median:	5.600
Mean:	5.472	Standard Error:	0.193
Variance:		0.297	
Standard Deviation:		0.545	

13-20
San Diego County's Acid Rain—Descriptive data.

t-test for a Difference from the Norm of 5.60

t-test of Location against the Norm (5.60)

La Jolla		Population
Mean:	5.525	5.600
Std. Deviation:	0.676	
Observations:	19	
t-statistic:	−0.482	Hypothesis:
Degrees of Freedom:	18	Ho: $\mu 1 = \mu 2$
Significance:	0.636	Ha: $\mu 1 \neq \mu 2$

Clairmont		Population
Mean:	5.618	5.600
Std. Deviation:	0.872	
Observations:	13	
t-statistic:	0.076	Hypothesis:
Degrees of Freedom:	12	Ho: $\mu 1 = \mu 2$
Significance:	0.940	Ha: $\mu 1 \neq \mu 2$

Hillcrest		Population
Mean:	5.472	5.600
Std. Deviation:	0.545	
Observations:	8	
t-statistic:	−0.662	Hypothesis:
Degrees of Freedom:	7	Ho: $\mu 1 = \mu 2$
Significance:	0.529	Ha: $\mu 1 \neq \mu 2$

13-21
San Diego County's Acid Rain—t-Test—Locations versus the norm.

The results showed that San Diego county rainfall generally falls within the normally accepted range for acidity. The statistics also proved that the rainfall from Tierra Santa and El Cajon, which are farthest from the ocean, are less acidic than the other rainfall samples. The rainfall from Hillcrest, which was the most geographically central, was the most acidic. This condition might exist because Hillcrest is close to downtown San Diego, an area with a great deal of traffic and smog.

An unexpected conclusion shows that the rainfall on the day after the clouds were seeded, on December 28, showed acidity of 4.97, which is above the normal range. This result is shown in Fig. 13-24.

t-test for a Difference Between Locations

	La Jolla	Clairmont
Mean:	5.525	5.618
Std. Deviation:	0.676	0.872
Observations:	19	13
t-statistic:	−0.340	Hypothesis:
Degrees of Freedom:	30	Ho: $\mu 1 = \mu 2$
Significance:	0.736	Ha: $\mu 1 \neq \mu 2$

	La Jolla	Tierra Santa
Mean:	5.525	5.915
Std. Deviation:	0.676	0.467
Observations:	19	11
t-statistic:	−1.689	Hypothesis:
Degrees of Freedom:	28	Ho: $\mu 1 = \mu 2$
Significance:	0.102	Ha: $\mu 1 \neq \mu 2$

	La Jolla	El Cajon
Mean:	5.525	6.017
Std. Deviation:	0.676	0.427
Observations:	19	6
t-statistic:	−1.664	Hypothesis:
Degrees of Freedom:	23	Ho: $\mu 1 = \mu 2$
Significance:	0.110	Ha: $\mu 1 \neq \mu 2$

13-22
San Diego County's Acid Rain—t-Test—Location versus location.

The backboard was constructed of painted cardboard (a really inexpensive solution—Catherine used leftover wall paint!). To title the panels, she used 2" and 3" vinyl letters. Besides her graphs and charts, she featured a map with the test locations color coded to the descriptive statistics for each location, shown in raindrop cutouts. The backboard is shown in Fig. 13-25.

Catherine enjoyed the project and anticipates doing another science project on acid rain. As a result of her unexpected conclusion, next year she will study the effects of cloud seeding on acid rain. She would also like to eliminate the stress of calculating the statistics at the last minute, but as long as she has to wait for the rain in Southern California, that problem might be unavoidable!

t-test for a Difference Between Dates

	11/28	12/28
Mean:	6.125	4.976
Std. Deviation:	0.284	0.827
Observations:	4	13
t-statistic:	2.677	Hypothesis:
Degrees of Freedom:	15	Ho: $\mu 1 = \mu 2$
Significance:	0.017	Ha: $\mu 1 \neq \mu 2$

	11/28	1/2
Mean:	6.125	5.600
Std. Deviation:	0.284	0.071
Observations:	4	2
t-statistic:	2.437	Hypothesis:
Degrees of Freedom:	4	Ho: $\mu 1 = \mu 2$
Significance:	0.071	Ha: $\mu 1 \neq \mu 2$

13-23
San Diego County's Acid Rain

	11/28	1/7
Mean:	6.125	5.458
Std. Deviation:	0.284	0.395
Observations:	4	6
t-statistic:	2.886	Hypothesis:
Degrees of Freedom:	8	Ho: $\mu 1 = \mu 2$
Significance:	0.020	Ha: $\mu 1 \neq \mu 2$

Results

After running the data I discovered that the rain water for 12/28 was the only rain water that is outside the range for normal rain water, which is 5.00–6.50.

12/28		Observations: 13
Minimum: 3.800		Maximum: 5.950
Range: 2.150		Median: 5.250
Mean: 4.976	Standard Error: 0.229	
Variance:		0.684
Standard Deviation:		0.827

Most of the other dates were more alkaline than the regular 5.60, although none of them were outside the range. These dates were 11/28, 1/13–1/14, 1/14, 1/14–1/15, and 1/16–1/17.

13-24 *San Diego County's Acid Rain—Statistics for 12/28/89.*

The locations were all in this range also. Although Tierra Santa and El Cajon were statistically more alkaline than the norm of 5.60, they both still fell within the range of normal rain water.

Tierra Santa		Population
Mean:	5.915	5.600
Std. Deviation:	0.467	
Observations:	11	
t-statistic:	2.242	Hypothesis:
Degrees of Freedom:	10	Ho: $\mu 1 = \mu 2$
Significance:	0.049	Ha: $\mu 1 \neq \mu 2$

13-24 *Continued.*

13-25 *San Diego County's Acid Rain—Backboard.*

Helpful hints

- While doing research, organize your facts, either by using index cards or by identifying each fact by category. It will make writing your paper easier.
- Do your experiment yourself, but do take advantage of any resources that are available to you, either for information, assistance, or equipment.
- If you're working with a large topic, narrow it down to an area that's more manageable. If your original idea is too limited, use more samples or trials to make the results more conclusive.
- Your experimental log can be handwritten, as long as you can read it when it's time to compile your results.

14 Green thumb

Most people have plants around the house, and many of us would love to have them grow green and strong instead of brown and soggy. This next project suggests that water drainage might be the key.

Jennifer Lynne Ade was always interested in plants. When her teacher assigned a science project, she saw a presentation featuring a botany project and realized that she could work in one of her favorite areas. At first she decided to do an experiment testing different types of soils. However, because a classmate had already submitted that topic, her teacher helped her develop another idea, an experiment relating water drainage to plant growth.

Jennifer conducted her research over a period of five to six weeks. She used her local library, the school library, and several encyclopedias and plant books at home. She also got information from seed packages.

As Jennifer did research, she took notes on sheets of paper. When she had collected all her information, she then identified similar facts and copied them to separate sheets, which organized the material by subject. She did not need a written outline because the note sheets by category were sufficient. After the material was organized, Jennifer wrote the paper in about three weeks. "Because I don't like to write," said Jennifer, "the research paper was the worst part of the project."

Based on her research, Jennifer developed the question and hypothesis shown in Fig. 14-1. The variables and controls for the project are shown in Fig. 14-2, and the experimental and control groups are shown in Fig. 14-3.

Jennifer's experiment was conducted entirely at home, using the materials listed in Fig. 14-4. She grew radishes because they can flourish at any time of year in Southern California, and also because they sprout rapidly, within one week after planting.

The entire experiment ran for four weeks during November and December, 1989. During the first week, however, Jennifer prepared the experiment. She divided the cups into three groups—labelled, fast, medium, and slow—and

Question	Hypothesis
Does water drainage adversely affect plant growth?	A moderate rate of drainage promotes plant growth.

14-1 *Water Drainage and Plants—Question and hypothesis.*

Variables	Controls
Experimental Drainage	• Amount of water
	• Amount of sunlight
Measured Growth of plants	• Type and amount of soil

14-2 *Water Drainage and Plants—Variables and controls.*

Experimental Groups	Control Group
1. Plants with 2 drainage holes	None
2. Plants with 4 drainage holes	
3. Plants with 6 drainage holes	

14-3 *Water Drainage and Plants—Experimental and control groups.*

Materials
1. 120 styrofoam cups
2. 240 Cherry Belle radish seeds
3. 1-cup measuring cup
4. Nail set to punch drainage holes in cups
5. Potting soil
6. 1-foot ruler

14-4 *Water Drainage and Plants—Materials.*

numbered every cup in each group. In the bottom of the slow cups, she punched two holes, in the bottom of the medium cups, she punched four holes, and in the bottom of the fast group, she punched six holes. Into each cup, she placed ½ cup of soil, then two seeds, then ½ cup of soil. She then placed all seedlings in one small area in the backyard to ensure that each plant would receive the same amount of sunlight and rain.

Once each week during the remaining three weeks of the experiment, Jennifer measured and recorded the height of each plant, and she watered each plant with ½ cup water. The procedures are summarized in Fig. 14-5.

At the end of the experimental period, Jennifer used her logs to build tables showing the growth of each plant group. Figures 14-6, 14-7, and 14-8 show the growth of the plants with slow, medium, and fast drainage, respectively. She also calculated the average growth for each group and created a combined graph, shown in Fig. 14-9.

The results showed that the plants with the slowest drainage produced no growth at all, and the plants with the fastest water drainage had the greatest plant growth. Jennifer concluded that with slower drainage, more water remained in the soil and drowned the plants.

Jennifer used a pegboard for her display, which she covered with green fabric. For titles, she stencilled lettering, cut out the strips, and pasted them on the backboard. Besides the written material, Jennifer added a seed packet on the display. The backboard is displayed in Fig. 14-10.

On the whole, although she did not like writing the research paper, she enjoyed the project. "The best part," she said, "was taking care of the plants." However, Jennifer felt that if she had started earlier, she could have conducted the experiment over a longer period of time, and perhaps she would have had more conclusive results. If she does another project, she will pick a different topic. "I've already done this," she said, "but the next one will also be about plants."

Procedures

1. Separated cups into three groups
2. Labelled each group: FAST, MEDIUM, SLOW, and numbered each cup in the group (1–40)
3. Punched holes in bottoms of cups
   - 6 in FAST
   - 4 in MEDIUM
   - 2 in SLOW
4. Into each cup, placed:
   - ½ cup soil
   - 2 radish seeds
   - ½ cup soil
5. Each week:
   - Measured and recorded height of each plant.
   - Watered each plant with ½ cup of water.

14-5 *Water Drainage and Plants—Procedures.*

PLANT GROWTH—SLOW WATER DRAINAGE

Height in Inches

PLANT	WEEK 1	WEEK 2	WEEK 3	PLANT	WEEK 1	WEEK 2	WEEK 3
1	0	0	0	21	0	0	0
2	0	0	0	22	0	0	0
3	0	0	0	23	0	0	0
4	0	0	0	24	0	0	0
5	0	0	0	25	0	0	0
6	0	0	0	26	0	0	0
7	0	0	0	27	0	0	0
8	0	0	0	28	0	0	0
9	0	0	0	29	0	0	0
10	0	0	0	30	0	0	0
11	0	0	0	31	0	0	0
12	0	0	0	32	0	0	0
13	0	0	0	33	0	0	0
14	0	0	0	34	0	0	0
15	0	0	0	35	0	0	0
16	0	0	0	36	0	0	0
17	0	0	0	37	0	0	0
18	0	0	0	38	0	0	0
19	0	0	0	39	0	0	0
20	0	0	0	40	0	0	0

14-6 *Water Drainage and Plants—Growth with slow drainage.*

PLANT GROWTH—MEDIUM WATER DRAINAGE

Height in Inches

PLANT	WEEK 1	WEEK 2	WEEK 3	PLANT	WEEK 1	WEEK 2	WEEK 3
1	0	0	0	**21**	0	1/2	1
2	0	0	0	**22**	0	0	0
3	0	1/4	1/2	**23**	0	1/2	1
4	1/4	1/2	1	**24**	0	0	0
5	1/4	3/4	1	**25**	0	0	1/4
6	1/4	1/2	1	**26**	0	0	0
7	3/4	1 3/4	2	**27**	0	3/4	1
8	1/4	3/4	1	**28**	0	1/2	3/4
9	1/2	1	1 1/2	**29**	0	1/2	1
10	0	1/2	1	**30**	0	0	1/4
11	0	3/4	1	**31**	0	0	0
12	0	1/4	1/2	**32**	0	0	0
13	1/4	1/2	3/4	**33**	0	0	0
14	0	3/4	1	**34**	1/4	1/4	1/2
15	0	0	1/4	**35**	0	0	0
16	0	1/2	1	**36**	0	0	0
17	1/4	3/4	1	**37**	0	0	0
18	0	1/4	1/2	**38**	0	0	0
19	0	3/4	1 1/2	**39**	0	0	0
20	0	3/4	1	**40**	0	0	0

14-7 *Water Drainage and Plants—Growth with medium drainage.*

PLANT GROWTH—FAST WATER DRAINAGE

Height in Inches

PLANT	WEEK 1	WEEK 2	WEEK 3	PLANT	WEEK 1	WEEK 2	WEEK 3
1	0	0	0	**21**	0	1/4	1/2
2	0	0	0	**22**	0	0	1/4
3	0	0	0	**23**	1/2	1	1 1/2
4	0	0	1/4	**24**	1/4	3/4	1
5	1/2	3/4	1	**25**	1	2	2 1/4
6	0	0	1/4	**26**	1/4	1/2	1
7	0	0	0	**27**	1/2	1	1 1/4
8	0	0	0	**28**	1/4	3/4	1
9	0	0	0	**29**	1/4	3/4	1
10	0	0	0	**30**	1/2	1	1 1/4
11	1/2	3/4	1	**31**	0	1/2	1
12	1/4	3/4	1	**32**	1/4	3/4	1
13	0	1/4	1/2	**33**	1/4	3/4	1
14	0	0	0	**34**	1 1/4	2 1/2	3
15	1/4	1/2	3/4	**35**	1	1 3/4	2
16	0	0	0	**36**	1/4	1	1 1/2
17	1/4	3/4	1	**37**	0	1/2	1
18	0	0	0	**38**	1/4	3/4	1
19	0	0	0	**39**	1/2	1	1 1/2
20	0	0	1/4	**40**	3/4	1 1/2	2

14-8 *Water Drainage and Plants—Growth with fast drainage.*

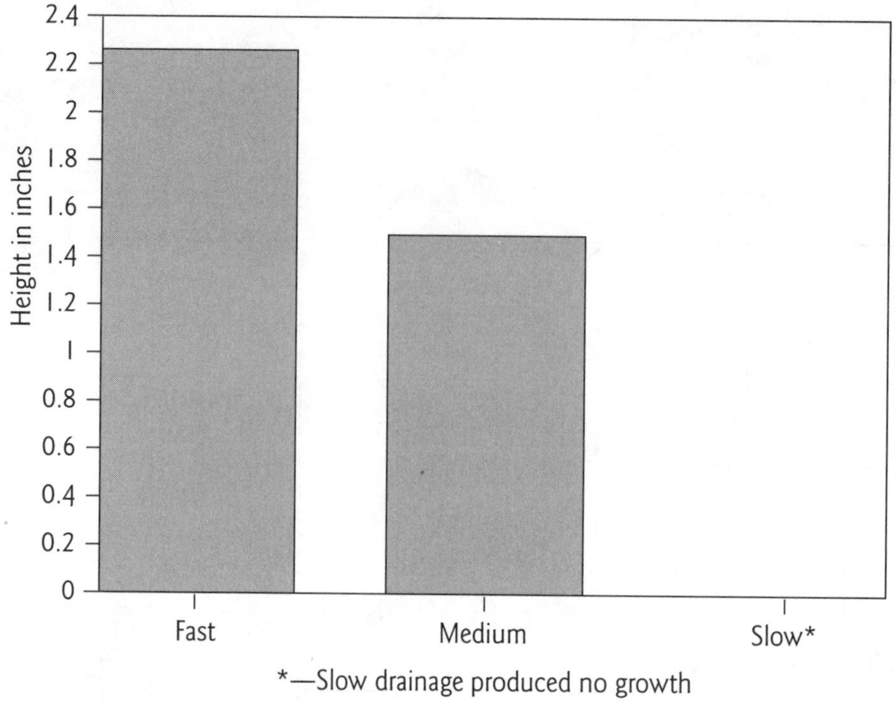

14-9 *Water Drainage and Plants—Combined graph.*

14-10 *Water Drainage and Plants—Backboard.*

Another project that deals with plants is Teri Vertullo's "Why do Plants Grow Up?" Teri's always been interested in plants because she has several relatives involved the field. Once she'd decided on a botany project, she focused on a project that would display well.

The object of this experiment is to determine whether plants grow up due to gravity, light, water, or air. The hypothesis of the experiment, shown in Fig. 14-11, was that gravity would cause the roots to grow down, and therefore make the plant grow up.

INTRODUCTION

At the start of the project the main goal was to find out why plants grow up. To do so, the experiment was conducted.

Are plants attracted to light? Are they attracted to air? Or do they grow up because of the laws of gravity? That's what the present author wanted to know. So the experiment was conducted to help answer these questions.

The present author hypothesized that seeds will grow down because gravity won't let them grow up.

14-11 *Why Do Plants Grow Up?—Hypothesis.*

To conduct the experiment, Teri started 32 seedlings from quick-growing seeds. She and her father then built an apparatus that would expose some of the plants to the light and keep some of them in darkness. Using a small motor, they were able to turn parts of the apparatus so that 16 plants were stationary and 16 were rotating. Half of each group was under direct light, and half of each group had no light. The apparatus is shown in Fig. 14-12, the project procedures are shown in Fig. 14-13, and the observations are shown in Figs. 14-14 and 14-15. See Fig. 14-16 for the backboard.

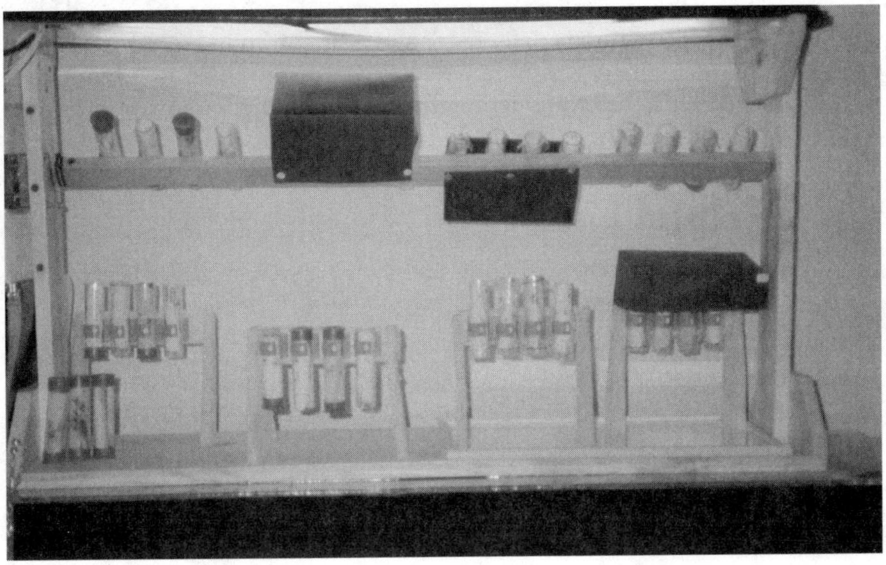

14-12 *Why Do Plants Grow Up?—Apparatus.*

1—Chose the variables: Light, no light, light bottom, light top, air, no air, air bottom, air top, gravity, and no gravity

2—Bought needed equipment: 32 clear tubes
1 very slow moving motor
2 mirrors
16 clear lids (that fit the tubes)
16 solid lids (that fit the tubes)
1 ultraviolet light

3—Folded and rolled stuffed paper towels

4—Spread few seeds on rolled paper towels

5—Stuffed rolled paper towels into tubes

6—Watered the towels in tubes

7—Covered tubes with clear lids, solid lids, or no lid

8—Placed tubes in places where they get their correct amount of light

9—Started up the project

14-13 *Why Do Plants Grow Up?—Procedures.*

Teri did the experiment four times with different types of seeds. During each experimental process, the experiment was running constantly. The results showed that the stationary plants always grew up, and in the rotating group, the seedling went toward the light. If no light was present, the plants grew in random direction, regardless of whether they were stationary or rotating. She concluded that the plants grew up first because of gravity, and where gravity was absent, they grew toward the light.

Teri's project display attracted attention because she included the apparatus used to run the experiment, as previously shown in Fig. 14-12. It was obviously the right kind of attention because Teri won a Third award in a crowded category. Her future plans definitely include another botany project. "Next time," she said, "I'll go for a more difficult one. After all, I'm experienced now."

Helpful hints

- Remember the KISS principle (keep it simple, stupid). Sometimes the simplest ideas are best.
- Do your experiment a sufficient number of times (or for a long enough period of time) to get adequate results.
- Including part of your experiment on your backboard can make your display more interesting.

GROUP A

	1	2	3	4
GRAVITY				
NO GRAVITY	√	√	√	√
AIR				√
NO AIR			√	
TOP AIR	√			
BOTTOM AIR		√		
LIGHT				
NO LIGHT				
TOP LIGHT	√	√	√	√
BOTTOM LIGHT				
DAY: 1	None	None	None	None
DAY: 2	None	None	None	None
DAY: 3	None	None	None	None
DAY: 4	Toward light	Toward light	Toward light	Toward light
DAY: 5	Same	Same	Same	Same
DAY: 6	Same	Same	Same	Same
DAY: 7	Same	Same	Same	Same

14-14 *Why Do Plants Grow Up?—Observations, group A.*

GROUP B

	1	2	3	4
GRAVITY				
NO GRAVITY	√	√	√	√
AIR				√
NO AIR			√	
TOP AIR	√			
BOTTOM AIR		√		
LIGHT				
NO LIGHT				
TOP LIGHT				
BOTTOM LIGHT	√	√	√	√
DAY: 1	None	None	None	None
DAY: 2	None	None	None	None
DAY: 3	None	None	None	None
DAY: 4	Toward light	Toward light	Toward light	Toward light
DAY: 5	Same	Same	Same	Same
DAY: 6	Same	Same	Same	Same
DAY: 7	Same	Same	Same	Same

14-15 *Why Do Plants Grow Up?—Observations, group B.*

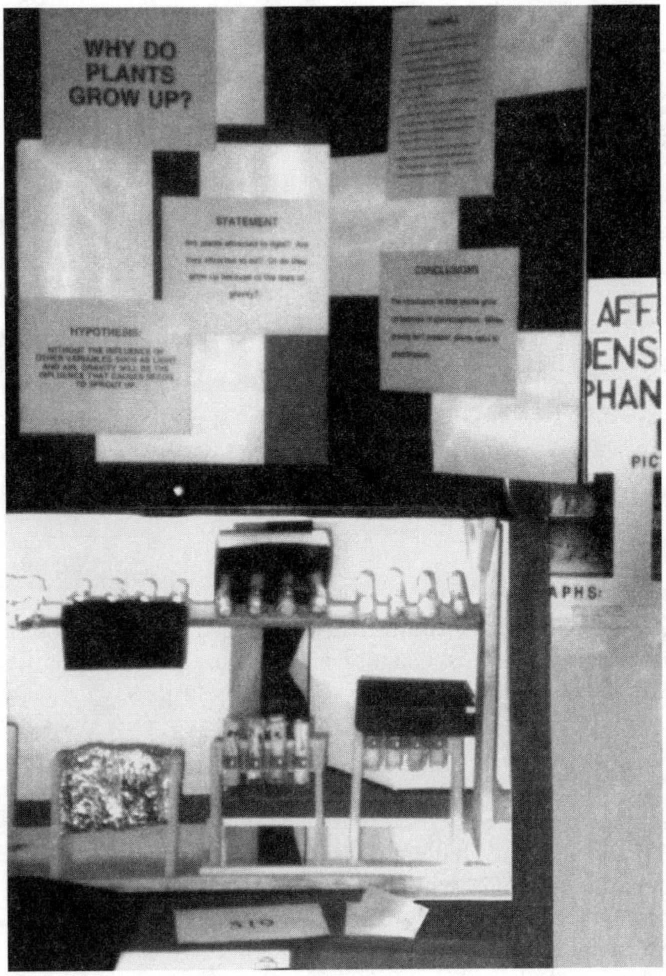

14-16 *Why Do Plants Grow Up?—Backboard.*

15 Results and conclusions

After the experiment is finished, you'll need to take a close look at what you learned. Now you must examine and organize your information, then interpret and analyze this data to formulate your conclusions.

Results

The results of a science project are what happened during the experiment. During this phase, the challenge is simply to present the results and not interpret them until you're ready to state the conclusion. At this point, you'll gather, organize, graph, chart, and analyze the material to make the results as clear and meaningful as possible. The results incorporate three elements: the raw data, the smooth data, and the analyzed data.

Raw data

The raw data is the information you recorded during the experiment. You might have been tempted to combine and analyze the information while you were doing the tests, especially if the experiment was proving your hypothesis. However, you must simply record your observations without an unconscious bias. This is really the hard part! You don't want to draw premature conclusions, but you want to be alert to any problems that might develop.

If you want, you can graph the raw data by creating bar and graphs for your variable and control group(s), extending over the life of the experiment. In Mike Iritz's project, "The Shaking Earth, The Burning Sky," the incidence of high-magnitude quakes for the period between 1932 and 1974 was correlated to solar activity. Each factor was graphed separately for a six-year period. (See Figs. 15-1, 15-2, and 15-3.)

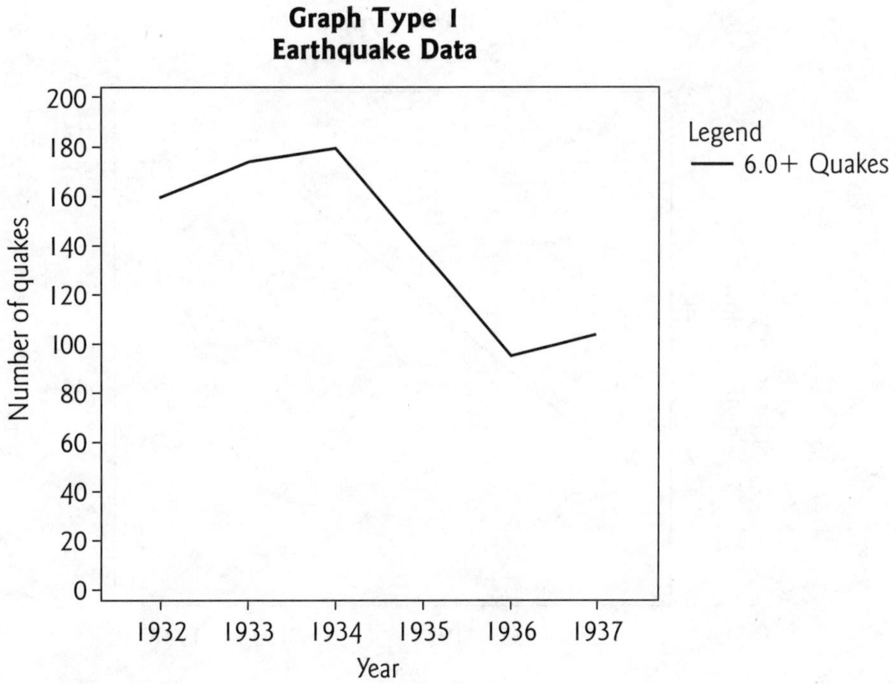

15-1 *6.0 Earthquake data.*

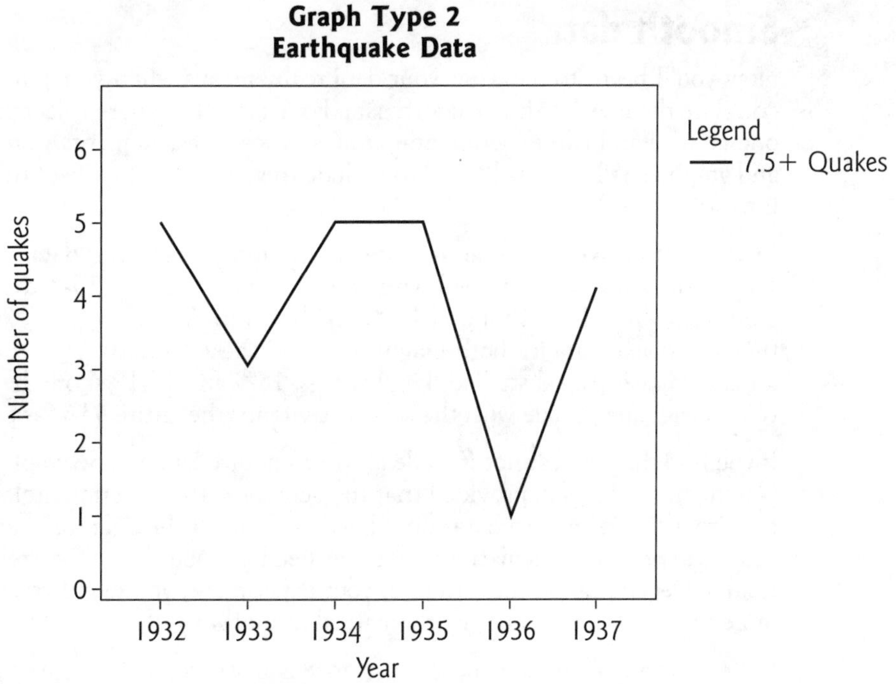

15-2 *7.5 Earthquake data.*

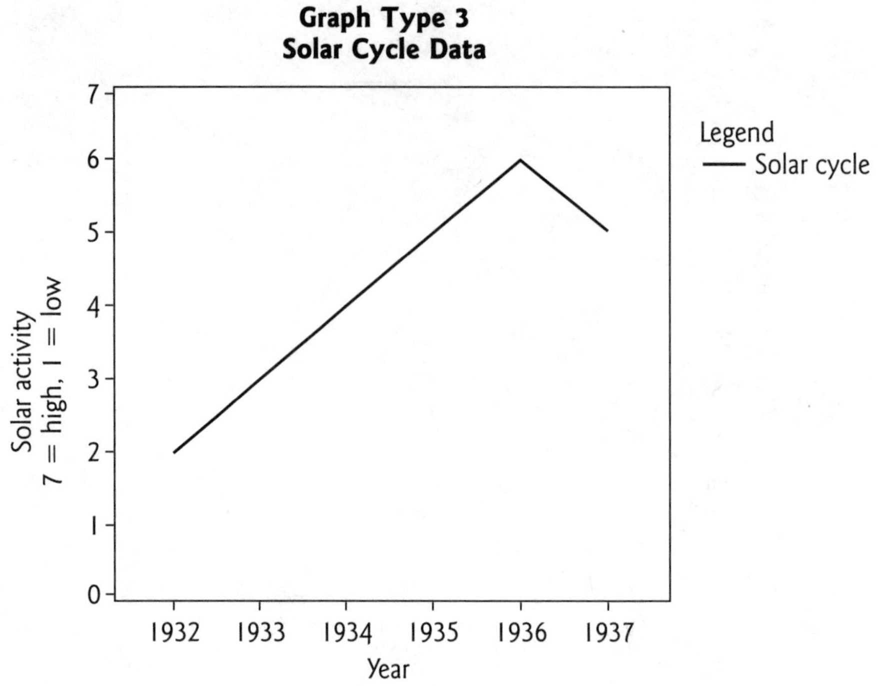

15-3 *Solar activity data.*

Smooth data

Now you'll begin to see what your data really means when you combine and correlate the raw data into smooth data. For example, if your project examined one control and two experimental groups, whose measurements were charted and graphed daily, you will need to include the data over the life of the project into your smooth data.

In the earthquake and solar activity correlation project, the data from Figs. 15-1 and 15-2 were combined with the data shown in Fig. 15-3 to form the graphs shown in Figs. 15-4 and 15-5. As shown in Figs. 15-6, 15-7, and 15-8, the earthquake data for both magnitudes and the solar activity were graphed for the 43-year period studied. Finally, Figs. 15-9 and 15-10 show the correlation of each magnitude with the solar activity for the entire 43-year period.

If you find that you cannot include all your smooth data on one graph or table, you might use several, provided that they combine the experimental and control groups. The smooth data should also include all the averages, totals, percentages, or other calculations that you need to tabulate and correlate your results. Depending on the nature of your experiment, you might require some more involved statistical or mathematical formulas.

If you haven't taken many math or science courses, you might need to consult with your math teacher to help select formulas that will appropriately analyze your raw data. When working with statistics, he or she can also provide guidance to determine how much variance, or which mathematical results, will prove or disprove your hypothesis.

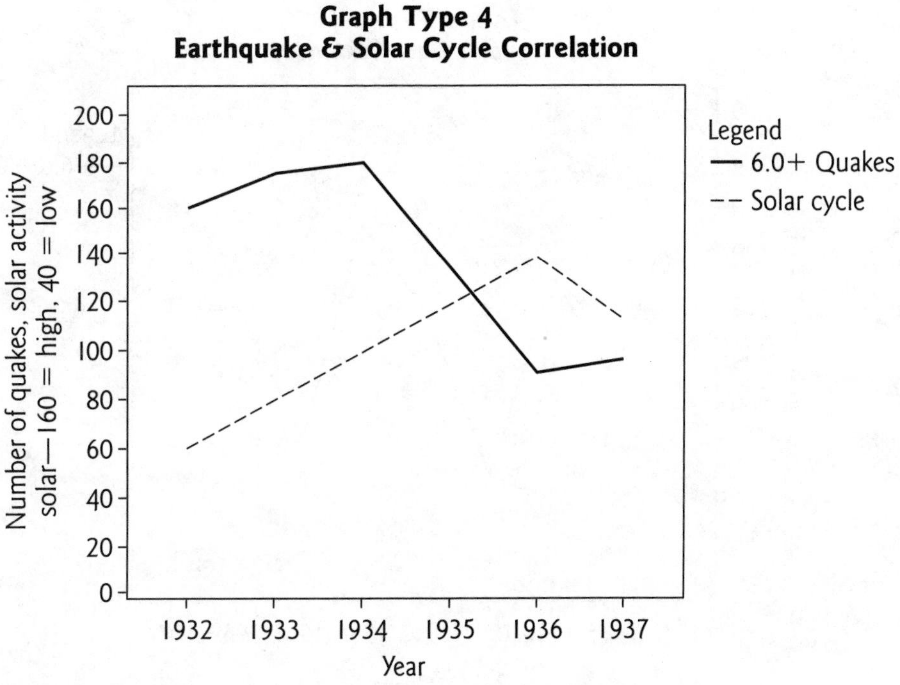

15-4 *Correlated 6.0 earthquake and solar activity data.*

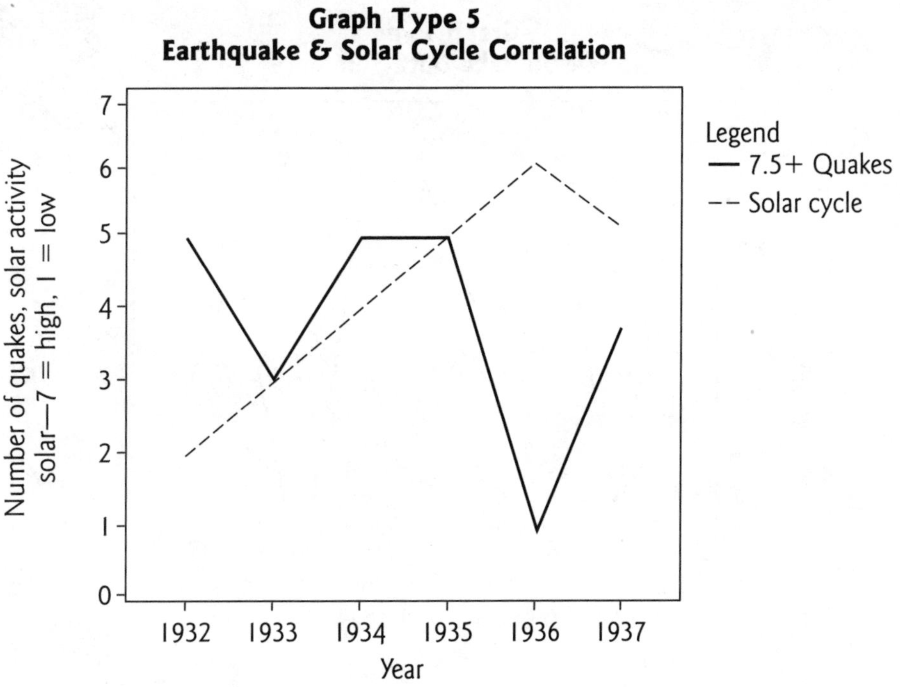

15-5 *Correlated 7.5 earthquake and solar activity data.*

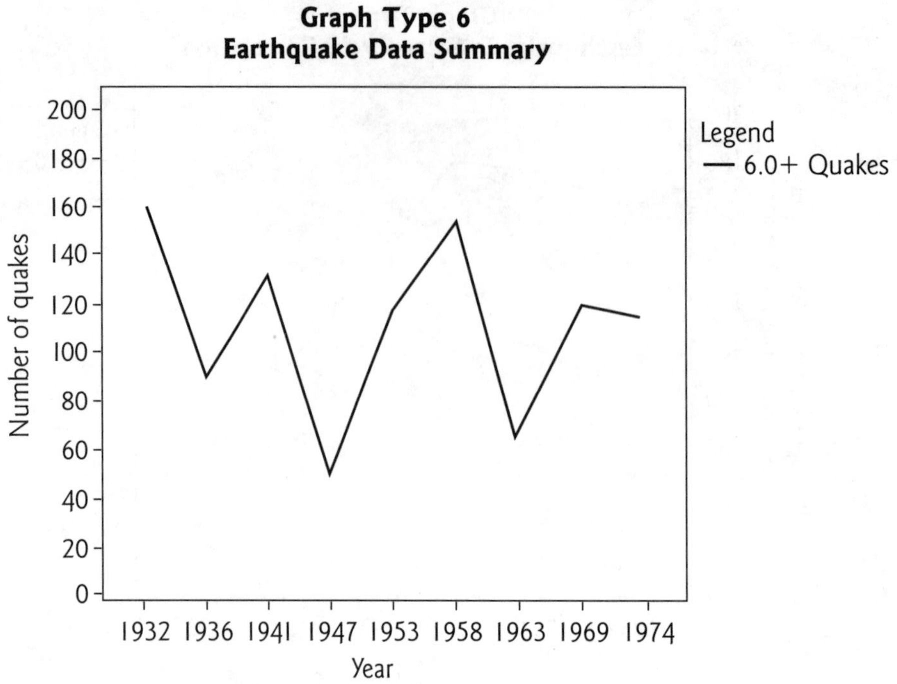

15-6 *Summarized 6.0 earthquake data.*

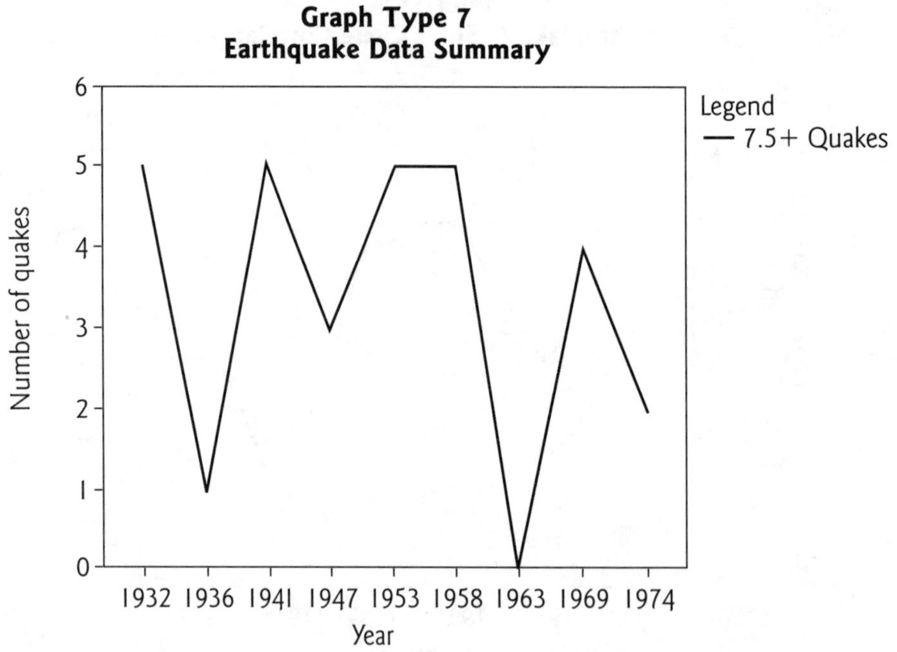

15-7 *Summarized 7.5 earthquake data.*

Results and conclusions

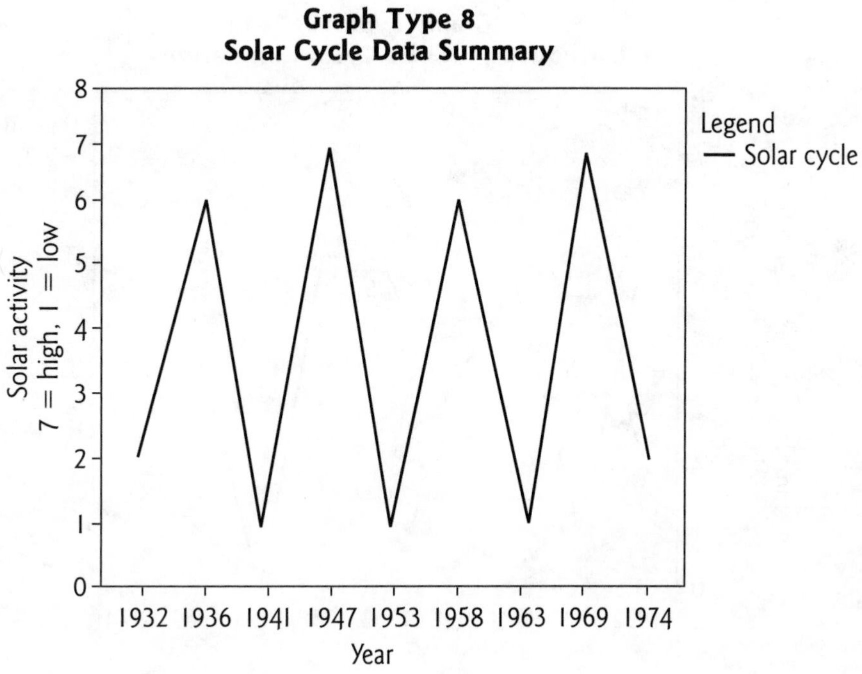

15-8 *Summarized solar activity data.*

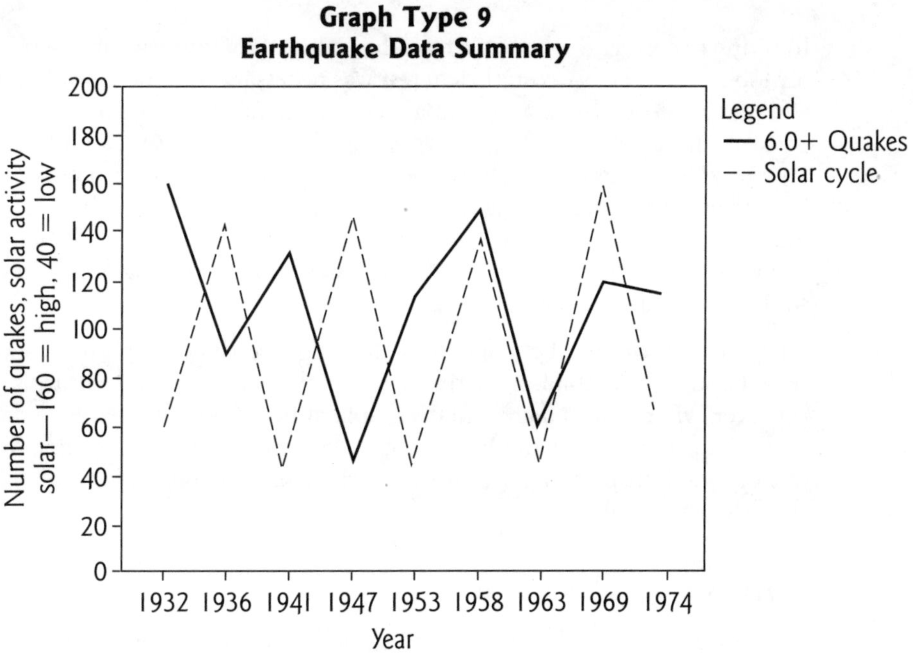

15-9 *Summarized correlated 6.0 earthquake and solar activity data.*

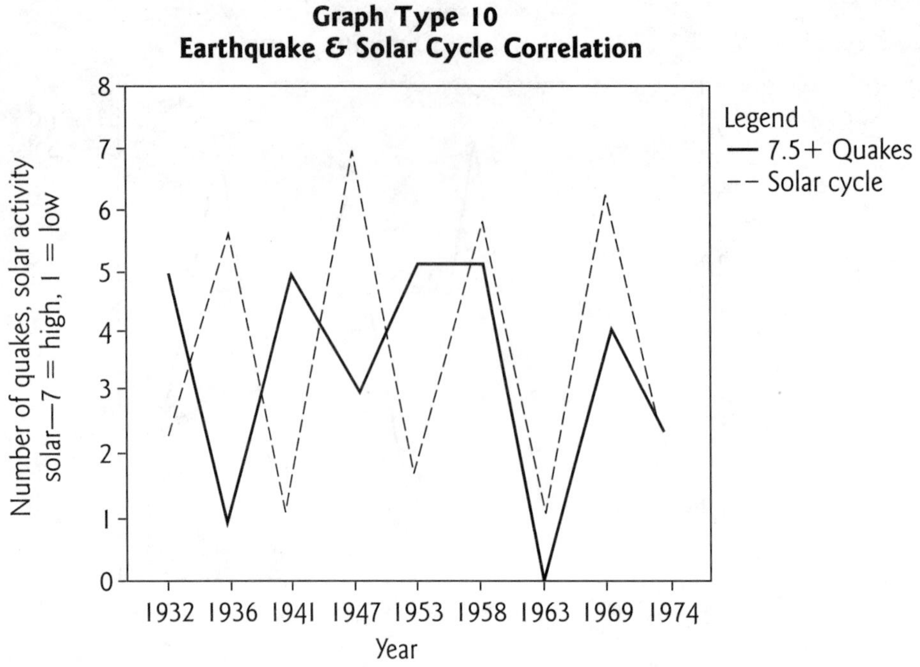

15-10 *Summarized correlated 7.5 earthquake and solar activity data.*

In trying to correlate solar activity with earthquakes, it was insufficient to simply look at the graphs. A statistical test was necessary, and the Correlation Coefficient Statistics Test was used. Based on the data in Fig 15-11, the statistical correlation was calculated, as shown in Figs 15-12 and 15-13. Don't forget that a spreadsheet program—such as Lotus 1-2-3, Excel, or QuattroPro—can also be very useful to calculate the results of an equation or to use built-in functions such as count, sum, average, minimum, maximum, or standard deviations. If you've studied programming, you can also write your own programs to compute statistical results.

Smooth data can also be graphed by drawing a separate graph for a specified time period while combining the data for the variables and controls. This, however, will result in a great many graphs if the experiment extended over a long period of time. At the bottom of each smooth data table or graph, write one or two short paragraphs that summarize the data and explain briefly what the facts and numbers show.

Analyzed data

The last element, analyzed data, will actually show the results, comparing the experimental groups with the control groups. The most effective method of presenting the analyzed data in a clear, accurate, and visually appealing way are charts and graphs. Line and bar graphs are the most common types of graphs used to present science project results. As shown in chapter 9, there are many variations on graph types to attractively present the data.

Year	6.0+ Quakes	7.5+ Quakes	Solar activity (1 = low, 7 = high)
1932	160	5	2
1933	175	3	3
1934	180	5	4
1935	135	5	5
1936	93	1	6
1937	97	4	5
1938	105	8	4
1939	96	5	3
1940	124	8	2
1941	132	5	1
1942	64	6	2
1943	93	11	3
1944	84	5	4
1945	64	2	5
1946	85	9	6
1947	49	3	7
1948	48	4	6
1949	94	6	5
1950	145	4	4
1951	125	2	3
1952	146	5	2
1953	117	5	1
1954	136	0	2
1955	132	0	3
1956	152	4	4
1957	183	11	5
1958	154	5	6
1959	148	3	5
1960	181	2	4
1961	156	3	3
1962	72	0	2
1963	63	0	1
1964	107	1	2
1965	167	3	3
1966	87	2	4
1967	104	1	5
1968	90	3	6
1969	118	4	7
1970	138	5	6
1971	133	7	5
1972	125	3	4
1973	108	7	3
1974	113	2	2

15-11 *Raw data—Earthquakes and solar activity.*

Correlating 6.0 Earthquakes and Solar Activity Using Correlation Coefficient.					
		y	X		
		6.0+ Quakes vs. Solar Activity			
Year	X_I	y_I	X_I^2	y_I^2	$X_I y_I$
1932	−1.837	41.097	3.374	1756.167	−076.983
1933	−0.837	56.907	0.701	3238.407	−047.631
1934	0.163	61.907	0.026	3832.477	0.10.091
1935	1.163	16.907	1.352	0285.847	019.663
1936	2.263	−25.093	4.678	0629.658	−054.276
1937	1.163	−21.093	1.352	0444.915	−024.531
1938	0.163	−13.093	0.026	0171.426	−002.134
1939	−0.837	−22.093	0.701	0488.101	018.492
1940	−1.837	05.907	3.374	0034.892	−010.851
1941	−2.837	13.907	8.048	0193.404	−039.454
1942	−1.837	−54.093	3.374	2926.053	099.368
1943	−0.837	−25.093	0.701	0629.658	021.003
1944	0.163	−34.093	0.026	1162.332	−005.560
1945	1.163	−54.093	1.352	2926.053	−062.901
1946	2.163	−33.093	4.678	1095.146	−071.580
1947	3.163	−69.093	10.004	4773.843	−218.541
1948	2.163	−70.093	4.678	4913.028	−151.611
1949	1.163	−24.093	1.352	0580.472	−028.020
1950	0.163	26.907	0.026	0723.986	004.386
1951	−0.837	06.907	0.701	0047.706	−005.781
1952	−1.837	27.907	3.374	0778.801	−051.265
1953	−2.837	−01.093	8.048	0001.195	003.101
1954	−1.837	17.907	3.374	0320.661	−032.895
1955	0.837	13.907	0.701	0193.404	−011.640
1956	0.163	33.907	0.026	1149.684	005.526
1957	1.163	64.907	1.352	4121.918	075.486
1958	2.163	35.907	4.678	1289.313	077.667
1959	1.163	29.907	1.352	0894.428	034.781
1960	0.163	62.907	0.026	3957.291	010.253
1961	−0.837	37.907	0.701	1436.941	−031.728
1962	−1.837	−46.903	3.374	2124.564	084.672
1963	−2.837	−55.903	8.048	3035.238	156.298
1964	−1.837	−11.093	3.374	0123.054	020.377
1965	0.837	48.907	0.701	2391.894	−040.935
1966	0.163	−31.093	0.026	0966.774	−005.068
1967	1.163	−14.093	1.352	0198.613	−016.390
1968	2.163	−28.093	4.678	0789.216	−060.765
1969	3.163	−00.093	10.004	0000.008	−000.294
1970	2.163	19.907	4.678	0396.288	043.058
1971	1.163	14.907	1.352	0222.218	017.336
1972	0.163	06.907	0.026	0047.706	001.125
1973	−0.837	−10.093	0.701	0101.868	008.477
1974	−1.837	−05.093	3.374	0025.939	009.355

E = SIGMA = the sum of . . .

$$0.143 = \frac{Ex_I y_I}{\sqrt{(Ex_I^2)\,(Ey_I^2)}}$$

"No Correlation, Statistically"

15-12 *6.0 Earthquakes and solar activity correlated using correlation coefficient.*

Results and conclusions

Correlating 7.5 Earthquakes and Solar Activity Using Correlation Coefficient.

y X

7.5 + Quakes vs. Solar Activity

Year	X_1	y_1	X_1^2	y_1^2	X_1y_1
1932	−1.837	0.907	3.374	00.823	-01.666
1933	−0.837	−1.093	0.701	01.194	00.915
1934	0.163	0.907	0.026	00.823	00.148
1935	1.163	0.907	1.352	00.823	01.055
1936	2.263	−3.093	4.678	09.576	−06.690
1937	1.163	0.093	1.352	00.008	−00.108
1938	0.163	−3.907	0.026	15.265	00.637
1939	−0.837	0.907	0.701	00.823	−00.759
1940	−1.837	−1.093	3.374	01.194	02.008
1941	−2.837	0.907	8.048	00.823	−02.573
1942	−1.837	1.907	3.374	03.637	−03.503
1943	−0.837	6.907	0.701	47.707	−05.781
1944	0.163	0.907	0.026	00.823	00.147
1945	1.163	−2.903	1.352	04.381	−02.434
1946	2.163	4.907	4.678	24.079	10.614
1947	3.163	−1.093	10.004	01.194	−03.457
1948	2.163	−0.903	4.678	00.008	−00.201
1949	1.163	1.907	1.352	03.637	02.217
1950	0.163	3.907	0.026	15.265	00.636
1951	−0.837	−2.093	0.701	04.381	01.752
1952	−1.837	0.907	3.374	00.823	−01.666
1953	−2.837	0.907	8.048	00.823	−02.573
1954	−1.837	−4.093	3.374	16.753	07.519
1955	0.837	−4.093	0.701	16.573	03.425
1956	0.163	−0.093	0.026	00.008	−00.015
1957	1.163	6.907	1.352	47.707	08.033
1958	2.163	0.907	4.678	00.823	01.962
1959	1.163	−1.093	1.352	01.194	−01.271
1960	0.163	−2.093	0.026	04.781	−00.341
1961	−0.837	−1.093	0.701	01.194	00.915
1962	−1.837	−4.093	3.374	16.753	07.519
1963	−2.837	−4.093	8.048	16.753	11.612
1964	−1.837	−3.093	3.374	09.576	05.682
1965	−0.837	−1.093	0.701	01.194	00.915
1966	0.163	−2.093	0.026	04.381	−00.341
1967	1.163	−3.093	1.352	09.576	−03.597
1968	2.163	−1.093	4.678	01.194	−02.364
1969	3.163	−0.093	10.004	00.008	−00.294
1970	2.163	0.097	4.678	00.823	01.962
1971	1.163	2.907	1.352	08.451	03.381
1972	0.163	−1.093	0.026	01.194	−00.178
1973	−0.837	2.907	0.701	08.451	−02.433
1974	−1.837	−2.093	3.374	04.381	03.845

E = SIGMA = the sum of . . .

$$0.182 = \frac{Ex_1Y_1}{\sqrt{(Ex_1^2)\ (Ey_1^2)}}$$

"No Correlation, Statistically"

15-13 *7.5 Earthquakes and solar activity correlated using correlation coefficient.*

Regardless of whether you've used graphs in your raw and smooth data sections, here is where graphs can be used to their best advantage to show the continuity of the results. The objective is to combine as much as possible on one graph to show the correlation of data without a loss of clarity. Consider the use of color, if possible, to distinguish among the various elements. If not, design can be used.

Pie charts, a very attractive way of diagramming results, will only lend themselves to projects that measure the division of a predetermined, specified quantity—for example, showing the percentage of a group of specimens. If your experiment uses that type of data, pie charts are appropriate and effective.

If you like working with graphs and your data lends itself to this method of presenting results, you might combine several graphing techniques. Remember, however, that as attractive as they are, graphs can only enhance the results; they will not compensate for deficiencies in research or experimentation.

Be sure to title each graph or chart. Describe the data being analyzed and compared. Clearly and accurately label each axis, column, or row, including the unit of measurement used. For illustration, review the graphs shown earlier in this chapter.

To show what happened, the results section can also include any photographs you took during the experiment. If the subject is easily and clearly photographed, this can be an excellent way to present information about what happened during experiments that were conducted over several weeks. Using a series of photos would, for example, lend itself to a project using plants, where the changes occur slowly over a period of time.

Although sketches can add a great deal to the appearance of your project notebook, they are not considered as factual as a photograph. However, if you're talented in that area, by all means, add drawings to liven up your project when you start working on the final notebook or the project display.

Besides the raw, smooth, and analyzed data, you'll need to write up your results, including a statement of your observations and measurements. You can also describe how you got your results by explaining any statistical work you've done and any correlations between the experimental and control groups. Don't draw your conclusions yet. This short statement should clearly and simply explain what happened and what the results showed.

Conclusions

Now that you've done your experiment and organized your results, you might wonder, "How do conclusions differ from results?" Your results showed what happened in your experiment, including any necessary mathematical or statistical interpretations and data correlation. To illustrate the data and make it easier to understand, you've also created charts, tables, and graphs.

The word "interpret" defines the last scientific step in your project—the conclusions. Through researching the background material and executing your experiment, you were trying to answer a question and prove a hypothesis. In conclusion, you will analyze the results to determine the effect of your experiment—what you really learned from the trials and testing you performed.

You should be able to present the project conclusions in a paper of approximately three pages. The conclusions will interpret the data and compare your results to the original hypothesis. Here you'll also critique your own project techniques and procedures, describing their impact on the results and conclusions. If appropriate, you can also evaluate your experimental design and suggest future improvements.

Begin your conclusion paper by restating your question or hypothesis. Next compare the results to your hypothesis. The data might concretely establish your theory to be true or false, or the results might be inconclusive. Inconclusive results usually mean that although there might be a trend in your data, it is not strong enough to prove or disprove your hypothesis.

In formulating conclusions, patterns are what you're looking for. Closely examine your tables, graphs, and charts to see if a trend clearly emerges. The most important thing is to review your results critically and without bias in order reach a definitive conclusion.

If the results show a conclusive direction, you can happily state either that your assumption was correct and you've proven your hypothesis, or that the experiment failed to demonstrate that your theory was true. In any event, explain why your results occurred. This is important even if the hypothesis was correct.

You'll also want to explain results that disprove the hypothesis. The most likely reason is that the theory was incorrect. That's fine; a hypothesis is simply an educated guess, and refuting it is as scientifically valid as conclusive proof. In the earthquake and solar correlation project, although the graphs seemed to indicate a relationship, the Correlation Coefficient Statistical Test did not. The statistical test required +.82 or –.82 to indicate a relationship. Since the calculated result, as shown in Fig. 15-12, was .143, and in Fig. 15-13 the calculated result was .182, there was no statistical correlation at all.

Another possible reason for inconclusive results is a weakness in the experimental design itself. In the course of a science project lasting several weeks, which is conducted in a home environment rather than a fully equipped lab, it is sometimes impractical to perform a sufficient number of tests on enough specimens to overwhelmingly prove something.

One experiment hypothesized that an orthodontic adhesive would weaken in various substances that were high in sugar. With one exception, the bonds did not break under pressure. The participant concluded that although the theory was disproved, it might have been because the trials were not carried on long enough, or the pull to loosen the bond was too weak.

In writing your conclusions, use your research and your results to explain the conclusions reached. The clearest and easiest way to do this is to discuss each fact or occurrence in a separate paragraph, referring to the experimentation and analysis that was done to reach the conclusion. Finally, write a summary that restates the hypothesis and conclusion as supported by the results.

Improvements and enhancements

Regardless of whether the project achieved its objectives, you'll need to analyze your experiment. Realistically reexamine your procedure in light of your results. Discuss the strengths and weaknesses of the design. Be honest; there are always some of each! Finally, suggest future modifications or improvements.

If this project has inspired you to continue research and experimentation in this field, briefly state how you plan to proceed. Even if you do not intend to pursue the subject, perhaps because it is beyond your resources or abilities, speculate on further work that could be done. However, remember that several of the big winners at the International Science and Engineering fairs had been working on variations of the same project for many years, refining and developing their work, each year building on the strengths and weaknesses of their prior year's projects.

"Real-life" applications

A powerful ending to your conclusions paper is a discussion of any potential practical value that your experiment might have. This will show teachers and judges not only your analytical ability as it relates to scientific reasoning, but also a well-rounded approach, relating your work to other fields of endeavor. Looking at those types of relationships have brought a great deal of personal satisfaction to many students. In some instances, there is even the potential for professional recognition and commercial reward. Some participants have been awarded patents for the work they've done on science projects.

On the other hand, other students have received less tangible but very real rewards. I spoke with several students whose projects developed computer systems for the physically challenged. Students can take particular satisfaction in the possible contribution their projects can make towards using the growing computer technology to make a better life for others.

16 All about us

Medical science is a field of big dreams—finding the cause of birth defects or the cure for a deadly disease. However, most of these discoveries are not the result of sudden inspiration or a quick bump on the head in the middle of the night. Instead, they are made after years of hard work doing patient research and experimentation. While you're spending a few months doing a science project, it's very unlikely that you'll have the resources, the know-how, or the time to address those kinds of issues.

However, there are important, though less spectacular, areas of medical science that you can explore to create a successful and rewarding science project.

Seeing (even sideways) is believing

At first, Yolanda Lockhart was not thrilled about doing a project, since science is not her primary interest. "I want to be a writer," she told me at our first meeting. However, because a project was required as part of her Life Sciences class, Yolanda set out to find a suitable topic. She couldn't seem to find anything she was interested in, and running out of time, decided to do an experiment on mold. However, her teacher discouraged her, since that was an idea that had been done too many times. Back to square one.

Then Yolanda remembered an experiment that she had done in fifth grade. At that time, each student had paired up with a partner to test peripheral vision. Using a board with a colored tab gradually moved from the edges towards the center, the subject looked straight ahead and noted when he or she first sighted the tab, while the partner recorded the number of degrees from the center.

Yolanda decided to expand this concept to perform the peripheral vision test on three groups of subjects—those with 20/20 vision, those who were nearsighted, and those who were farsighted—and compare the results. At first she wanted to conduct the experiment using adults and children. However, she soon realized that this would make the experiment more time-consuming and the record keeping too complicated. She therefore determined that she could get enough subjects by testing her own classmates.

Yolanda conducted her research using the encyclopedias in the school library. She found that although there was a great deal of material on the eye and on vision problems in general, there was very little about peripheral vision. However, she wrote her research paper concentrating on the generally available knowledge in the field.

While doing research, Yolanda simply took notes on sheets of paper. Because she had written several papers and essays before, organizing the material and writing the paper presented no problem for her.

When the research paper was done, Yolanda developed the project question and hypothesis shown in Fig. 16-1. The experimental and control groups are shown in Fig. 16-2.

Yolanda was able to do the entire experiment with simple and inexpensive materials, as shown in Fig. 16-3. To prepare for the experiment, she created the experimental field on a piece of white poster board. Using a compass and protractor, she marked off a semicircle where the subject would place his or her chin. She then measured the degrees from 0 through 90° on the left side of the board and 0 through 90° on the right side of the board, marked off in 5° increments. Finally, she made seven tabs of different colors out of construction paper.

Question	Hypothesis
What peripheral differences exist between 20/20 vision and visually impaired?	People who wear glasses have worse peripheral vision than those who do not.

16-1 *Peripheral Vision—Question and hypothesis.*

Experimental Groups	Control Group
1. Students with 20/20 vision 2. Nearsighted students 3. Farsighted students	None

16-2 *Peripheral Vision—Experimental and control groups.*

Materials
1. Oak tag 2. Black marker 3. Compass 4. Protractor 5. 7 colored tabs, made from construction paper

16-3 *Peripheral Vision—Materials.*

Yolanda conducted the experiment in her science classroom, between January 23 and February 5, 1990, as shown in her project log displayed in Fig. 16-4. Her three subject groups were divided between male and female, and between those who are nearsighted, those who are farsighted, and those with 20/20 vision.

DECEMBER 7, 1989—Developed an idea.
DECEMBER 17, 1989—Began research.
DECEMBER 26, 1989—Continued research.
JANUARY 13, 1990—Purchased materials to arrange peripheral vision test.
JANUARY 21, 1990—Designed a peripheral vision testing board.
JANUARY 23, 1990—Began testing.
JANUARY 24, 1990—Tested five subjects.
JANUARY 25, 1990—Tested three subjects.
JANUARY 26, 1990—Tested seven subjects.
JANUARY 29, 1990—Tested five subjects.
JANUARY 31, 1990—Tested eleven subjects.
FEBRUARY 1, 1990—Tested six students.
FEBRUARY 5, 1990—Tested five students.
FEBRUARY 8–FEBRUARY 23—Designed display board, cumulated data, and formulated research folder.

16-4 *Peripheral Vision—Project log.*

"I had no trouble finding subjects," said Yolanda. "In fact, once my friends saw what I was doing, they volunteered to be part of my experiment." At times, a classmate helped by recording the test results while Yolanda worked with the test subject. However, if no one was available to assist, she was able to conduct the tests and record the data by herself.

Each subject went through the entire experiment once. To begin, the subject placed his or her chin on the marked area, with eyes kept straight ahead. Yolanda placed a colored tab at the 0° marking on the rightmost side of the board, and she moved along the degree markings towards 90°, the center of the board. As the tab moved, the subject kept his or her eyes forward and indicated when he or she first sighted the tab and identified the color. The test was repeated for each of the seven colored tabs for both the left and right sides of the board.

A view of the actual experiment is exhibited in Fig. 16-5. Each trial took approximately 15 minutes, and the findings were recorded in the experimental log. The procedures are summarized in Fig. 16-6.

Once the experiment was complete, Yolanda averaged the scores for each student. She then constructed four graphs to display the average for farsighted subjects, shown in Fig. 16-7, nearsighted subjects, shown in Fig. 16-8, 20/20 females, shown in Fig. 16-9, and 20/20 males, shown in Fig. 16-10. Based on her results, Yolanda's concluded that there is a difference in peripheral vision between those with 20/20 vision and those with visual impairment.

16-5 *Peripheral Vision—Photo of experiment.*

Procedures
1. Subject placed chin on marked area, with eyes forward.
2. Placed colored tab at the rightmost 0° marking on the board.
3. Gradually moved tab towards 90°, the center of the board.
4. Subject indicated when tab first sighted, and when color first identified.
5. Placed colored tab at the leftmost 0° marking on the board.
6. Gradually moved tab towards 90°, the center of the board.
7. Subject indicated when tab first sighted, and when color first identified.

16-6 *Peripheral Vision—Procedures.*

The backboard for the project, entitled "Comparison of Peripheral Vision in Persons with 20/20 and Impaired Vision," contained the graphs and charts and a photo of her experiment. The backboard panels are shown in Figs. 16-11, 16-12, and 16-13.

Since Yolanda already knows she'll have to do another project next year, she's decided to expand on this idea. For the continuation of the experiment, she will conduct more extensive research, perhaps using medical references or consulting with professionals in the field.

Yolanda has already thought of several ways of building on her project. One idea is to analyze the differences in peripheral vision based on the color of tab because Yolanda observed that the yellow tab was more easily noticed. Another plan is to use the subject groups she had originally wanted to use, adults and children. A third possibility is to compare differences in peripheral vision between the left and right eye.

"Even though I wasn't enthusiastic to begin with," said Yolanda, "I began to enjoy the project as time went on, especially the testing. I think it will be fun to take advantage of what I've learned and take the project a step further."

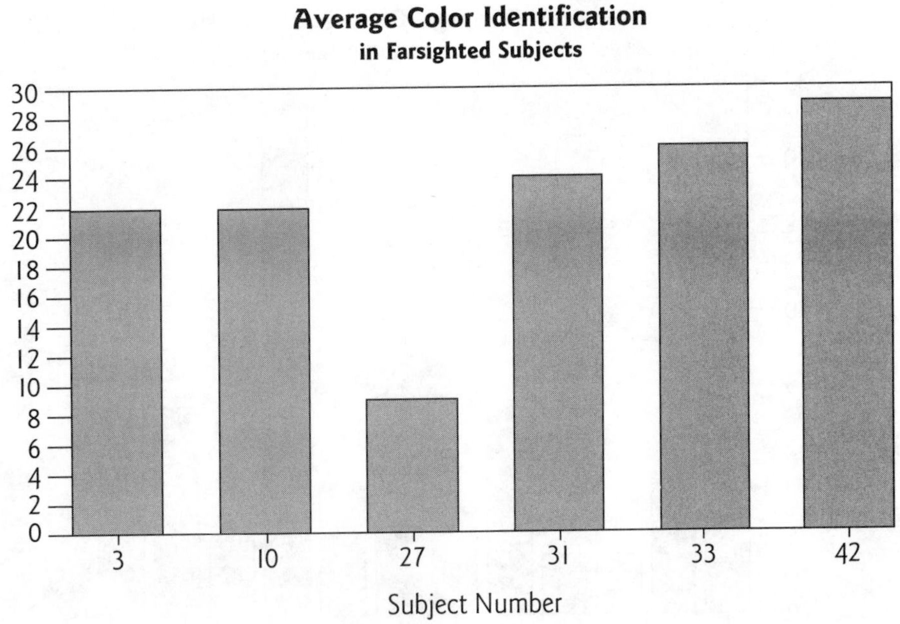

16-7 *Peripheral Vision—Graph, farsighted subjects.*

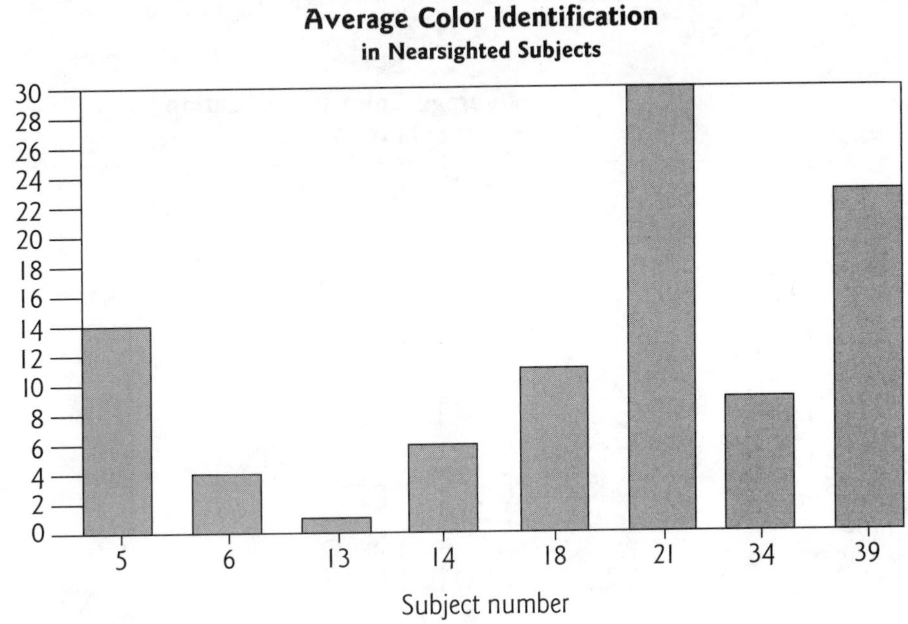

16-8 *Peripheral Vision—Graph, nearsighted subjects.*

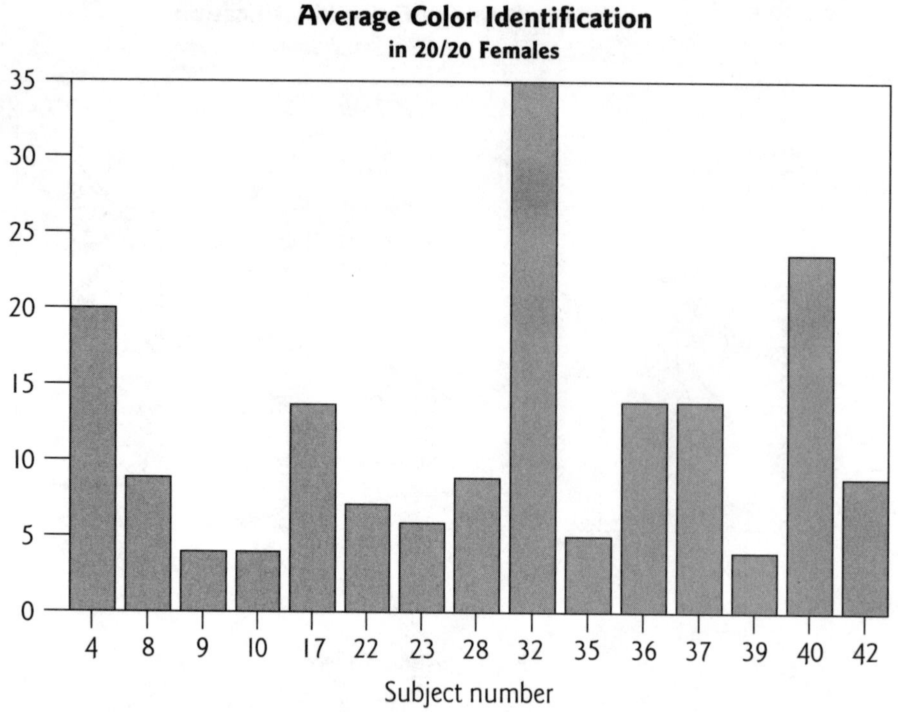

16-9 *Peripheral Vision—Graph, 20/20 female subjects.*

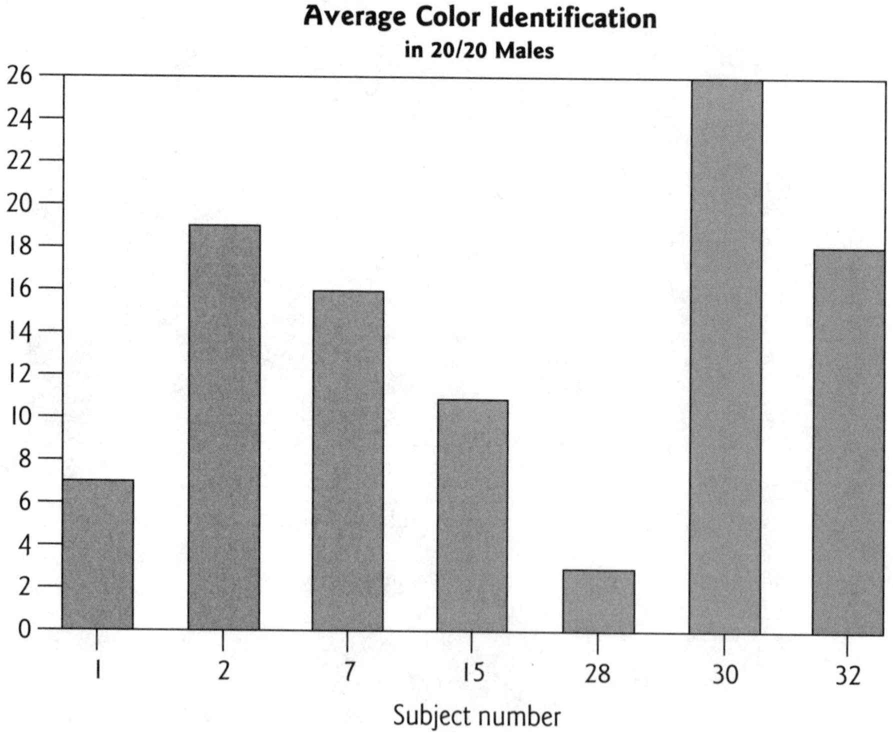

16-10 *Peripheral Vision—Graph, 20/20 male subjects.*

16-11
Peripheral Vision—Backboard.

16-12
Peripheral Vision—Backboard.

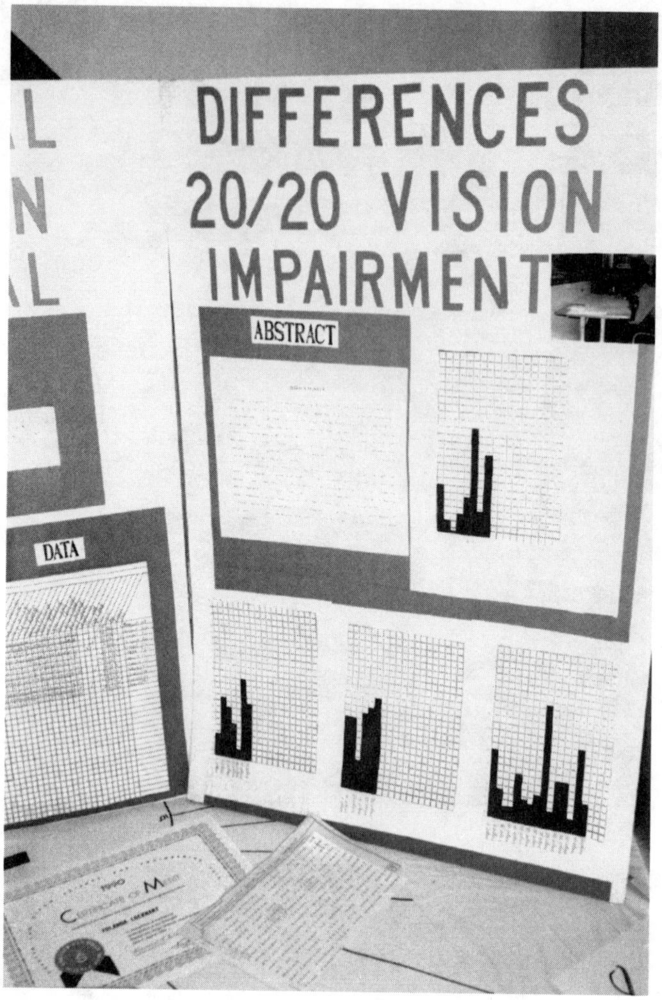

16-13 *Peripheral Vision—Backboard.*

"Where there's smoke, there's . . ."

When Daryl Smith found he had to do a science project, he didn't have any particular subject in mind. In order to find a topic, he started brainstorming and listing subjects until he had a list of about ten ideas. Most of them were in the medical field, which is not surprising, since his father is a physician.

He then talked with his science teacher, and together they narrowed the list down to three ideas. Armed with this smaller list, Daryl hit the libraries to find out which topic had the most information available. Based on this preliminary research, he decided to test the effects of second-hand smoking. Until then, he hadn't read a lot about this topic, but he knew that smoking had become socially unacceptable. Also, since some of his friends' parents smoke, and some do not, he planned to test children of smokers and nonsmokers.

Daryl did most of his research at the school library, a local branch library, and the central library. He also used some references that were available at his father's office, and the Surgeon General's report on smoking.

Daryl borrowed the books he needed, and he tagged relevant pages with post-it notes. "This might not have been quite legal," he said, "but I just kept renewing the books until I got my research done."

He outlined his paper by writing down the various subjects he wanted to include, such as the physiology of lungs, carcinogens, and the effects of smoking. After he wrote the opening sentence for a paragraph, he went through his references to find all the facts that pertained to that particular subject, and added them to the paragraph. He wrote his background research paper on an IBM PC, using PC Write. While conducting his research, Daryl developed the question and hypothesis shown in Fig. 16-14.

To conduct the experiment, Daryl tested 100 students, 50 whose parents are smokers, and 50 whose parents are nonsmokers. The subjects were equally divided between males and females.

Before testing, each subject filled out a questionnaire to make sure he or she did not have asthma or any other condition that would affect the results. To assure a constant environment, Daryl conducted all tests in the same classroom, and he did no testing on excessively hot, cold, dry, or humid days. The project variables and controls are shown in Fig. 16-15, and the experimental and control groups are shown in Fig. 16-16. To conduct the experiment, Daryl used the materials shown in Fig. 16-17.

As each subject began the experiment, Daryl explained what would happen during the test. Twice, he had the subject take a deep breath and exhale through the sterilized mouthpiece of the respirometer, shown in Fig. 16-18, until he or she was unable to continue. He then recorded the higher set of all six respirometer measurements.

Question	Hypothesis
Does involuntary smoking cause decreased lung capacity?	Children of smokers will have less lung capacity than children of non-smokers.

16-14 *Involuntary Smoking—Question and hypothesis.*

Variables	Controls
Experimental Whether parents smoked	• Room temperature between 72° and 80°F
Measured FEV[1]	• Subjects were free of respiratory disease or allergy

16-15 *Involuntary Smoking—Variables and controls.*

Experimental Groups	Control Group
Students whose parents are smokers (Must have been exposed to smoke for at least seven years)	Students whose parents are non-smokers
Note: Both the experimental and control groups must meet the following requirements: • Must be in Junior High School (grades 7, 8, and 9) • Must be at rest for at least 10 minutes prior to beginning test • Must have no recent respiratory illness.	

16-16 *Involuntary Smoking—Experimental and control groups.*

Materials
1. One Respiradyne (Pulmonary Function Monitor), which measures lung capacity in liters, as follows: • FEV^1, which measures the forced expiratory volume in one second • FVC, the forced vital capacity • Peak flow • FEF 25–75, which measures 25–75% of the forced expiratory flow • Volume extra percent • FEV^1 / FVC
2. Four hollow mouthpieces, with flow control at the end
3. Twenty hollow mouthpiece adapters
4. One hundred alcohol swabs to sterilize the mouthpiece

16-17 *Involuntary Smoking—Materials.*

A summary of experimental procedures are shown in Fig. 16-19. When all subjects were tested, Daryl researched the meaning of all six measurements. He determined that FEV^1 was the best overall indication of lung condition, and decided to base his results on that measurement.

Daryl then listed the total and mean of all the high scores, as shown in Fig. 16-20. He noted that the zero scores, shown for subjects 31 and 40 in the nonsmoking group, "would mean that the people were dead." He therefore did not include these measurements when computing average or mean scores. He also graphed the scores for children of smokers and nonsmokers, as shown in Figs. 16-21 and 16-22. After analyzing the data, Daryl con-

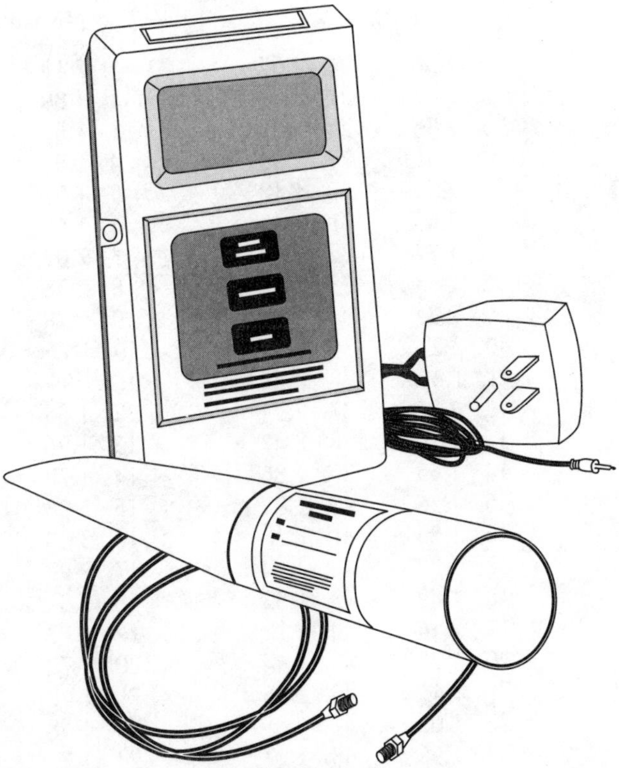

16-18 *Involuntary Smoking—Respirometer.*

Procedures
1. Subject seated and instructed on procedures for test.
2. Subject took mouthpiece, and after inhaling as much air as possible, exhaled through sterilized mouthpiece as forcefully as possible until unable to continue.
3. Recorded Forced Expiratory Volume in one second (FEV^1)
4. Repeated test.

16-19 *Involuntary Smoking—Procedures.*

cluded that the children of smokers actually had higher FEV^1 scores, which disproved his hypothesis.

One possible reason for the unexpected results was the fact that the testing was done during flu season. "Even though I eliminated anyone who was sick," said Daryl, "they might have been in an incubation period at the time." Another factor was that in homes where parents smoke, Daryl did not know what the smoking patterns were. For example, in some homes, smoking is restricted to a certain area of the house, or outdoors on a patio or balcony. In the homes where the parents did not smoke, he didn't know what other exposure students might have

Smokers		Nonsmokers	
1. 2.56	26. 1.52	1. 2.13	26. 1.74
2. 1.77	27. 1.38	2. 1.89	27. 1.67
3. 2.86	28. 1.95	3. 1.68	28. 2.68
4. 2.41	29. 2.94	4. 1.84	29. 1.68
5. 2.4	30. 1.18	5. 1.57	30. .81
6. 3.06	31. 1.26	6. 1.65	31. .0
7. 1.72	32. 1.44	7. 2.02	32. 3.34
8. 2.33	33. 2.02	8. 2.56	33. 2.03
9. 2.2	34. 1.24	9. 1.78	34. 2.5
10. 3.2	35. 1.52	10. 1.76	35. 1.3
11. 1.81	36. 4.24	11. 1.99	36. 1.98
12. 2.52	37. 2.2	12. 1.85	37. 1.27
13. 1.11	38. 2.42	13. 1.96	38. 1.29
14. 1.65	39. 1.86	14. 1.72	39. 2.58
15. 1.36	40. 2.82	15. 3.08	40. .0
16. 1.84	41. 1.21	16. 3.38	41. 1.99
17. 3.34	42. 2.14	17. 2.92	42. .79
18. 1.49	43. 1.82	18. 2.3	43. 2.0
19. 2.16	44. 2.78	19. .83	44. 2.74
20. 2.23	45. 1.44	20. .72	45. 1.53
21. 1.43	46. 2.96	21. 1.49	46. 2.03
22. 1.02	47. .81	22. 1.58	47. 2.0
23. 1.95	48. 1.47	23. 1.25	48. 2.45
24. 2.94	49. .88	24. 1.3	49. 1.96
25. 1.18	50. 2.3	25. 1.74	50. 2.54
TOTAL = 98.82152		TOTAL = 90.371529	
MEAN = 1.9764304		MEAN = 1.8827401	

All volumes were measured in liters. The higher of two scores is shown in the table above.

16-20 *Involuntary Smoking—Mean and high scores.*

had, such as friends and relatives who smoke. The backboard for the project, entitled "Effect of Involuntary Smoking on Children," is displayed in Fig. 16-23.

Next year, Daryl intends to keep building on the same topic. He will use the same background research, but he plans to use a new group of students and also consult a specialist for the precise meaning of the measurements. He also plans to analyze all six measurements in his results and conclusions, instead of just FEV^1. Despite the results of the experiment, Daryl believes that second-hand smoking is dangerous. Next year, he hopes to prove it.

The next project takes the same subject, second-hand smoke, but tests and analyzes it in a completely different way. Pippa Munro, who did a project last year about the effects of direct smoke, modified it to address this issue. She was attracted to this topic not only because it was current and controversial, but be-

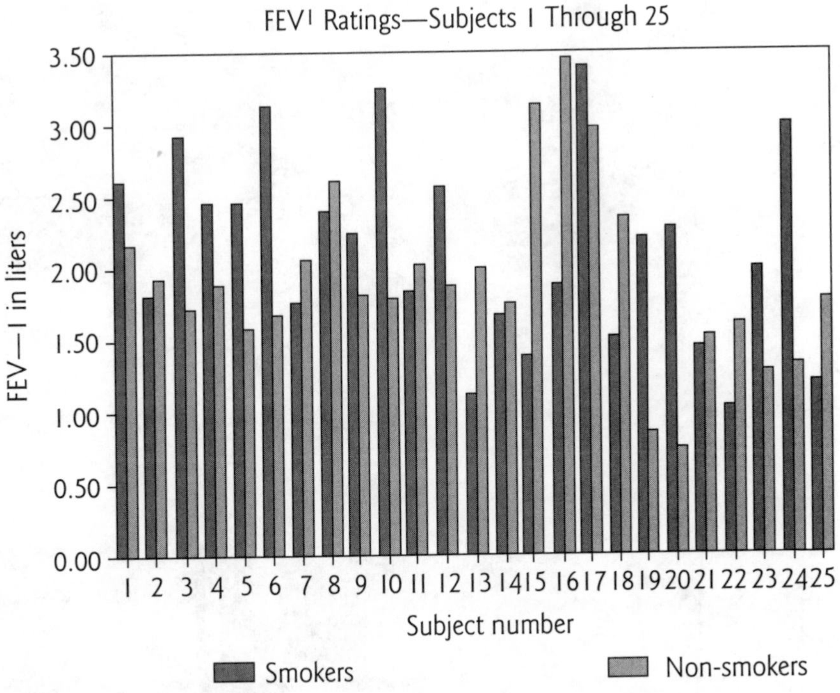

16-21 *Involuntary Smoking—Graph of smokers and nonsmokers.*

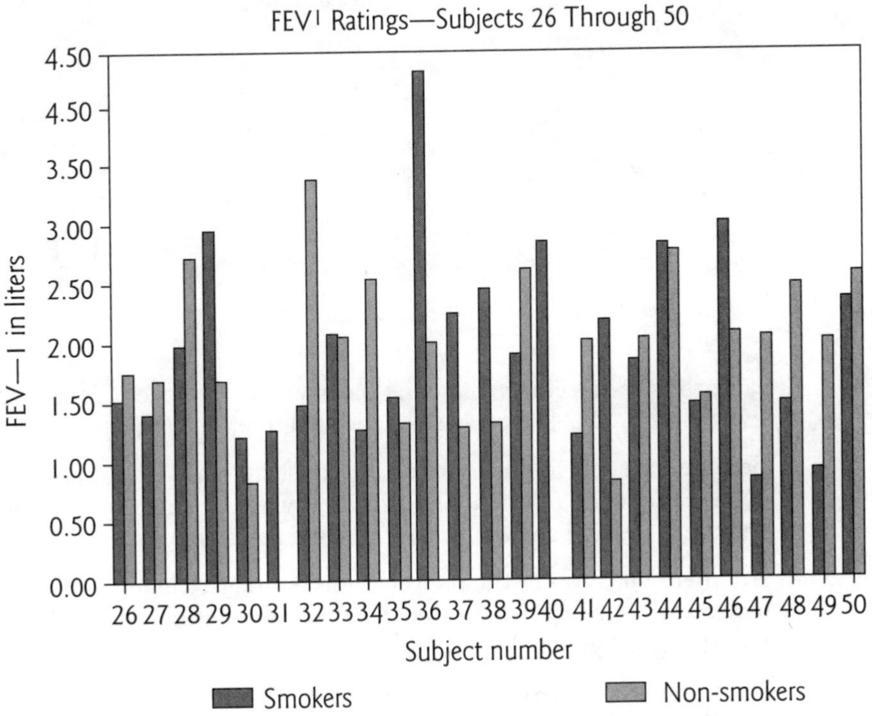

16-22 *Involuntary Smoking—Graph of smokers and nonsmokers.*

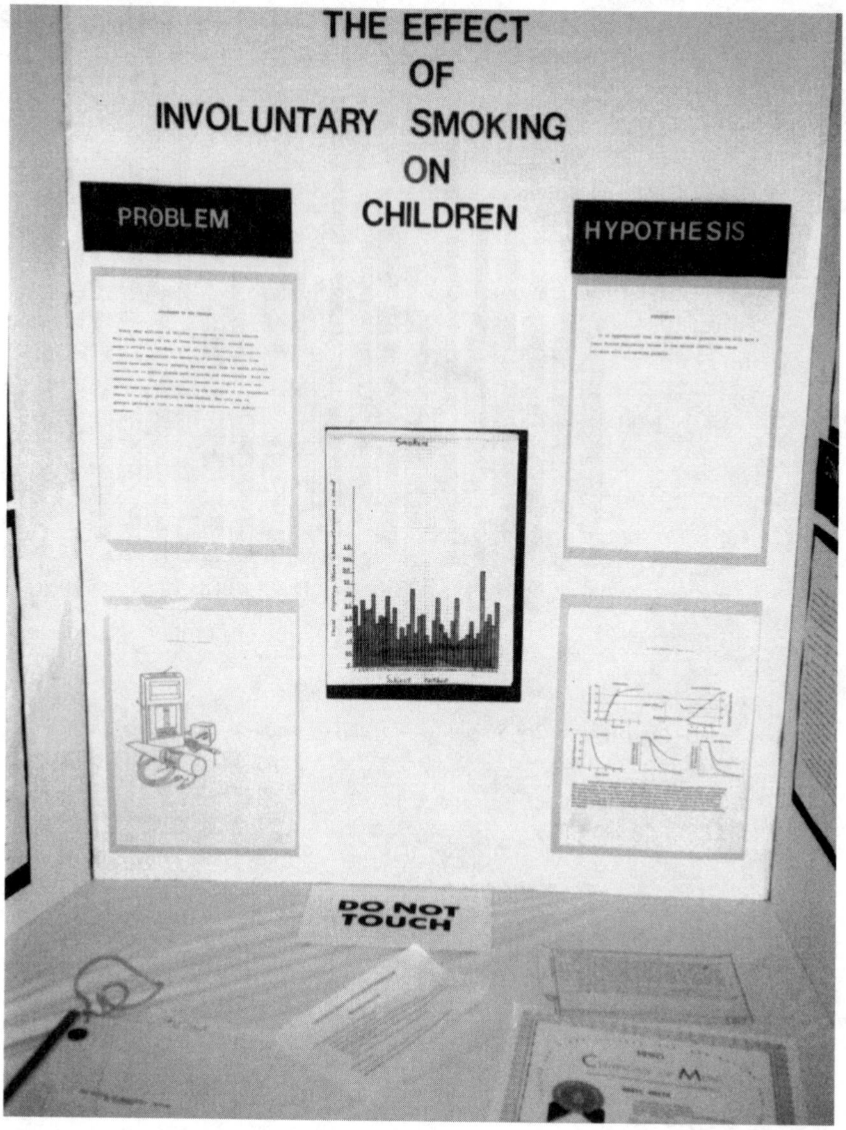

16-23 *Involuntary Smoking—Backboard.*

cause she's been trying to discourage a parent who smokes. Her stated purpose, shown in Fig. 16-24, expresses her personal interest in this project.

Because Pippa did a similar project last year, she was able to capitalize on a lot of her background research. She also knew where to find the smoking machine and the scales that she would need to measure the results.

Another dimension to the project was the product claims by cigarette manufacturers that their products were the lowest in tar and nicotine, as shown in Fig. 16-25, the project hypothesis.

To execute the experiment, Pippa "smoked" four packs of cigarettes, using a smoking machine. The filter in the machine represented the lungs. A household air purifier represented a person breathing second-hand smoke. The fan filter from the air purifier was weighed before and after each pack of cigarettes. A fifth filter was used to clean the machine between each pack. Figs. 16-26 and 16-27 show the detailed materials list and the procedures for the experiment.

Purpose

This project is being done to find out how much particulate matter, or tar-nicotine, is in secondhand smoke. It is also being done to see if "low-tar" cigarettes make a difference when it comes to secondhand smoke. This will be measured by the amount of particulate matter collected on the filters.

This project can benefit people by showing how much harm smoking cigarettes can do. Hopefully it will encourage many people to quit smoking, and not to breathe in the smoke of others. Again, hopefully it will also help to prevent young children from ever starting to smoke.

16-24 *Effects of Secondhand Smoke—Purpose.*

Hypothesis

If four different brands of cigarettes, two low-tar and two regular, are tested through a smoking machine and then through a fan filter, then Marlboro Regular cigarettes will have the highest amount of particulate matter in the secondhand smoke.

16-25 *Effects of Secondhand Smoke—Hypothesis.*

Materials

1) one (1) smoking machine
2) one (1) filter fan
3) one (1) Satorius Top Balance scale
4) one (1) Mettler AE 160 scale
5) twenty (20) Marlboro Light cigarettes
6) twenty (20) Marlboro Regular cigarettes
7) twenty (20) Camel Light cigarettes
8) twenty (20) Camel Regular cigarettes
9) five (5) fan filters
10) four (4) paper filters
11) eighty (80) square decimeters of tin foil
12) one (1) surgical mask
13) one (1) pair of latex medical gloves
14) one (1) pair of tweezers
15) one (1) cigarette lighter
16) four (4) petri dishes
17) nine (9) plastic zip-lock bags
18) ten (10) non-abrasive low-lint wipes

16-26 *Effects of Secondhand Smoke—Materials.*

Procedure

1) Preweigh fan filters
2) Preweigh paper filters
3) Set up smoking machine
4) Set up filter fan
5) Clear air with designated fan filter
6) Insert into smoking machine designated paper filter
7) Change fan filter with designated testing fan filter
8) Wrap cigarettes in tin foil
9) Test twenty (20) Marlboro Light cigarettes through smoking machine
10) Run filter fan while testing
11) Repeat steps five through ten (5–10) for each brand of cigarettes
12) Weigh fan filters
13) Weigh paper filters

16-27 *Effects of Secondhand Smoke—Procedure.*

The experiment showed that the regular cigarettes yielded more particulate matter than the low-tar and nicotine brands, as shown in Figs. 16-28 and 16-29. However, even these brands showed a measurable amount of particulate matter. This might be due to either the amount of tobacco in the cigarette or the strength of the cigarette filter.

Possible project improvements would be to test more brands of cigarettes and to do more research to find additional background information. Pippa's already thinking about her next project, and most likely, it too will deal with smoking. Potential future project ideas are shown in Fig. 16-30.

Chart

Filter Type	Before	After	Difference
Fan 1	9.67 g	9.69 g	0.02 g
Fan 2	9.49 g	9.52 g	0.03 g
Fan 3	9.44 g	9.46 g	0.02 g
Fan 4	9.92 g	9.97 g	0.05 g
Paper 1	16.3857 g	16.6749 g	0.2892 g
Paper 2	16.4038 g	16.7712 g	0.3674 g
Paper 3	16.6555 g	16.9479 g	0.2924 g
Paper 4	16.3719 g	16.7036 g	0.3317 g

16-28 *Effects of Secondhand Smoke—Results.*

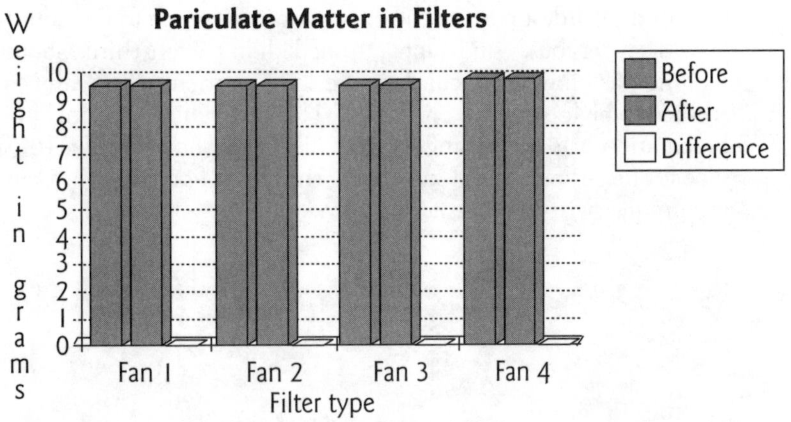

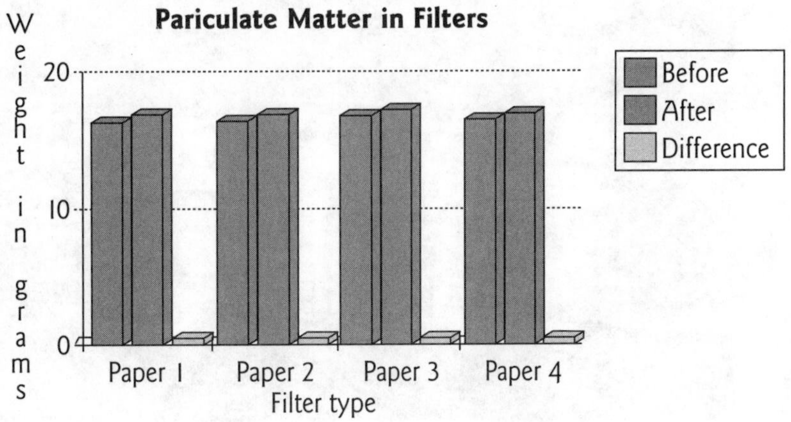

16-29 *Effects of Secondhand Smoke—Conclusions.*

Suggestions for Further Research

1) Which country has the highest amount of tar-nicotine in their cigarettes?
2) Which cigarettes take the longest to burn?
3) Is the difference in low-tar cigarettes in the tobacco or the filter?
4) Which brand of cigarettes has the most tar-nicotine?
5) Which brand of cigarettes has the most tobacco in their cigarettes?
6) Which brand of cigarettes has the strongest filters?
7) How much smoke does it take to set off smoke detectors?

16-30 *Effects of Secondhand Smoke—Future project ideas.*

One of the hardest parts of the experience was going to the county science fair. "I was so nervous," said Pippa, "that I didn't even think about awards. The judging was kind of difficult because some of them were really easy and others seemed to be looking for problems." The experience certainly pointed out that preparation was everything. Pippa's display is shown in Fig 16-31. Pippa's advice for first-timers? Find something that lots of people are discussing, but give it a unique twist to make it your own.

16-31 *Effects of Secondhand Smoke—Backboard.*

Helpful hints

You might want to see how much information is available before you begin.

- Dig into your past. There might be some good ideas there.
- Look at your results! Dead subjects don't breathe!
- Record keeping can sometimes be tedious, but without good records there is no project.
- An experiment that disproves the hypothesis is as valid as one that comes out the way you expect.
- You can use some similar techniques for behavioral and social science projects, where you need to survey a large number of people and control the results. Keeping experimental and control groups of equal size helps validate the results.

17 The project display

"You never get a second chance to make a first impression," says the expression in many how-to-sell books. Now that you've done the research, completed your experiment, analyzed and graphed the results, and formulated your conclusions, you're ready to present your project. You are, in fact, marketing your project, and your target audience is the science fair judges. These judges are professors, scientists, engineers, consultants, and business people—in other words, a judge could be anyone with knowledge and interest in your field.

Whenever you market a complex product, you first need to attract attention in order to convince your future customers to take a closer look. Then, when your prospects are interested, you need to present all the facts that they need to make their decision. To accomplish these objectives, you'll use your science fair notebook, and a project display or backboard.

The science fair notebook

The science fair notebook will contain all the written and visual materials that you've developed for your project. If you've seen other students' notebooks, you'll realize that this is a fairly hefty piece of work, but the good news is that you already have most of the material. You've done the research paper, posed your question and hypothesis, kept your logs, outlined your procedures, and formulated your results and conclusions. Now you'll need to do some editing and revision to get everything into the most attractive and presentable form.

Appearances count, so plan to use an attractive and appropriate cover. Your teacher might have his or her own specific requirements for the size and type of folder, but if not, a good guideline is to use three-hole, 8½-x-11 paper and folder.

If you're typing, use regular bond paper, since erasable bond smudges, and thin, onion-skin paper might cause the reader to see double. Regardless of how you create the written material, double-space all of your work, with the possible exception of tables, bibliography entries, or footnotes written in standard form, as shown in chapter 8.

Some teachers might allow handwritten notebooks. Make sure that your handwriting is completely legible. If you have any doubts, print. Use ink only. (No erasables, please. They smudge!) The only possible exception is the log section, which represents raw data. However, type or use computer printout wherever possible. The easier your work is on the teacher's eyes, the happier he or she will be. And a happy teacher usually gives better grades! Now let's review the items to be included in your science fair notebook:

- Required forms. If you needed any ISEF forms (described in chapter 7 and appendix B) you must include them in your notebook.
- Title page.
- Table of contents. Remember that although this goes right in the beginning of the notebook, it will probably be the last thing you'll create, once the pages are numbered. If you're using a word processor, your program can create a table of contents for you.
- Abstract. The abstract is a summary of your project, including the background research paper, the hypothesis, the procedure, and the results. Because you'll need to fit a version of the abstract on your entry form, keep it to approximately 200 words.
- Background research. Basically, this is the research paper you wrote at the beginning of the project. Now, however, you can polish it to make it look more professional. You can also incorporate any comments or suggestions that your teachers made, in order to fix, clarify, and edit your work. If you gathered any additional information during your project, such as advice from your teachers or mentors, or new information that appeared in the newspapers or magazines, you can include that data as well.
- Bibliography. For the most part, this will be the bibliography you submitted with your original research paper. This, too, should be updated for format, grammar, and spelling. Be sure to credit any new or additional sources.
- Statement of the problem or question. The question or problem that expresses the purpose of the experiment.
- The hypothesis. The theory that your project was designed to prove. Make sure that you identify the subject of the experiment, the experimental and control groups, the dependent and independent variables, and the controls. Again, edit for grammar and spelling. (Do I sound like a broken record? If so, it's because a few too many errors will make your excellent project look unprofessional and badly prepared.) Even if your experiment disproved the hypothesis, be honest and state your original hypothesis. Do not change your original theory to fit the results. Remember that a disproved hypothesis is just as valuable as a proven one.
- Procedures. Include a sequential list of all your procedures. If you revised the procedures while doing the experiment, be sure to modify them before including the list in your final notebook. Your procedures should reflect the way you actually performed the project steps.

- Materials list. Include anything and everything you used for your project, regardless of whether you bought, borrowed, or built it.
- Variables and controls. Fully describe each variable and control and its role in the experiment. Show how you managed and monitored the variables and how you measured and recorded what happened.
- Results. Include raw, smooth and analyzed data, including all the charts, graphs, tables, photographs, and diagrams. Be sure that all results are neat, legible, and accurately and clearly labeled. Also, describe your observations, which summarize the raw, smooth, and analyzed data.
- Conclusions. Edit, spell-check, and revise!
- Acknowledgments. Now you can thank everyone who helped with your project. However, try not to identify teachers, school or family by name because you're required to remain anonymous when you compete in science fairs.
- Project log. Here neatness doesn't count; you just want to show the detailed progress of your science project, including your diary, working log, rough notes, and drafts of tables and graphs.

When you've reprinted and collected everything, review the entire notebook. Make sure that you have all the sections in order, and that the pages within each section are in proper sequence. Make sure that the pages are numbered, and then create the table of contents. Remember that if you're using a word processor, the program will do it all for you. Otherwise, you can type or write (legibly, please) the numbers on each page. When you're done, have someone review the notebook. After all your hard work, you don't want to be tripped up by pages (or worse yet, entire sections) out of sequence.

The science fair display

The final step is to create your project exhibit, the thing that will advertise and call attention to your research and experiment. Remember, though, that once you've invited the judges to look at your notebook, its contents must live up to the promise of your marketing. Just as with the notebook, the most polished presentation in the world won't substitute for mediocre work. However, since you've followed this step-by-step guide, your project will be excellent, your notebook will be neat and professional, and your exhibit will be first-class.

The purpose of the display is to summarize your project. Read that sentence again and remember the key word—summarize. Do not try to recreate your entire project notebook. Instead, simply cover the main points and the highlights.

Most science project displays are three-sectioned, freestanding backboards. The sections are normally folded or hinged for easier transporting to the science fairs where you'll be competing. However, backboards can have as few as two or as many as five sections to successfully display the material.

Backboards can be made from a variety of elements, from cardboard to Plexiglas. You can also try prefabricated backboards, which are commonly made of foam core or other art materials and can be bought in many colors. Besides being easier and quicker than constructing your own backboard, using a prefab assures that your display will meet exhibit requirements. If, however, you decide to build your own, consider using rigid, durable, fireproof material, such as Masonite, pegboard, plywood, or Plexiglas. Some science fairs might prohibit displays made of cardboard or other paper products, due to fire regulations. Although the actual construction might require some time and effort, the basic backboard can later be stripped of the display materials and used for subsequent science projects.

Science fair displays are normally between 3 and 5 feet. When deciding, first check to see if the science fair has restrictions on overall size. Occasionally, you'll see a display that is so large that it cannot be placed on a table and needs to set on the floor. This happens most often with engineering projects. Be sure to get permission from your local fair officials before designing a floor display. In any event, determine how much material needs to go on the backboard before deciding on the size.

Next decide whether you will cover the basic backboard or keep it bare. If you're using pegboard, you might want to use hooks to attach material. Some students paint their backboards, while others glue Velcro strips to the backboard and attach materials later. If you plan to cover the panels, consider the dimensions of the covering material, such as the width of construction paper or self-adhesive papers.

Your display must include summaries of the problem, hypothesis, procedures, results, and conclusions. You can do this using all written material, but you might include graphs, photographs, drawings, tables, or other artwork that will make the display more attractive. Remember, however, that all this information must fit onto the backboard you have selected.

Some students have very creatively solved the problem of too much material and too little room on a backboard. You can use several panels to display graphs and samples on the backboard, as shown in Fig. 17-1. You can also create a "minidiorama" in front of the backboard to display parts of your experiment, as Brian Berning and Teri Vertullo did. Figures 17-2 through 17-6 show everything from computers to models in front of a backboard.

The best way to ensure a well-designed backboard is to make a map or blueprint of your project display. Decide what to put on each of the panels, including the estimated sizes. When calculating, remember to account for the size and style of the lettering you will use. As you can see from the photographs throughout the book, there are infinite combinations and permutations of where and how to place the materials.

If you plan to display anything on the table in front of your backboard, make sure that these items will not block an important part of the display. Of course, if your material can be placed flat on the display table, you need not allocate any extra space for it. Important: no animal specimens, please.

As you've noticed, at least some portions of your display will consist of written material. The problem and hypothesis, which are already short statements, can

17-1 *Backboard with hinged panels.*

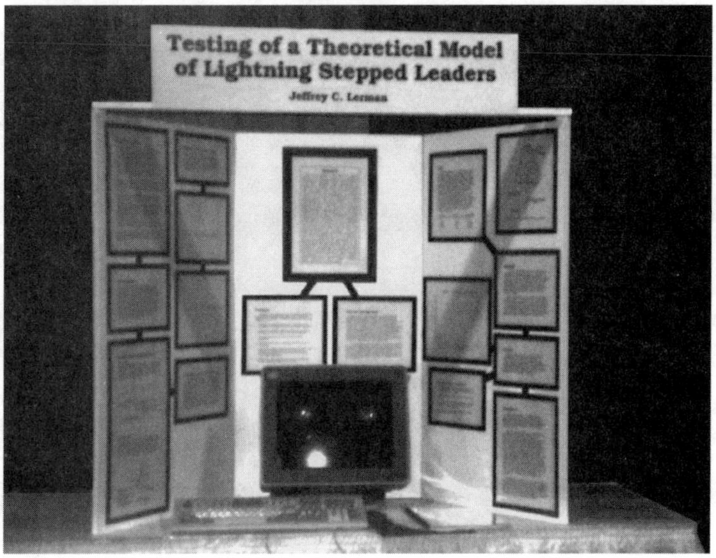

17-2 *Testing of a Theoretical Model of Lightning Stepped Leaders Backboard.*

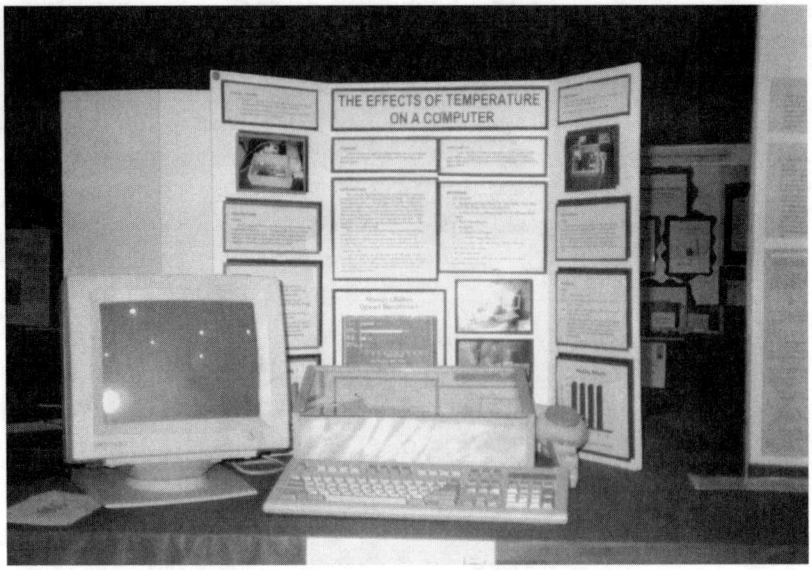

17-3 *Effects of Temperature on a Computer—Backboard.*

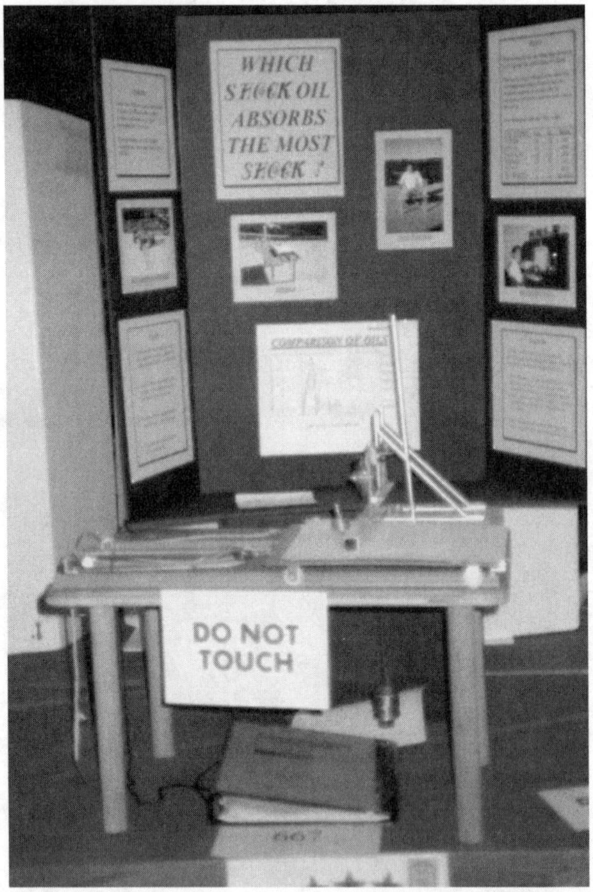

17-4 *Which Shock Oil Absorbs the Most Shock?—Backboard.*

17-5 *Can the Effects of an Earthquake on a Cable-Stayed Bridge be Reduced?—Backboard.*

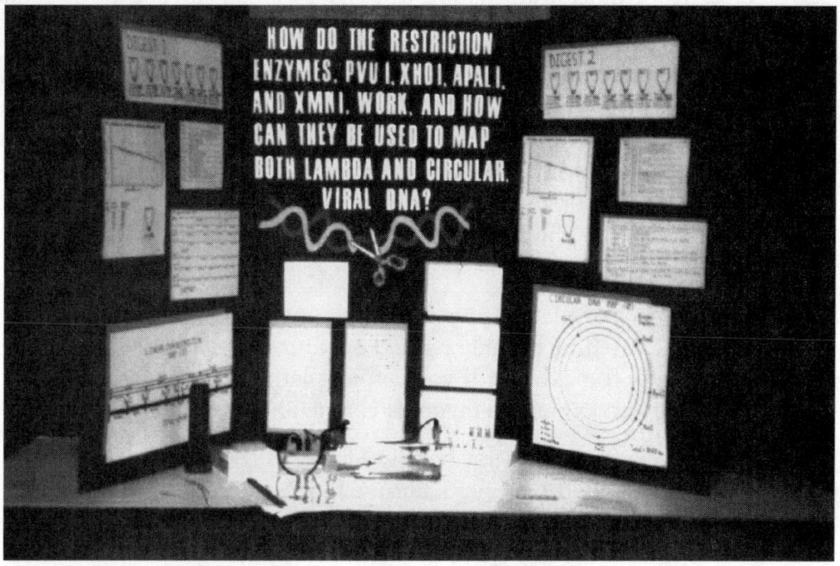

17-6 *How do the Restriction Enzymes PVU1, XHO1, APPAL1, and XMN1 Work, and How Can They Be Used to Map Both Lambda and Circular Viral DNA?—Backboard.*

probably be used without any further editing. However, you can display printed matter in several ways:

- Typewritten.
- Computer printout. Using word processing, desktop publishing or graphics programs, you can experiment with different sizes and fonts.
- Hand lettering.
- Stenciling or press-on letters.
- Lettering made on a Kroy or other labeling machine.

As shown in the samples, be sure to title everything you display, using larger lettering to make it stand out. When doing the written material, you will become an expert in the art of summarizing.

Some participants create backboards that consist mainly of written material. However, using different fonts and including some illustrations or graphs with the text can liven up the text display.

The main thing to remember here is that "less is more." Strive for maximum accuracy and clarity with minimum words. Remember that this is a summary. You don't need to show all the facts on the display. The judges will take the time to examine the notebook and interview you to find out the details. Including too much information will make your backboard look busy and difficult to read, perhaps discouraging a closer look.

If you include graphs, charts, or tables, try to create enlarged versions, using color for added interest. If you're not using a computer for graphs and charts, there are several ways to do this. Wide, colored tape can make excellent lines on a graph, and thin, black tape can be used to show gradations. Remember to make them accurate and attractive. If you used computer-generated graphs in your notebook, you might be able to produce larger, colored versions for the backboard.

Photographs or illustrations can be mounted using hinges, corners, or glue. Be sure that anything pasted or glued on your backboard will stay in place for the duration of the exhibit. If your project lends itself to it, line drawings (hand-sketched or computer generated) can be an eye-catching addition.

A good cement useful for bonding paper is the best way to paste things on a backboard. Buy the proper adhesive for the material you are using, and follow the manufacturer's directions. For example, ventilate the room properly when working with certain types of glue. Also, investigate using staples, nails, push pins, or other methods of attaching material to your display.

Also, it is a good idea to plan and coordinate the colors for the display. Contrasting colors, which attract attention without being loud or garish, usually work well. Metallics are good attention-getters. Many students have also used colors that reflect the project itself, such as green for botany projects or blue for astronomy or oceanography projects. In any event, if you're using several colors, check out how they look together before making a final decision.

Always (no exceptions), always have extra material on hand. A Sunday night, when the display is due first period on Monday morning, is the worst possible time to find that you've misspelled something on the very last sheet of construction paper. It's a mistake that has often reduced panicked families to rummaging through wastepaper baskets for an even halfway respectable scrap.

Careful planning and measuring, however, will reduce the need for such last-minute resourcefulness. Lettering seems to be the area most vulnerable to errors, so here are a few hints that are useful, regardless of whether you're using press-ons, stencils, or doing your own.

First, plan exactly what you're going to say, and check the spelling of everything to be included. Decide on capitalization and punctuation, and check that for accuracy and completeness, too.

Next, check the number of lines the text will occupy. To do this, decide on the size of lettering you'll use. If you're using computer-generated text, you're ahead of the game. You can print your message in several fonts and sizes to find the one that best suits your display. If you're using another method, you'll need to verify that what you need to say will fit across the panel. If not, reach for a thesaurus to find alternate ways of stating the needed information.

If you're buying press-on letters, count how many of each letter, in each size, that you'll need for the entire display. Although this might seem like a tedious task, it might save money for buying extra sheets "just in case," or even worse, running out of Es at the last minute. If, however, Murphy's law takes effect and you run out of letters after the store has closed, remember that with a good eye, a steady hand, a sharp razor blade, and fragments from unused Js and Zs, an F can become an E, a V can be transformed into an A, and an P can be made from a R!

When you're finally ready to place all the material on your backboard, follow these steps for a professional display. Lightly draw lines across the sheet to be sure that your lettering is level and mark the center of each line. Place the center letter(s) of your text on that spot and work outward until you've completed your line. If you're using stencils, you might want to outline these in pencil and check the line before filling the forms with marker or paint. If you're gluing anything, or using press-ons, keep them lightly attached in case you need to remove them later.

When placing the rest of your written and visual materials, follow similar steps. Lightly mark exactly where each item will go, and make sure it creates the effect you really want before gluing it into place.

Attach your notebook to the lower left corner of the center panel, and the display is done. Open up the backboard, step back, and enjoy. You've done a great job!

18 The fair

The big day is approaching. You've done your best work, created an attractive presentation, and you're ready for your first science fair.

Setting up

On the day before judging, you'll need to set up your display in the exhibit hall. This area can be as simple as a school lunchroom or as elaborate as a civic center or convention hall. Regardless of where it's held, however, some things remain the same.

When you enter the exhibit area, your display will be checked for size and then assigned a number, which will indicate your spot. Projects in the same category are always grouped together. This is for convenience, since there are often different judges for each category. Within a category, places on the exhibit tables are usually assigned in alphabetical order, so your location is the luck of the draw. The only exceptions are oversized displays or those needing electrical power.

Most science fairs have some fairly stringent safety rules. Here are the ISEF rules:

- If your exhibit produces temperatures greater than 100°C, you must adequately insulate it from its surroundings.
- You may not display batteries with open-top cells.
- To prevent accidental contact, you must shield high-voltage equipment with a grounded metal box or cage.
- Properly shield large vacuum tubes or dangerous ray-generating devices.
- Place high-voltage wiring, switches, and metal parts well out of reach with adequate overload safety factors.

- Electric circuits for 110-volt ac must have a UL approved cord, at least 9 feet long, of the proper load bearing capacity.
- You must properly insulate all wiring. Do not use nails or uninsulated staples to fasten wiring.
- You may use bare wire or exposed knife switches only on circuits of 12 volts or less; otherwise, you must use standard enclosed switches.
- Electrical connections in 110-volt circuits must be soldered or fixed under approved connectors. Connecting wires must be properly insulated.
- Follow the standard safety precautions for chemicals outlined in the booklet *Safety in the High School*. You can get a copy from:

  American Chemical Society
  Career Publications
  1155 16th Street NW
  Washington, DC 20036
  (202) 872-6168
- Also, remember that you may not display any live or preserved animal or animal parts, or photographs of live vertebrates under abnormal conditions.

Installing your project can be easier and quicker if you're prepared. Wear old clothes if setting up involves crawling or climbing. Just in case, bring a small collection of tools—such as a hammer, nails, and a screwdriver—to fix anything that breaks in transport. A glue stick to fix corners of your display material that have become dog-eared might also be helpful. If you use light bulbs that can burn out or glassware that can break, it's a good idea to have extras on hand for the duration of the science fair. If you need an extension cord, pack it together with your other tools. Incidentally, having your own tool kit might make you the most popular person in the hall on setup day.

Don't worry about the safety of your materials because at most fairs, the exhibit area is guarded by professional security personnel. Be assured that everything possible is done to protect your property.

Judging at the fair

To take some of the stress out of the judging process, it might help to understand what judges are looking for. Although local and state science fairs might be somewhat different, we'll discuss the general process based on ISEF guidelines.

First of all, who are the judges? They're experts in their field from your community, and representatives sent by the organizations involved in presenting special awards. Although the judges certainly bring their own interests to the experience, ISEF guidelines are specific about what the judges should be evaluating. A representative of Science Service (the folks who run the ISEF) said, "It's no secret. We want the students to know what we're looking for, so that they're better prepared."

Overall, the judges are comparing all the projects in a single category. Sometimes, if a category has a great many entries, they might divide into subcategories. Judges will neither view your project as an isolated entity, nor will they compare it with projects in other categories. Mainly, they will evaluate the quality of the work, always keeping in mind that it is work done by students, not by professional scientists or engineers.

However, an important aspect to the judging (which we'll get to in more detail in a bit) is the knowledge, understanding, and insight that you show, both of your own project and of other work in your field. Although most ISEF participants have had some help, and some, as we've discussed, have worked extensively with a mentor, your intelligence and understanding of the area in which you've been working indicates the degree to which the project is your own work. The judges will also assess whether the project is relevant—a real solution to a real problem, and not some outrageous gadget like a device that will automatically walk your dog.

To make the judging process as fair as possible, judges rate projects in the following areas:

- Creative ability.
- Scientific thought or engineering goals.
- Thoroughness.
- Skill.
- Clarity.

Let's examine the judging criteria in a little more detail.

Creativity

The project should show creative ability and originality in terms of the question, the approach to solving the problem, the analysis and interpretation of data, and the selection and use of equipment. When looking at how you got your idea, they might want to know whether you simply took your idea from a book you read or developed your idea by interpreting and developing a concept that you read about. They will also be looking closely at any adult help (particularly by engineers or scientists) that you've received, and how you used that help. For example, you won't be penalized for getting help once you've posed your hypothesis and developed your procedures. That's how professional scientists and engineers work "in the real world."

Warning: A few "don'ts" to keep in mind—collections and bizarre inventions are not considered creative, unless there is an especially innovative aspect to them.

Scientific thought or engineering goals

Obviously, this will be applied differently, depending on whether it is a science or engineering project. For a science project, the judges evaluate your use of the scientific method by looking at the following points:

- Have you clearly stated the problem?
- Was the project at the appropriate level of complexity for your grade?
- Were the procedures well defined?

- ➢ Have you recognized and defined the project variables and controls (if necessary)?
- ➢ Did you obtain adequate data to support your conclusions?
- ➢ Do you understand the limitations of the data?
- ➢ Do you understand how your project relates to other research in the field?
- ➢ Do you have plans for future research, or, if not, have you at least identified what further work is needed in the field?
- ➢ Have you used scientific literature in your work?

For an engineering project, the judges are looking for the identification of the problem and a clear, relevant, feasible, practical solution to that problem. To evaluate the project, they will look at the following factors:

- ➢ Do you have a clear objective?
- ➢ Is the objective relevant to the potential users' needs?
- ➢ Do you have an economically feasible, practical solution that is acceptable to the user (in other words, is it a "real-life" solution to a "real-life" problem)?
- ➢ Can the solution be successfully incorporated in the design or construction of some end-product? (Have you actually created "the better mousetrap?")
- ➢ Is your solution an improvement over previous alternatives?
- ➢ Have you tested the solution under actual conditions?

Thoroughness

Judges will be rating how completely you did your research, conducted your experiments, and took notes. They will want to make sure that, as far as possible, you covered the scope of your original problem. They'll check your sample size and the number of tests you conducted if that's relevant to your project. They'll look at your logs and notes to see that you were a conscientious record keeper.

Skill

The judges will evaluate the knowledge and abilities you brought to the project, such as laboratory, computational, design, and observational skills, taking into account the resources that you had to work with—whether you did your experiment at home, a school laboratory, or a professional or university facility, and the type of equipment and professional assistance that was available to you.

Clarity

The best ideas will go unnoticed if no one understands them, so this criterion will evaluate your written and verbal communication abilities. What the judges are looking for is evidence that you have a clear understanding of your project. They will also be impressed by your ability to discuss the project clearly and concisely. (Incidentally, some genuine enthusiasm wouldn't hurt; don't strive so hard to look "professional" that you sound like you've memorized a speech.)

When looking at your display and project notebook, judges will want a clear presentation of the data. They will also want to be reassured that you have prepared the written material. Although looks aren't everything, keep in mind that the judges will be examining the exhibits before they get a chance to meet and talk with you. Therefore, try to make your exhibit as attractive, clear, and self-explanatory as possible.

Take the interview time as an opportunity to discuss your work with professionals in your field of interest. Many exhibitors feel that they don't have enough opportunity to talk to the judges and learn from them.

As nervous as you might be, keep in mind that although good presentation (oral, written, and visual) can only help your cause, it is the quality of the research and experimentation, and the creativity and use of good scientific practices, that will impress the judges. If you've done your best up to this point, your project will stand on its own merits.

Unfortunately (and this is another student complaint) participants get no feedback from the judging process. Unless you receive an award, you won't know what was good or bad in your project or presentation, and you might lack a good handle on how to improve your work for next year. The best suggestion I can offer is to examine the award-winning projects in your category, keeping in mind that judging is a comparative process that might put your very excellent project behind several others that the judges considered better. If you can, find out what they did to get the recognition that their projects earned. Perhaps it was more thorough research, more detailed record keeping, or a more impressive presentation. After all, learning some techniques is not a lack of creativity; it's a show of initiative, a quality that will always be well judged!

Be prepared

Now that you know what judging's all about, you're probably still nervous. You know your project is good and your display is attractive, but you don't know what the judges are looking for. While you set up, you might have seen some other projects in your category, and you might feel that everyone else's project is better than yours. Don't panic, though; opening-night jitters are normal. However, a bit of common-sense preparation might make it a little less stressful.

If possible, sleep well the night before. Fatigue and stress do not mix well when trying to make a good impression. Next, look well. You don't need to wear expensive clothes on judging day, but neat, conservative clothes help create a positive image. Also, act well. Don't eat, chew gum, clutch a soft drink, or slouch when the judges are walking through the exhibit area. Finally, speak well, both verbally and nonverbally. Smile and be upbeat. Although your project is being evaluated, not your manners or appearance, remember that the judges are only human. They'd rather spend time with an agreeable exhibitor than an unpleasant one.

Take the interview time as an opportunity to discuss your work with those who are professionals in your field of interest. Many exhibitors feel that they don't have enough opportunity to talk to the judges and learn from them. If someone asks a question, don't wave your arm and say, "It's all here on the backboard." The judge already knows that. He or she wants to hear you express yourself. Review your notebook the night before so that you'll have the information at your fingertips. Some questions commonly asked are:

- How or why did you get interested in the topic?
- Are there any aspects of the experiment or research that you might have changed or corrected, if you had the time?
- Do you intend to continue work in this area? If so, how? If not, why not?
- What practical applications or future use does your work have in "the real world?"
- Have you seen the article last month in the Blah-de-blah Magazine by Dr. Such-and-such dealing with the further implications of etcetera and so forth?

First of all, don't be afraid to admit that you don't know an answer or that you haven't read the article or book. You'll make a far better impression with your honesty than with a futile attempt to "snow" an expert.

Science fair judges agree that the factors that come across most positively are knowledge and enthusiasm. A student who takes the path of least resistance by selecting a topic requiring a minimal amount of work is unlikely to rate high marks, even if he or she has a beautiful display. However, someone who has really worked to learn as much as possible and has made an effort to follow good scientific procedures will impress the judges, even if the experiment has not worked out well. As we've all heard before, enthusiasm is contagious. Participants who are excited about their experiment and research show that they've gained the true benefit of doing a project and being in a science fair.

When the talk or the question-and-answer period is over, smile, shake hands, and thank the judge. When he or she has moved on to the next backboard, you can breathe a sigh of relief. Now it's only a few more hours until you find out if you've won an award and the chance to advance to the next level.

Whether or not you get an award, you're a winner before you even get to the awards ceremony. In fact, you've been a winner from the moment you made the commitment to do a science project, decided to do your best, stuck with it through the difficult times, and showed your flexibility in considering "alternate plan B" when your experiment seemed to be failing. Your creativity, curiosity, and talents have won you new knowledge and confidence, and perhaps even a lifelong enthusiasm.

However, awards are nice, and there are lots to go around! There is usually a wide variety of awards. There are the awards of the particular science fair itself, which consist of first, second, and third place in each category; there are sweepstakes winners, who are judged to have the best overall projects. Finally, various private companies, research institutes, and military representatives give awards to projects that enhance the knowledge in their particular area.

Meet me at the fair

Once the excitement and tension of judging and awards night is over, enjoy yourself. Most science fairs go on for several days to allow both school children and the public at large the opportunity to review the projects.

If you like meeting and talking with people, this might be fun, especially if you have the kind of project that generates many questions. Some exhibitors even prepare handouts describing their work to give out to interested viewers. Elizabeth Eubanks, who did the project on cars following too closely, handed out the DMV guidelines. Most students I've spoken to, especially first-time participants, have spoken with pride of meeting an acquaintance who didn't even know they were in the fair.

You'll also get the chance to look at others' projects. For comparison, interest, or perhaps ideas on future projects, most participants enjoy looking at others' work.

Finally, in many cities, museums, hospitals, universities, and other institutions join together to congratulate and celebrate the participants in their local science fair. In San Diego, California, the fair is held in Balboa Park, the site of most of the city's museums. For the duration of the fair, an exhibitor badge gains the student free admission to any museum. There are also lectures and guided tours, especially for participants. The university observatory, a behind-the-scenes look at the zoo, or a trip to a medical center can be fun and informative. Counseling sessions, given by professionals to advise students about various scientific careers, are also available.

You'll be required to keep your project on exhibit until the specified end of the fair, or suffer the consequences. This is to ensure each student will check out his or her own project materials when the fair is over.

If you've won an award, congratulations! Hopefully, it's the first of many. But if you didn't get a prize, don't let your disappointment spoil the science fair for you or dampen your enthusiasm for future competition. Whatever you come away with, you've gained a working knowledge of the scientific method and an insight into an area of science.

Appendix A
ISEF project categories

Behavioral and social sciences:

Psychology, sociology, anthropology, archaeology, ethology, ethnology, linguistics, animal behavior (learned or instinctive), learning, perception, urban problems, reading problems, public-opinion surveys, and educational testing, etc.

Biochemistry:

Molecular biology, molecular genetics, enzymes, photosynthesis, blood chemistry, protein chemistry, food chemistry, hormones, etc.

Botany:

Agriculture, agronomy, horticulture, forestry, plant biorhythms, palynology, plant anatomy, plant taxonomy, plant physiology, plant pathology, plant genetics, hydroponics, algology, mycology, etc.

Chemistry:

Physical chemistry, organic chemistry (other than biochemistry), inorganic chemistry, materials, plastics, fuels, pesticides, metallurgy, soil chemistry, etc.

Computer science:

New developments in hardware or software, information systems, computer systems organization, computer methodologies and data (including structures, encryption, coding and information theory).

Earth and space sciences:

Geology, geophysics, physical oceanography, meteorology, atmospheric physics, seismology, petroleum, geography, speleology, mineralogy, topography, optical astronomy, radioastronomy, astrophysics, etc.

Engineering:

Civil, mechanical, aeronautical, chemical, electrical, photographic, sound, automotive, marine, heating and refrigerating, transportation, environmental engineering, power transmission and generation, electronics, communications, architecture, bioengineering, lasers, etc.

Environmental sciences

Pollution (air, water, land), pollution sources and their control, waste disposal, impact studies, environmental alteration (heat, light, irrigation, erosion, etc.), ecology.

Mathematics:

Calculus, geometry, abstract algebra, number theory, statistics, complex analysis, probability, topology, logic, operations research, and other topics in pure and applied mathematics.

Medicine and health:

Medicine, dentistry, pharmacology, veterinary medicine, pathology, ophthalmology, nutrition, sanitation, pediatrics, dermatology, allergies, speech and hearing, optometry, etc.

Microbiology:

Bacteriology, virology, protozoology, fungal and bacterial genetics, yeast, etc.

Physics:

Solid state, optics, acoustics, particle, nuclear, atomic, plasma, superconductivity, fluid and gas dynamics, thermodynamics, semiconductors, magnetism, quantum mechanics, biophysics, etc.

Zoology:

Animal genetics, ornithology, ichthyology, herpetology, entomology, animal ecology, anatomy, paleontology, cellular physiology, animal biorhythms, animal husbandry, cytology, histology, animal physiology, neurophysiology, invertebrate biology, etc.

Category interpretations

The following are project areas about which questions frequently arise. The list is included only to provide some basis for interpretation of the category descriptions.

Instruments:

The design and construction of a telescope, bubble chamber, laser, or other instrument would be engineering if the design and construction were the primary purpose of the project. If a telescope were constructed, data gathered using the telescope, and an analysis presented, the project would be placed in earth and space sciences.

Marine biology:

Behavioral and social sciences (schooling of fish), botany (marine algae), zoology (sea urchins), or environmental sciences (plant and animal life of sea, river, pond).

Fossils:

Botany (prehistoric plants), chemistry (chemical composition of fossil shells), earth and space sciences (geological ages), and zoology (prehistoric animals).

Rockets:

Chemistry (rocket fuels), earth and space sciences (use of a rocket as a vehicle for meteorological instruments), engineering (design of a rocket), or physics (computing rocket trajectories). A project on the effects of rocket acceleration on mice would go in medicine and health.

Genetics:

Biochemistry (studies of DNA), botany (hybridization), microbiology (genetics of bacteria), or zoology (fruit flies).

Vitamins:

Biochemistry (how the body deals with vitamins), chemistry (analysis), and medicine and health (effects of vitamin deficiencies).

Crystallography:

Chemistry (crystal composition), mathematics (symmetry), and physics (lattice structure).

Speech and hearing:

Behavioral and social sciences (reading problems), engineering (hearing aids), medicine and health (speech defects), physics (sound), zoology (structure of the ear).

Radioactivity:

Biochemistry, botany, medicine and health, and zoology could all involve the use of tracers. Earth and space sciences or physics could involve the measurement of radioactivity. Engineering could involve design and construction of detection instruments.

Space-related projects:

Note that many projects involving "space" do not go into earth and space sciences. Botany (effects of zero G on plants), medicine and health (effects of G on human beings), Engineering (development of closed environmental system for space capsule).

Computers:

If a computer is used as an instrument, the project should be considered for assignment to the area of basic science on which the project focuses. As examples: If the computer is used to calculate rocket trajectories, then it would be assigned to physics. If the computer is used to calculate estimates of heat generated from a specified inorganic chemical reaction, then it would be entered in chemistry, or if the computer is used as a teaching aid, then it would be entered in behavioral and social sciences.

Appendix B
ISEF rules and certifications

The following pages contain information you will find extremely helpful as you prepare for the science fair. Included are flowcharts that indicate which forms are required for certain kinds of projects. Then you'll find a checklist that you can use to make sure you've covered all the bases, as well as a matrix you can use to double-check yourself. Finally, you'll see copies of all required forms. Note: Because the following forms were taken directly from ISEF documentation, you will see two page numbers on the following pages. Also, note that these forms should be used as general guide only; they should not take the place of the most current edition of the ISEF rules.

TEACHER-SUPERVISOR/RESEARCH PLAN/SAFETY REVIEW CERTIFICATION #1

(COMPLETION OF FRONT AND BACK OF FORM IS REQUIRED FOR ALL PROJECTS)

Student's Name (type) ______________________________

Student's School ______________________________

Student's Signature ______________________________

Parent/Guardian's Signature ______________________________

Project Title ______________________________

ISEF Affiliated Fair ______________________________

TEACHER APPROVAL—PRIOR TO RESEARCH

I agree to sponsor the student named above and assume the responsibility for compliance with all existing ISEF Rules and approve the research plan on the reverse side. I have also conducted a safety review as outlined on page 26.

Teacher-Supervisor Name (type) ______________________________

Work Phone ______________________________

Work Address ______________________________

City ____________________ State __________ Zip Code __________

Starting date of laboratory or field research ______________________________

Name and address where laboratory or field research will be done

____

Teacher-Supervisor Signature ____________________ Date __________

Signed for all projects prior to the start of experimental research.

SRC APPROVAL—PRIOR TO RESEARCH (WHEN NECESSARY)*

SRC Review - I certify that the committee has carefully studied this research proposal and certify that all required certifications are included. My signature indicates approval of this research proposal prior to the beginning of experimental work by the student.

Signature ____________________ Date __________
Local Fair SRC Chairperson or Affiliated Fair SRC Chairperson

* Signature required for all projects involving vertebrate animals, humans, recombinant DNA, tissue or pathogenic agents/controlled substances prior to the start of experimental research.

Note: Major deviations from the original plan must be approved prior to changes in experimental procedures being used by the student.

SRC APPROVAL—PRIOR TO COMPETITION AT AN ISEF-AFFILIATED FAIR

I certify that this project complies with all ISEF Rules.

Signature ____________________ Date __________
Affiliated Fair SRC Chairperson

Signed for all projects, before competition at the affiliated fair.

This form, with all signatures, must be submitted to the ISEF Scientific Review Committee for students named as ISEF Finalists.

43rd ISEF Rules - Page 28

B-1

RESEARCH PLAN—PART II OF CERTIFICATION #1

MUST BE COMPLETED PRIOR TO RESEARCH
(see instructions on page 25)

Student's name ______________________________

NOTE: You are to start each section here and add additional sheets as necessary.

1. Problem and Hypothesis:

2. Methods or Procedures (use additional sheets and include your complete procedure):

3. Bibliography (minimum of 3 major sources):
(Vertebrate animal experiments must include at least one animal care reference source.)

43rd ISEF Rules - Page 29

VERTEBRATE ANIMAL CERTIFICATION #2

MUST BE COMPLETED FOR ALL VERTEBRATE ANIMAL RESEARCH PRIOR TO THE RESEARCH

TYPE OR PRINT

Student's name ____________________

Student's school ____________________

NOTE: COMPLETE EACH SPACE - BE SPECIFIC

(Modify form appropriately for aquatic animals)

A. Genus, species and common name of animals to be used ____________________

____

B. Number of animals to be used ____________________

C. Animals to be obtained from ____________________

(pet store animals are not appropriate)

D. Describe proposed animal care ____________________

*1. Cage size ____________________

Number of animals per cage ____________________

2. Temperature range in degrees Celsius of room where animals are to be kept from ________ to ________

3. Frequency of feeding and watering ____________________

4. Indicate type of food ____________________

5. Frequency of cleaning cage ____________________

6. Type of bedding to be used (do not use cedar chips or newspapers)

____

7. Where will animals be housed? (Animals infected with pathogenic organisms must be housed in institutional settings, however, such studies are discouraged.)

____

** 8. Will animals be sacrificed? ________ Yes ________ No

If yes, by what method and by whom? ____________________

If no, what will happen to the animals upon termination of research?

____

E. Teacher-Supervisor Signature ____________________ Date ________

* See note on page 27.

** See note on page 27.

43rd ISEF Rules - Page 30

B-1 Continued

ANIMAL CARE SUPERVISOR CERTIFICATION #3

TYPE OR PRINT

MUST BE COMPLETED FOR ALL VERTEBRATE ANIMAL RESEARCH
PRIOR TO THE START OF THE RESEARCH

Student's name ____________________

Research Title ____________________

____

____

I certify that I have discussed this research with the student prior to its start and will supervise and will accept primary responsibility for the quality of care and handling of the live vertebrate animals used by the above named student. I further certify that I am knowledgeable in the proper care and handling of laboratory animals, meet prevailing animal care supervisory requirements and, when an animal must be sacrificed, I certify that I will be present and will perform or direct the procedure, using such agents as are recommended.

Signature ____________________ Date __________
(Animal Care Supervisor)

TYPE OR PRINT

Name ____________________
(Animal Care Supervisor)

Position ____________________

Institution ____________________

Address ____________________

____

Office phone (______) ____________________
area code

43rd ISEF Rules - Page 31

QUALIFIED SCIENTIST CERTIFICATION #4

TYPE OR PRINT

Student's name ______________________________

Research Title ______________________________

____

Scientist's name ______________________________

Earned Degrees ______________________________

Position ______________________________

Institution ______________________________

Address ______________________________

____

Phone (______) ______________________________
area code

1. Animals used? yes __________ no __________
2. Human Subjects used? yes __________ no __________
3. Controlled substance used? yes __________ no __________ DEA # __________
   a. If controlled substance used: ______________________________
   (name of substance)
   b. Controlled substances were used according to existing local, state, and federal laws:
   yes __________ no __________
4. Pathogenic agents used? yes __________ no __________
   a. If yes, pathogenic agents were used according to accepted procedures?
   yes __________ no __________

I certify that I have reviewed and approved the Research Plan prior to the start of the research, that if the student or Designated Adult Supervisor is not trained in the necessary procedures I will ensure his/her training, that I will provide advice and supervision during the research, and that I am a Qualified Scientist with a working knowledge of the techniques to be used by the student in this Research Plan. I understand that a Designated Adult Supervisor is required when the student is not conducting his/her research in my laboratory.

Scientist's signature ______________________________ Date __________
Earned Doctoral Degree required
(Ph.D., M.D., D.V.M., D.D.S., or D.O.)

Designated Adult signature ______________________________ Date __________

Student's signature ______________________________ Date __________

43rd ISEF Rules - Page 32

B-1 Continued

DESIGNATED ADULT SUPERVISOR CERTIFICATION #5

TYPE OR PRINT

Student's name ____

Research Title ____

____

I certify that I have been trained in the techniques to be used by this student prior to the start of the research and will provide direct supervision.

Signature ____________________________
(Designated Adult Supervisor)

Date ______________

TYPE OR PRINT

Name ____
(Designated Adult Supervisor)

Position ____

Institution ____

Address ____

____

Office Phone (______) ____________________

43rd ISEF Rules - Page 33

HUMAN SUBJECTS AND INSTITUTIONAL REVIEW BOARD (IRB) CERTIFICATION #6

MUST BE COMPLETED FOR ALL RESEARCH INVOLVING HUMANS AND SIGNED BY: INSTITUTIONAL REVIEW BOARD OR SCIENTIFIC REVIEW COMMITTEE PRIOR TO THE ONSET OF EXPERIMENTAL RESEARCH.

TYPE OR PRINT

Student's name ______________________________

Student's school ______________________________

PART I—TO BE COMPLETED BY THE STUDENT

A. Explain why human subjects are proposed or necessary for this research. ______________________________

____

B. Describe and assess any potential risk (physical, psychological, social, legal or other).

____

____

C. Describe consent procedures to be followed (attach sample of completed form to be used). Informed consent recommended for all human subjects.

____

____

D. Describe procedures to minimize risks.

____

____

E. Describe benefits to the individual or society.

____

____

F. Explain how the benefits exceed the risks.

____

____

PART II—TO BE COMPLETED BY INSTITUTIONAL REVIEW BOARD OR SCIENTIFIC REVIEW COMMITTEE PRIOR TO EXPERIMENTAL RESEARCH:

________ No risks involved. (Informed consent for all human subjects recommended.)
________ Acceptable risks involved. Certifications #4, #5, and #7 are required.
________ Unacceptable risks involved. Project must be revised.

Please circle to the right of the signature the person who served as Chairperson:

			Chairperson (circle one)
Signature ____________ Member of IRB or SRC	Position ____________ Scientist/Medical/Nurse	Date ________	yes no
Signature ____________ Member of IRB or SRC	Position ____________ Science Teacher	Date ________	yes no
Signature ____________ Member of IRB or SRC	Position ____________ Administrator, and others as designated.	Date ________	yes no

43rd ISEF Rules - Page 34

B-1 Continued

INFORMED CONSENT CERTIFICATION #7*

TYPE OR PRINT

Researcher's name ______________________________

Researcher's school ______________________________

Research Title ______________________________

____

A. Research procedures involving you are: ______________________________

____

B. Risks

1. Possible discomforts or risks you may reasonably expect by participation in this research.

____

2. Procedures to be used to minimize risks ______________________________

____

C. Possible benefits you may reasonably expect ______________________________

____

D. If you have any questions regarding this research, please contact Teacher-Supervisor

______________________________ at ____________/______________________

Name of Teacher-Supervisor area code/phone number

I have read and understand the conditions stated above and consent to participate in this research procedure. You are free to withdraw your consent and to discontinue participation in this research activity at any time without prejudice toward you.

Participant's signature ______________________________ Date ______________

Parent's or guardian's signature if participant is a minor (under age 18) or a protected special needs person (see page 39, definition 23).

______________________________ Date ______________

(Parent's/guardian's signature)

Qualified Scientist's signature** ______________________________

* If the institution where the project is to be conducted has a different Informed Consent Statement that contains essentially this same information, the form of the institution may be used and will be accepted by the ISEF.

** When this form has been approved and signed by the Qualified Scientist, then it should be reproduced and signed by each research participant.

43rd ISEF Rules - Page 35

TISSUE CERTIFICATION #8

TYPE OR PRINT

MUST BE COMPLETED FOR ALL PROJECTS USING
TISSUE, ORGANS, HUMAN PARTS, OR ANIMAL PARTS, INCLUDING BLOOD
BLOOD PRODUCTS, TEETH, CELL CULTURES, AND BODY FLUIDS
(PLANT TISSUE IS EXCLUDED)

Student's name (type or print) ______________________________

(Signature) ______________________________

Student's School ______________________________

Teacher-Supervisor (type or print) ______________________________

(Signature) ______________________________

Tissue(s), organ(s), or part(s) used ______________________________

____

Vertebrate tissue:

a. Where was the tissue obtained? ______________________________

b Why had the animal been sacrificed? ______________________________

Institution or Company of Acquisition ______________________________

____

Human blood and blood products have been tested and documented free of AIDS and hepatitis antibodies and antigens. Human teeth are certified free of blood and blood products.

Signature ______________________________ Date ______________
(Certifying Authority)

I certify that the above listed materials were provided by me and that the student listed was not involved in the direct acquisition of the samples provided or purchased.

Signature ______________________________

Title ______________________________

Date ______________________________

43rd ISEF Rules - Page 36

B-1 Continued

SUPERVISING SCIENTIST CERTIFICATION #9

Student's name ____

A Supervising Qualified Scientist of a Summer Institute, Science Training Program, or a Scientist's Laboratory Attended by Science Fair Participants Must Answer the Following Questions:

1. How did the student get the idea for his/her project?
   Was the project assigned, was it picked from a list of possible research topics, did it come out of discussion with a scientist, did it arise from some work in which the student was engaged, or did the student suggest it?

2. Did the student work on the project as part of a team or a group?
   If so, how big was the team, what kind of a team was it (student, group of adult researchers, etc.), and what was the student's role on the team?

3. How independently did the student work on the project?
   What parts did the student do on his/her own, and what parts did he/she receive help on (in the experimental design, choice of techniques, use of special instruments or equipment, construction of equipment, gathering data, evaluation of data, arriving at conclusions, etc.)?

4. What did the student do that showed creativity and ingenuity?
   Do you know of any examples? If so, were they creative in terms of science, or what is more likely, was it creative for a high school student? Was it in experimental design, construction or use of equipment, evaluation of data, etc.?

5. Has the student received a salary or other compensation for doing his/her research?

6. Other comments?

____

Signature Title

____

Institution Date

THIS COMPLETED FORM MUST BE SUBMITTED WITH THE RESEARCH PLAN AND BE DISPLAYED WITH THE PROJECT AT THE ISEF.

43rd ISEF Rules - Page 37

MATRIX FOR REQUIRED DOCUMENTATION/CERTIFICATIONS

	DOCUMENTATION & CERTIFICATIONS REQUIRED	RESEARCH PLAN & CERTIFICATIONS SIGNED		DOCUMENTATION & CERTIFICATIONS SUBMITTED TO SRC		FOR REVIEW OR DISPLAY AT THE FAIR SITE
		BEFORE RESEARCH BEGINS	BEFORE FAIR/ ISEF	BEFORE RESEARCH BEGINS	BEFORE FAIR/ ISEF	
ALL PROJECTS	ABSTRACT				X	X
	CERT. #1	X			X	X
	CERT. #9*		X		X	X
	Plus, ANY REQUIRED GOVERNMENT PERMITS*	X			X	X
RESEARCH INVOLVING VERTEBRATE ANIMALS	Same as ALL PROJECTS (see above), Plus:					
	CERT. #1**	X		X	X	X
	CERT. #2	X		X	X	X
	CERT. #3	X		X	X	X
	CERT. #4	X		X	X	X
	CERT. #5*	X		X	X	X
RESEARCH INVOLVING HUMAN SUBJECTS	Same as ALL PROJECTS (see above), Plus:			X	X	
	CERT. #1**	X		X	X	X
	CERT. #6	X		X	X	X
	And, if required by IRB:					
	CERT. #4	X		X	X	X
	CERT. #5*	X		X	X	X
	CERT. #7	X		X	X	X
RECOMBINANT DNA RESEARCH	Same as ALL PROJECTS (see above), Plus:			X	X	
	CERT. #1**	X		X	X	X
	CERT. #4	X		X	X	X
	CERT. #5*	X		X	X	X
TISSUE RESEARCH	Same as ALL PROJECTS (see above), Plus:			X	X	
	CERT. #1**	X		X	X	X
	CERT. #8		X		X	X
PATHOGENIC AGENTS OR CONTROLLED SUBSTANCES	Same as ALL PROJECTS (see above), Plus:			X	X	
	CERT. #1**	X		X	X	X
	CERT. #4	X		X	X	X
	CERT. #5*	X		X	X	X

* If Applicable

** Note: In these cases, Certification #1 must be submitted to and signed by the Local Fair SRC Chairperson or Affiliated Fair SRC Chairperson prior to the onset of research.

43rd ISEF Rules-Page 42

B-1 Continued

ALL PROJECTS

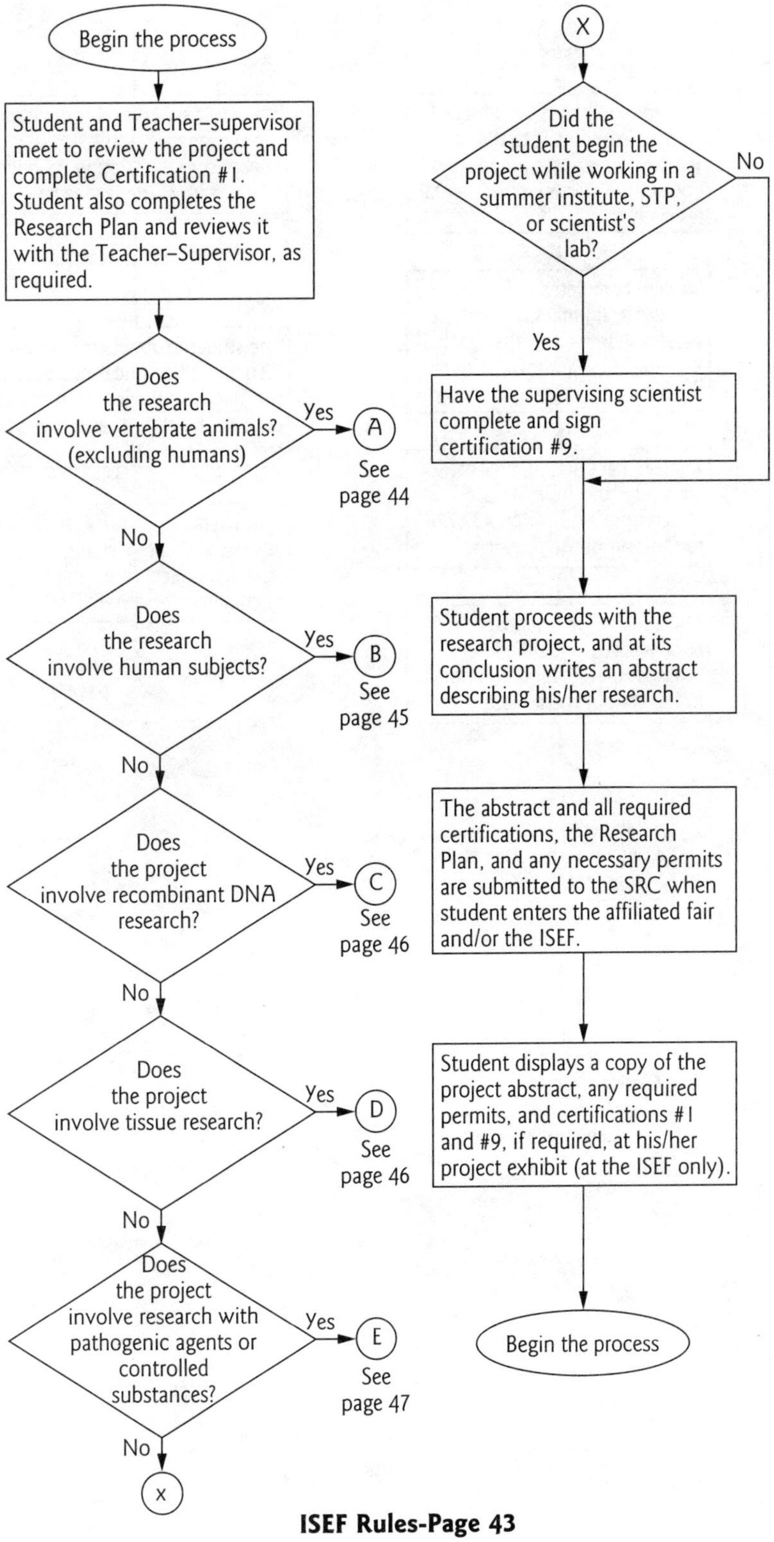

ISEF Rules-Page 43

VERTEBRATE ANIMAL RESEARCH

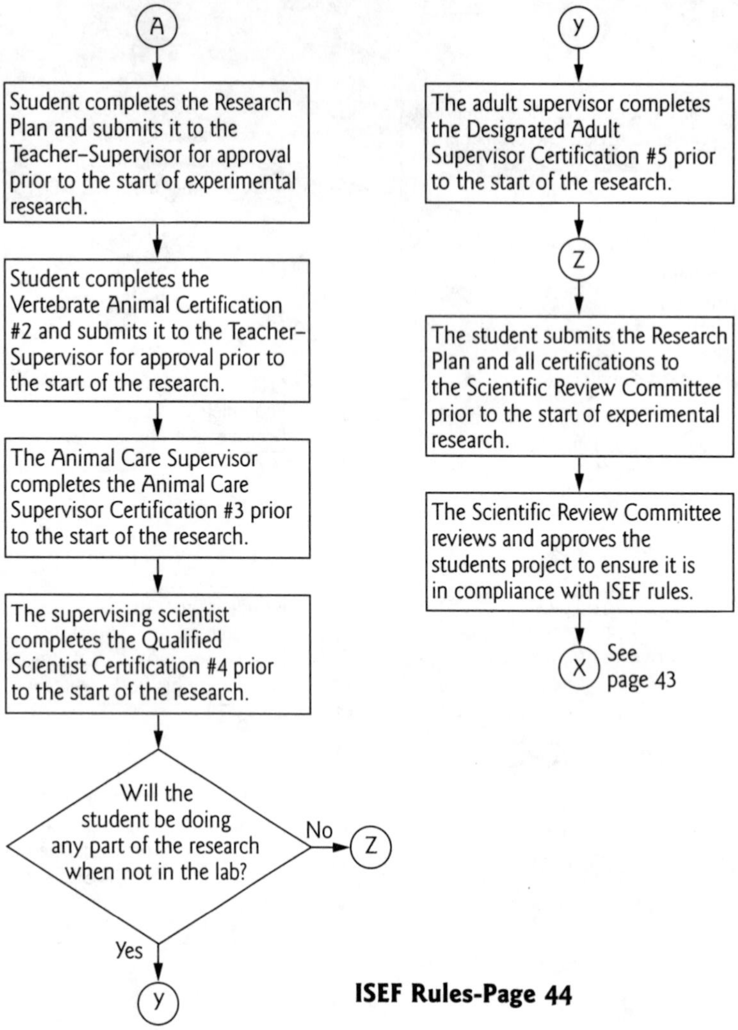

A
Student completes the Research Plan and submits it to the Teacher–Supervisor for approval prior to the start of experimental research.
Student completes the Vertebrate Animal Certification #2 and submits it to the Teacher–Supervisor for approval prior to the start of the research.
The Animal Care Supervisor completes the Animal Care Supervisor Certification #3 prior to the start of the research.
The supervising scientist completes the Qualified Scientist Certification #4 prior to the start of the research.
Will the student be doing any part of the research when not in the lab?
No
Z
Yes
Y
Y
The adult supervisor completes the Designated Adult Supervisor Certification #5 prior to the start of the research.
Z
The student submits the Research Plan and all certifications to the Scientific Review Committee prior to the start of experimental research.
The Scientific Review Committee reviews and approves the students project to ensure it is in compliance with ISEF rules.
X
See page 43

ISEF Rules-Page 44

B-1 Continued

HUMAN RESEARCH

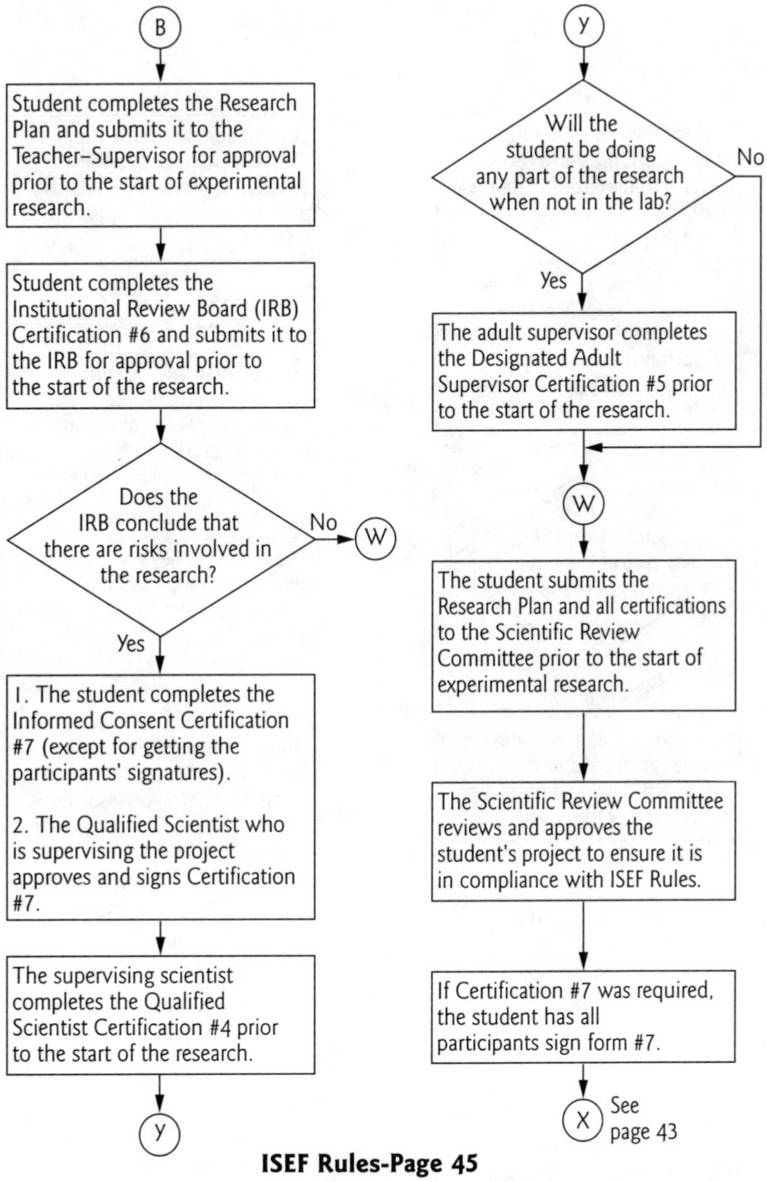
B
Student completes the Research Plan and submits it to the Teacher–Supervisor for approval prior to the start of experimental research.
Student completes the Institutional Review Board (IRB) Certification #6 and submits it to the IRB for approval prior to the start of the research.
Does the IRB conclude that there are risks involved in the research?
No
W
Yes
1. The student completes the Informed Consent Certification #7 (except for getting the participants' signatures).
2. The Qualified Scientist who is supervising the project approves and signs Certification #7.
The supervising scientist completes the Qualified Scientist Certification #4 prior to the start of the research.
Y
Y
Will the student be doing any part of the research when not in the lab?
No
Yes
The adult supervisor completes the Designated Adult Supervisor Certification #5 prior to the start of the research.
W
The student submits the Research Plan and all certifications to the Scientific Review Committee prior to the start of experimental research.
The Scientific Review Committee reviews and approves the student's project to ensure it is in compliance with ISEF Rules.
If Certification #7 was required, the student has all participants sign form #7.
X
See page 43

ISEF Rules-Page 45

RECOMBINANT DNA

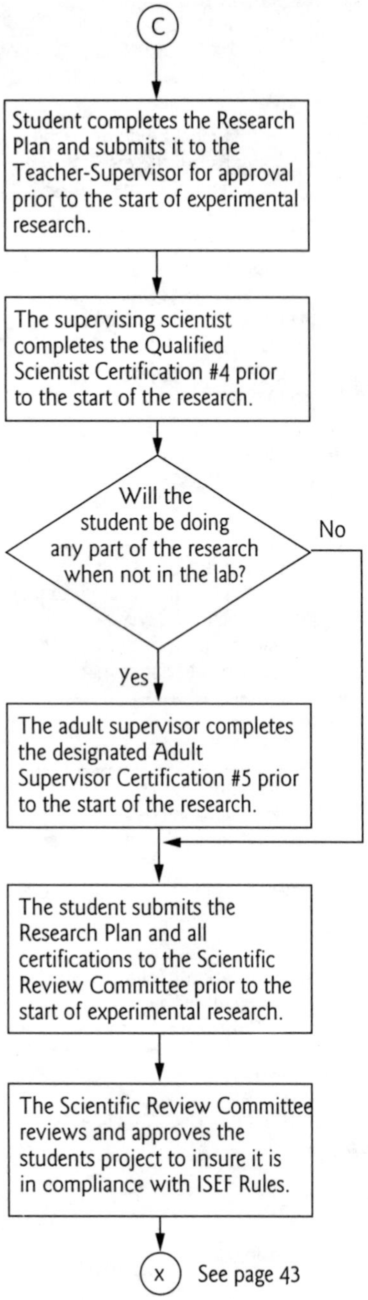

C
Student completes the Research Plan and submits it to the Teacher-Supervisor for approval prior to the start of experimental research.
The supervising scientist completes the Qualified Scientist Certification #4 prior to the start of the research.
Will the student be doing any part of the research when not in the lab?
No
Yes
The adult supervisor completes the designated Adult Supervisor Certification #5 prior to the start of the research.
The student submits the Research Plan and all certifications to the Scientific Review Committee prior to the start of experimental research.
The Scientific Review Committee reviews and approves the students project to insure it is in compliance with ISEF Rules.
X
See page 43

TISSUE

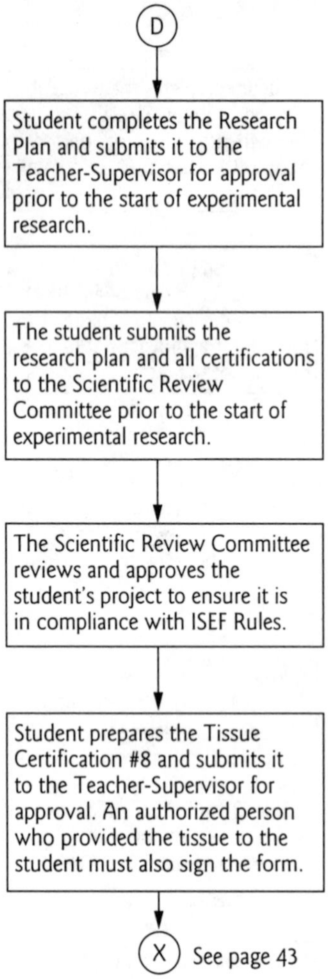

D
Student completes the Research Plan and submits it to the Teacher-Supervisor for approval prior to the start of experimental research.
The student submits the research plan and all certifications to the Scientific Review Committee prior to the start of experimental research.
The Scientific Review Committee reviews and approves the student's project to ensure it is in compliance with ISEF Rules.
Student prepares the Tissue Certification #8 and submits it to the Teacher-Supervisor for approval. An authorized person who provided the tissue to the student must also sign the form.
X
See page 43

ISEF Rules-Page 46

B-1 Continued

PATHOGENIC AGENTS OR CONTROLLED SUBSTANCES

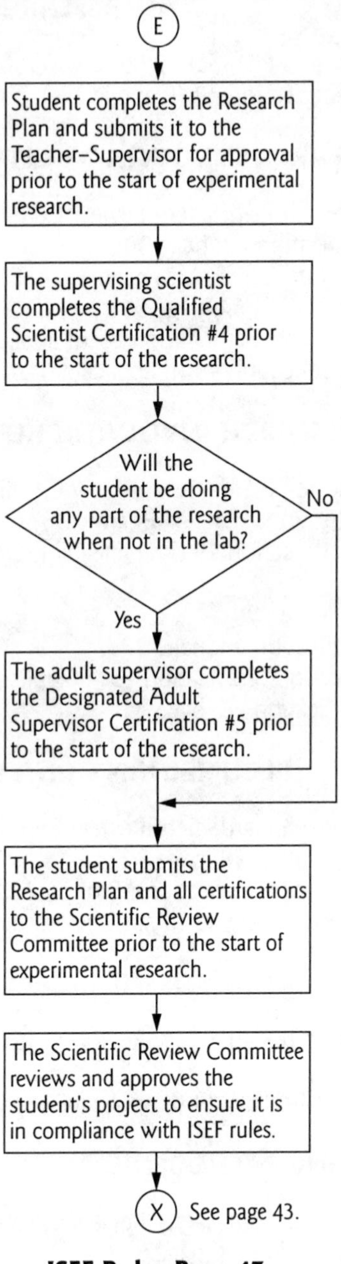

E
Student completes the Research Plan and submits it to the Teacher–Supervisor for approval prior to the start of experimental research.
The supervising scientist completes the Qualified Scientist Certification #4 prior to the start of the research.
Will the student be doing any part of the research when not in the lab?
No
Yes
The adult supervisor completes the Designated Adult Supervisor Certification #5 prior to the start of the research.
The student submits the Research Plan and all certifications to the Scientific Review Committee prior to the start of experimental research.
The Scientific Review Committee reviews and approves the student's project to ensure it is in compliance with ISEF rules.
X
See page 43.

ISEF Rules-Page 47

CHECKLIST SEQUENCE FOR REQUIRED DOCUMENTATION/CERTIFICATIONS

ALL RESEARCH

1. Teacher-Supervisor/Research Plan/Safety Review Certification #1, pp. 28–29
2. Supervising Scientist Certification #9 (if applicable), page 37

RESEARCH INVOLVING VERTEBRATE ANIMALS

1. Teacher-Supervisor/Research Plan/Safety Review Certification #1, pp. 28–29
2. Vertebrate Animal Certification #2, page 30
3. Animal Care Supervisor Certification #3, page 31
4. Qualified Scientist Certification #4, page 32
5. Designated Adult Supervision Certification #5 (if applicable), page 33
6. Supervising Scientist Certification #9 (if applicable), page 37

RESEARCH INVOLVING HUMAN SUBJECTS

1. Teacher-Supervisor/Research Plan/Safety Review Certification #1, pp. 28–29
2. Human Subjects & Institutional Review Board (IRB) Certification #6, p. 34
3. Supervising Scientist Certification #9 (if applicable), page 37

If required by IRB:

4. Qualified Scientist Certification #4, page 32
5. Designated Adult Supervisor Certification #5 (if applicable), page 33
6. Informed Consent Certification #7, page 35

RECOMBINANT DNA RESEARCH

1. Teacher-Supervisor/Research Plan/Safety Review Certification #1, pp. 28–29
2. Qualified Scientist Certification #4, page 32
3. Designated Adult Supervisor Certification #5 (if applicable), page 33
4. Supervising Scientist Certification #9 (if applicable), page 37

TISSUE RESEARCH

1. Teacher-Supervisor/Research Plan/Safety Review Certification #1, pp. 28–29
2. Tissue Certification #8, page 36
3. Supervising Scientist Certification #9 (if applicable), page 37

RESEARCH INVOLVING PATHOGENIC AGENTS OR CONTROLLED SUBSTANCES

1. Teacher-Supervisor/Research Plan/Safety Review Certification #1, pp. 28–29
2. Qualified Scientist Certification #4, page 32
3. Designated Adult Supervisor Certification #5 (if applicable), page 33
4. Supervising Scientist Certification #9 (if applicable), page 37

43rd ISEF Rules - Page 48

B-1 Continued

Glossary

abstract A short summary of the main points of a project. This is normally between 200–250 words in length.

analyzed data Data derived from raw and smooth data, from which conclusions can be drawn.

clip art Pictures that are included with many word-processing, graphics, and desktop-publishing software. These pictures can be incorporated into your documents and can sometimes be modified using graphics software.

conclusion Interpretation based on outcome of results and answering the question or comparison suggested by purpose.

control group Identical to the experimental group in all aspects, except that no variables are applied. This represents the test group that has all variables standardized and forms the basis for comparison.

controls This represents factors that are not to be changed, or variables that are to be controlled. Do not confuse with control group.

database Data files organized so that they can be manipulated and accessed in a variety of groups and sequences. Working with a database requires specialized software.

dependent variable The factor that changes as a result of altering the independent variable. Also, the change in events or results linked and controlled by another factor that has also been changed.

desktop publisher A system that performs printing functions, such as page layout and composition. A desktop publisher can incorporate files from many sources, such as spreadsheets, word processors, and graphics and photo-processing programs.

experiment A planned investigation to determine the outcome that would arise from changing a variable or from changing "natural" conditions.

experimental group A group of subjects to which independent or experimental variables are applied.

experimental variable See independent variable.

graphs Illustrated form of presenting raw, smooth, or analyzed data.

hypothesis Statement of an idea that can be tested experimentally, based upon research. States what experimenter believes will happen as a result of the experiment.

independent variable The item, quantity, or condition that is altered to observe what will happen; something that can be changed in an experiment without causing a change in other variables.

interpretation One's personal viewpoint based on the data. This can be based on either qualitative or quantitative analysis and might become a part of the project's conclusion.

materials All items used in the course of the experiment.

measured variable See dependent variable.

observation What one sees in the course of the experiment. Observations are often incorporated into raw data.

procedures Steps that must be followed to perform an experiment.

qualitative analysis Analysis made subjectively, without measurement.

quantitative analysis Analysis made objectively, with measurement devices.

question (or problem) The basis of the hypothesis or objective of the experiment.

raw data Logs, tables and graphs that represent data as it is collected in the course of the experiment.

research The process of learning facts or prior theories on a subject by reviewing existing sources of information.

results Graphs and tables that represent raw, smooth, and analyzed data.

scientific method Manner of conducting an experiment, using valid subjects, variables and controls, and accurately recording results.

smooth data Tables or graphs where all the averages, totals, or percentages are placed. These might combine the information from raw data tables and graphs.

spreadsheet A program that manipulates data laid out in columns and rows that contain cells of data. A spreadsheet can perform mathematical functions on the data and automatically recalculate results when any of the data changes. A spreadsheet program can also create a variety of graphs based on the data.

tables Written form of presenting raw, smooth, or analyzed data.

variable A condition that is changed to test the hypothesis, or a condition that changes as a result of testing the hypothesis.

word processor Software that allows you to create and edit written documents, including the ability to insert, delete, and change text, change fonts, layout tables, and print on a variety of paper sizes on different printers.

Index

G

H

I

J

K

L

M

N

O

P

About the author

Maxine Haren Iritz is a technical writer who has authored a number of successful children's science books, including *Science Fair: Developing a Fun and Successful Project*; *Blue-Ribbon Science Fair Projects*; and *Winning the Grand Award: Successful Strategies for International Science & Engineering Fair Competition*. An author of three computer software books and magazine and newspaper articles, she is also experienced in business and computer issues.